# ROCHESTER LIVES

*Emerson Klees*

*Friends of the Finger Lakes Publishing*

*Rochester, New York*

Other books about New York State by Emerson Klees

*Persons, Places, and Things In the Finger Lakes Region*
(1993, 2000)
*Person, Places, and Things Around the Finger Lakes Region*
    (1994, 2004)
*People of the Finger Lakes Region* (1995)
*Legends and Stories of the Finger Lakes Region* (1995)
*The Erie Canal in the Finger Lakes Region* (1996)
*Underground Railroad Tales With Routes Through the*
    *Finger Lakes Region* (1997)
*More Legends and Stories of the Finger Lakes Region* (1997)
*The Women's Rights Movement and the Finger Lakes Region*
    (1998)
*Wineries of the Finger Lakes Region* (2000, 2003)
*The Crucible of Ferment: New York's Psychic Highway* (2001)
*The Iroquois Confederacy: History and Legends* (2003)

Friends of the Finger Lakes Publishing
P. O. Box 18131
Rochester, New York 14618

Library of Congress Control Number: 2003195102

ISBN 1-891046-05-5

Printed in the United States of America
9 8 7 6 5 4 3 2 1

# *PREFACE*

"The history of the world is but the biography of great men [and women]." Thomas Carlyle, "The Heroes as Divinity," *Heroes and Hero Worship,* 1841

"There is properly no history, only biography." Ralph Waldo Emerson, "Essays, First Series," *History,* 1841

*Rochester Lives* provides profiles of people who founded Rochester and those who lived in New York's third largest city and made significant contributions to society.

A goal of this book is to relate Rochester's history through biographical sketches of its people. Selecting forty-five out of the hundreds of achievers who contributed to Rochester's beginning and growth is difficult; many others are worthy of inclusion.

A number of the individuals profiled in this book were not born and raised in Rochester but moved here later. Obviously, the city's pioneers, such as Nathaniel Rochester, made their accomplishments here in adulthood. Industrialist John Jacob Bausch and nurseryman George Ellwanger emigrated from Germany, and Ellwanger's partner, Patrick Barry, emigrated from Ireland. Activist Emma Goldman was an immigrant to the U.S. from the Ukraine.

Some of the achievers profiled in the book were not long-term residents but lived in Rochester only a short time: Brigham Young, who succeeded founder Joseph Smith as leader of the Mormons founded in nearby Palmyra, lived in Mendon as a young adult, Thomas J. Watson of IBM lived in the "Flower City" from 1899 until 1903, and Bishop Fulton J. Sheen lived here from 1966 through 1969. Revivalist Charles Grandison Finney, visited Rochester on three occasions; his longest stay was less than a year. However, his impact on boomtown Rochester in the mid-1800s was so profound that he is included in the book.

*Rochester Lives* provides forty-five biographical sketches of the City's natives and residents. Profiles are grouped into nine categories:

**R**eformers / Pioneers
**O**rganizers / Visionaries
**C**omposers / Authors / Educators
**H**umanitarians / Industrialists
**E**ngineers / Entrepreneurs
**S**portsmen / Notables
**T**hinkers / Politicians
**E**ccentrics / Architects
**R**eligious Leaders / Ecclesiastics

The Prologue describes Rochester as the western gateway to the Finger Lakes Region, and the Introduction is an overview of Rochester history through the twentieth century. The Epilogue highlights plans for the years ahead as described in Mayor William A. Johnson, Jr.'s Renaissance 2010 plan. Also included are twelve stories about Rochester. This book includes material edited and reprinted from *People of the Finger Lakes Region, Crucible of Ferment: New York's "Psychic Highway," Legends and Stories of the Finger Lakes Region, More Legends and Stories of the Finger Lakes Region,* and *Entrepreneurs In History—Success vs. Failure: Entrepreneurial Role Models.*

# LIST OF PHOTOGRAPHS

Front cover: Rochester skyline, Courtesy Greater Rochester
Visitors Association
Back cover: Statue of Mercury, Courtesy West, a Thompson
Company, formerly Lawyers' Cooperative Publishing

Page No.

Susan B. Anthony House, Madison Street.                           24
Statue of Frederick Douglass and Susan B. Anthony at Tea,
    Madison Street                                               26
Statue of Frederick Douglass, Highland Park                      30
Talman Building, East Main Street, Home of
    Frederick Douglass's *North Star*                            34
Sibley, Lindsay, and Curr Building, East Main Street             48
Wilder Building, Corner of Main and Exchange Streets             74
George Eastman House, East Avenue                                111
Mt. Hope Cemetery Gatehouse, Mt. Hope Avenue                     128
Powers Block, Corner of Main and State Streets                   171
Rochester Free Academy, Fitzhugh Street                          194
Warner's Castle, Mt. Hope Avenue                                 202
Chamber of Commerce, South St. Paul Street                       222
First Universalist Church, South Clinton Avenue                  224
Rochester Savings Bank Building, Liberty Pole Way                228
City Hall, Broad and Fitzhugh Streets, now Irving Place          230
Third Monroe County Courthouse, West Main Street,
    now the Monroe County Office Building                        232
Monroe County Courthouse, Church Street, now City Hall           233
First Presbyterian Church, South Plymouth Avenue,
    now Central Church of Christ                                 234
Statue of Mercury atop the Kimball Tobacco Factory,
    Courtesy West, a Thompson Company                            262

Cover design by Dunn and Rice Design, Rochester, New York
Map by Actionmaps, Rochester, New York

# TABLE OF CONTENTS

*Page No.*

*PREFACE*     3

*LIST OF PHOTOGRAPHS*     5

*PROLOGUE*     9

*MAP OF ROCHESTER*     12

*INTRODUCTION*     13

*CHAPTER 1—REFORMERS / PIONEERS*     19

   *Nathaniel Rochester*     19
   *Susan B. Anthony*     23
   *Frederick Douglass*     31
   *Amy Post*     37
   *Antoinette Brown Blackwell*     39

*CHAPTER 2—ORGANIZERS / VISIONARIES*     49

   *Hiram Sibley*     49
   *Seth Green*     52
   *Daniel Powers*     55
   *Frank Gannett*     58
   *Al Neuharth*     67

*CHAPTER 3—COMPOSERS / AUTHORS /*
       *EDUCATORS*     75

   *Alec Wilder*     75
   *Howard Hanson*     86
   *Lewis Henry Morgan*     90
   *Garson Kanin*     93
   *Rush Rhees*     95

*Page No.*

*CHAPTER 4—HUMANITARIANS /
        INDUSTRIALISTS*                107

   *George Eastman*                107
   *Henry Alvah Strong*            113
   *John Jacob Bausch / Henry Lomb*  116
   *Thomas J. Watson*              120
   *Joseph C. Wilson*              124

*CHAPTER 5—ENGINEERS / ENTREPRENEURS*    129

   *Elisha Johnson*                129
   *George B. Selden*              132
   *James Cunningham*              134
   *Kate Gleason*                  142
   *Chester Carlson*               149

*CHAPTER 6—SPORTSMEN / NOTABLES*         151

   *Walter Hagen*                  151
   *Cab Calloway*                  157
   *William Warfield*              163
   *George Ellwanger / Patrick Barry*  172
   *Maj. Gen. Elwell Otis*         177

*CHAPTER 7—THINKERS / POLITICIANS*       181

   *Marion Folsom*                 181
   *George Aldridge*               185
   *James Cutler*                  191
   *Hiram Edgerton*                195
   *Kenneth Keating*               198

*CHAPTER 8—ECCENTRICS / ARCHITECTS*      203

   *William Morgan*                203
   *Margaret Fox / Kate Fox*       206
   *"Red Emma" Goldman*            218
   *Claude Bragdon*                221
   *A. J. Warner / J. Foster Warner*  229

*Page No.*

**CHAPTER 9—RELIGIOUS LEADERS /
ECCLESIASTICS**     235

*Charles Grandison Finney*     235
*Brigham Young*     239
*Reverend Algernon Crapsey*     248
*Bishop Bernard McQuaid*     251
*Bishop Fulton J. Sheen*     254

**CHAPTER 10—ROCHESTER STORIES**     263

*The Statue of Mercury on the Rochester Skyline*     263
*Buffalo Bill's Rochester Connection*     265
*Sam Patch's Last Jump*     268
*Rattlesnake Pete's Cure for Goiters*     270
*The First McCormick Harvester*     271
*The Society of the Genesee*     272
*The Rochester Subway*     275
*Rochester's NBA Team—The Rochester Royals*     278
*Rochester, "Smugtown, U.S.A."*     281
*Rochester, the Friendliest City*     284
*Rochester's Ties to Hollywood*     286
*How Xerox Invented the Personal Computer
but Failed to Exploit It*     288

**EPILOGUE: ROCHESTER IN THE
TWENTY-FIRST CENTURY**     297

**BIBLIOGRAPHY**     301

**INDEX**     307

# PROLOGUE

"Rochester was never a prototypical company town, although its successive nicknames derive from whatever industry was dominant at a given time. 'The Flour City' of the early nineteenth century reflected the mills on the Genesee; after midcentury the more decorous 'Flower City' was attached, in deference to the growing nursery trade. By the early 1900s, it was definitely 'Kodak City' remaining to the present. Eastman's lifelong love affair with Rochester ... is unique in the annals of American communities. In few other places has a man, a company, and a city been so closely identified."        Elizabeth Brayer, *George Eastman: A Biography*

### Rochester—Western Gateway to the Finger Lakes Region
Rochester is located in Monroe County, south of Lake Ontario, where the Genesee River empties into the Lake. The County is one of fourteen counties of the Finger Lakes Region. The City extends along the lower Genesee River to the Port of Rochester on Lake Ontario. Rochester has three exits from the New York State Thruway, Exits 45, 46, and 47, and an inner loop and an outer loop of expressways that encircle the city.

The City of Rochester has a population of 220,000, according to the 2000 census; the twenty Monroe County suburban towns have 515,000 people, for a total Monroe County population of 735,000. The five-county Greater Rochester Region has a population of over one million.

Rochester, in the nineteenth century called the "Flour City" because of its flour mills at the waterfalls on the Genesee River, became known as the "Flower City" because of the nurseries—the largest in the United States at the time—of George Ellwanger and Patrick Barry, James Vick, and Hiram Sibley, which provided trees, bushes, seedlings, and seeds to worldwide markets.

Contemporary Rochester is called the "World Image Center" because it is home to the University of Rochester's Institute of Optics, Rochester Institute of Technology's College of Imaging Arts and Sciences, and over ninety imaging and optics firms, including Bausch & Lomb, Eastman Kodak, and Xerox.

The imaging industry employs almost 100,000 people in the Rochester region; half of U.S. workers who manufacture photographic equipment and supplies work in the area. Downsizings of major corporations have been more than offset by the growth of small and medium-sized companies, particularly high tech firms, in most years.

In a recent year, residents of Rochester were granted more U.S. patents than any other city except San Jose, California. Also, the City was ranked fourth in the world for its "knowledge-based economy" behind San Francisco, Austin-San Marcos, and Boston, according to the *World Knowledge Competitive Index* published by Robert Huggins Associates of the United Kingdom.

Rochester, a technologically progressive city with conservative social values known for the philanthropy of its citizens, has always been considered a good place to raise a family. A high percentage of its residents own their homes. In recent years, the Greater Rochester Visitors Association has promoted Rochester as "Made for Living."

Rochester has excellent medical facilities and ranks high nationally in health care. Area colleges include Monroe Community College, Nazareth College of Rochester, Roberts Wesleyan College, Rochester Institute of Technology, St. John Fisher College, State University of New York—College at Brockport, State University of New York—Empire State College, and the University of Rochester. The State University of New York—College at Geneseo is a half hour south of Rochester by expressway.

Monroe County has an outstanding park system. Including village, town, city, county, and state parks, the County has over 120 parks. Rochester has a nationally ranked symphony orchestra, the Rochester Philharmonic Orchestra, and the top-ranked Eastman School of Music of the University of Rochester. The Eastman School has many concerts, either free or at nominal cost, during the week in the Eastman Theatre and adjoining Kilbourn Hall. Rochester is also the home of GeVa Theater, a superb regional theater, and the highly regarded Garth Fagan Dance Company.

Rochester has a wealth of museums, including the International Museum of Photography at George Eastman House, the Memorial Art Gallery, Rochester Museum and Science Center, Strasenburgh

Planetarium, Strong Museum, and the Genesee Country Museum twenty miles southwest of the City. Rochester's festivals with more than a regional reputation include the Lilac Festival, the Corn Hill Arts Festival, the Memorial Art Gallery's Clothesline Art Festival, and the Park Avenue Summer Arts Festival. Also, Rochester has become a literary center with scores of local authors, and the City is known for its jazz festivals and movie festivals.

Rochester is home to the American Hockey League Rochester Americans, the International League Rochester Red Wings Triple-A baseball team, the Rochester Rhinos A-league soccer team, and the Knighthawks National Lacrosse League team. Oak Hill Country Club is a venue for national golf events such as the U.S. Open, the U.S. Senior Open, and the PGA Tournament.

The Buffalo Bills National Football League team conducts their preseason practices at athletic facilities at St. John Fisher College. In 2003, Rochesterian Tom Galisano, owner of the Buffalo Sabres National Hockey League Team, arranged for the first NHL game played in Rochester.

Rochester has the inherent advantages of a mid-sized city. It is large enough to offer a wide variety of events and activities, but small enough not to have traffic problems. Also, real estate values are considerably lower than the national average.

San Antonio, Texas, transformed a sleepy river flowing through town into Riverwalk, a premier tourist attraction. How many cities have, as Rochester does, three waterfalls on the river flowing through it, particularly on a river that flows north?

Rochester has a beautiful setting on a Great Lake; scenic beauty in the city, county, and region; enlightened high-tech organizations; and vital, civic-minded people. Rochester can fail to prosper and move forward only if comprehensive plans—that are in place—fail to be executed.

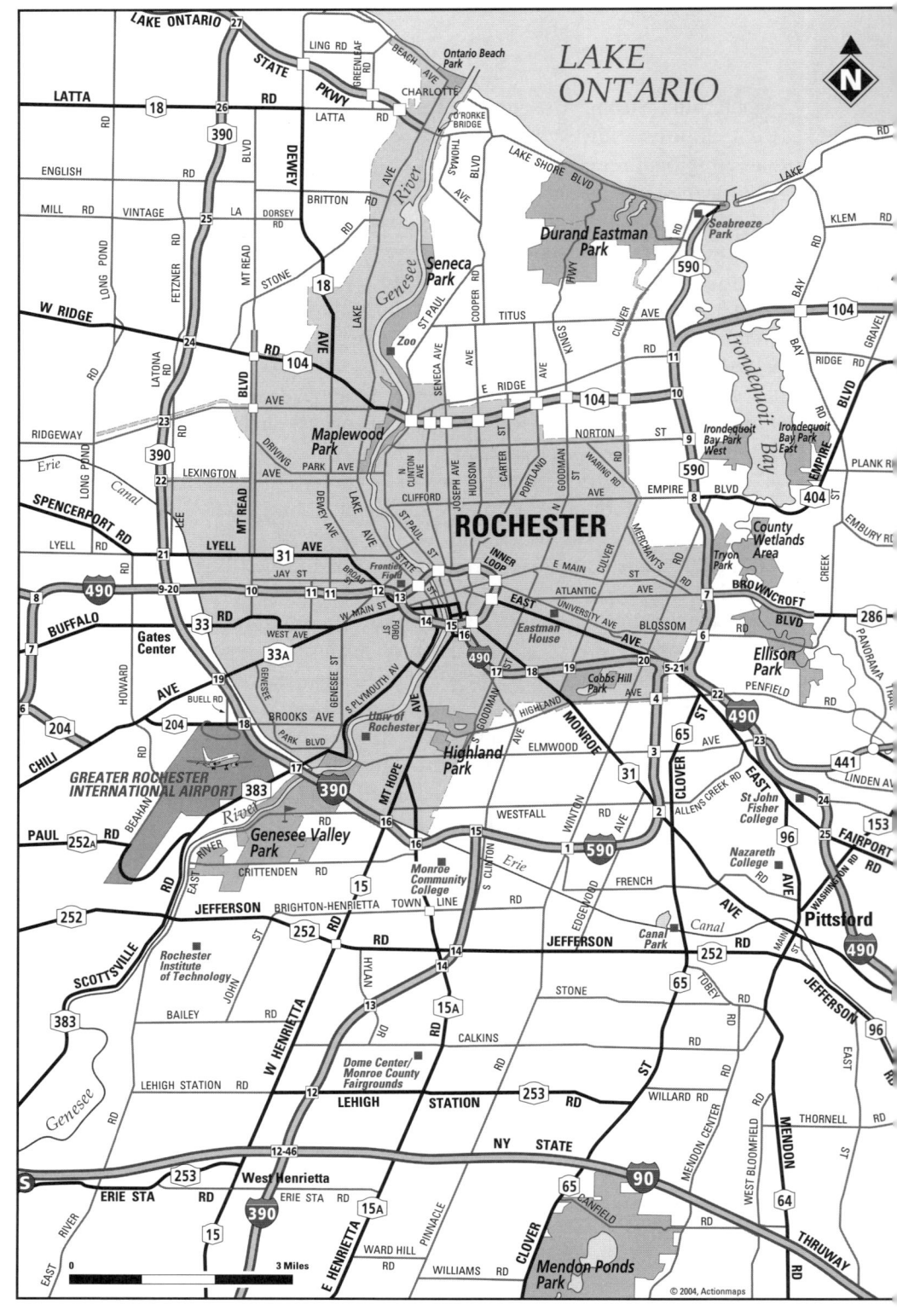

# *INTRODUCTION*

"It is interesting to see how pioneers finally settled on the Genesee falls as the proper site for a mill town; how the villagers there read-justed to the fact that it was becoming a city; how the Flour City gave way to the Flower City, and that, in turn, to a cosmopolitan city; how the emphasis on good government evolved; how Rochesterians responded to two World Wars and the Great Depression, as well as to new metropolitan problems; and, finally, how the present generation is handling its new diversity and its expanding regional and international horizons....

The successive waves of ethnic newcomers ... constituted a chal-lenging diversity to the generation of their arrival.... The strategy of their adjustments and the nature of their contributions differed, but both benefitted from the restless mobility that characterized Rochester's inhabitants both native and foreign-born as they moved in and out in search of fresh opportunities. The City's economic and technological shifts contributed to this mobility and fostered appro-priate social and cultural institutions."                    Blake McKelvey,
*Rochester on the Genesee: Growth of a City*

## *Overview of Rochester's Early History*
Ebenezer "Indian" Allan, who settled near Scottsville in 1786, was the first settler in Monroe County. Oliver Phelps, land agent for the Phelps-Gorham Purchase, promised Native Americans that he would build a gristmill and a sawmill at one of the falls on the Genesee River. He offered Allan 100 acres to fulfill that pledge. The mills were operating by November 1789, just west of the pre-sent location of Court Street Bridge.

Among the next settlers were Israel and Simon Stone, who cleared land in Pittsford, sowed wheat, and convinced five families of their old neighbors from New England to join them in 1791. Orringh Stone built a home and tavern, the Stone-Tolan House, on East Avenue about 1790.

Indian Allan sold his 100-acre tract in 1792, and his mills fell into disrepair. One mill was carried away in a flood. In 1803, three men from Maryland bought the Allan property. Nathaniel Rochester and his partners, Charles Carroll and William Fitzhugh, had a profound influence on an evolving Rochester. Hamlet Scrantom, from Lewis County, was the first settler on Colonel Rochester's 100-acre tract.

Rochester petitioned the State to incorporate the settlement as a county in 1817. The State Legislature rejected the petition, but granted a charter for the Village of Rochesterville. Finally, Monroe County, named for President James Monroe, was formed on February 23, 1821.

Rochester's second gristmill was built at Middle Falls in 1807. It burned down in 1818, and the Phoenix Mill, one of the large flour mills that contributed to Rochester's reputation as the "Flour City," was built on its foundation.

Excavation for the Erie Canal began near Rome, New York, in 1817. The Canal reached Bushnell's Basin by 1821, and that village served as the temporary western terminus until 1823. The Canal was finished in 1825 when the complex, multilevel locks at Lockport were completed. An 802-foot-long aqueduct carried the Erie Canal over the Genesee River at Broad Street. The completion of the Erie Canal made Rochester, which had an 1825 population of 5,000, the first inland boomtown in the United States. Wheat flour was one of the principal Rochester area products shipped via the Erie Canal; corn was another. Rochester shipped 200,000 barrels of flour in 1826.

In 1834, Rochester, with a population of 12,000, received its city charter from the State Legislature. Laying of railroad track was completed between Rochester and Batavia in 1837, and by 1842 it was possible to cross the State by rail. Ultimately, twenty-one flour mills along the Genesee River ground 500,000 barrels of flour each year. The first Rochester nursery and seed farm, Mt. Hope Nurseries, was established in 1839 by George Ellwanger, who was joined by partner Patrick Barry in 1840.

In 1850, Rochester was the fourth largest city in the State with a population of 51,000. By the 1850s, over 4,000 acres of land in the suburbs had been planted with flowers, shrubs, and trees. The area supplied almost half of the U.S. commercially produced trees in the 1870s and 1880s.

Susan B. Anthony began her participation in the Women's

Rights Movement in 1851; she was arrested for voting in the 1872 presidential election, decades before women won the right to vote. Frederick Douglass, editor of the abolitionist newspaper *North Star* and leader in the antislavery movement and the underground railroad, lived in Rochester from 1847 to 1872. Clothing and shoe manufacturing moved into the area, and Cyrus McCormick's reapers, manufactured in Brockport, revolutionized the agriculture industry in the late 1800s.

John Jacob Bausch and Henry Lomb began their partnership in the Reynolds Arcade, where Hiram Sibley planned the combination of many small, competing telegraph companies to form the Western Union. In 1878, George Eastman, a young bank clerk, founded the Eastman Dry Plate Company, which was the predecessor of the Eastman Kodak Company. The Haloid Company was founded in 1906 and expanded rapidly once office copiers were introduced in volume in the early 1960s. It became the Xerox Corporation in 1961. One of the fastest growing Rochester companies in the 1970s through 1990s was Paychex, Inc., founded by Thomas Galisano.

### The Burned-over District
The Burned-over District was the name applied to western New York State from the Adirondacks to Lake Erie during the first half of the nineteenth century. The name "Burned-over District," which refers to an area that experienced a large number of religious revivals, was given to the region by Charles Grandison Finney, the most dynamic evangelist of his day. In his book, *Listen for a Lonesome Drum*, Carl Carmer views it as a "Spirit Way":

> Across the entire breadth of York State, undeviatingly, a hilly strip scarcely twenty-five miles wide invites the world's wonder. It is a broad psychic highway, a thoroughfare of the occult whose great stations number the mystic seven. For where, in its rolling course from east of Albany to west of Buffalo, it has reached one of seven isolated and lonely heights, voices out of other worlds have spoken with spiritual authority to men and women, and the invisible mantles of the prophets have been laid on consecrated shoulders.

In no other area of the Western Hemisphere have so many evidences of an existence transcending mortal living been manifest. It is impossible to reckon the number of listeners who on the plateaus of this strange midstate adventure have knelt before seen or unseen supernatural visitants to hear counsel. And the sum of those whose lives have been affected by that counsel, save for the fact that it is in the millions, is incalculable.

Five of the seven instances referred to by Carmer involved the Finger Lakes Region: Jemima Wilkinson, the Publick Universal Friend, and her community at Jerusalem, near Branchport; Margaret and Kate Fox and their experiences with Spiritualism at Hydesville, near Newark; founding of the Mormon religion at Palmyra by Joseph Smith; Mother Ann Lee and the Shakers near Albany, who had settlements at Sodus and Groveland in the Finger Lakes Region; and William Miller, who made predictions of the end of the world, and the Millerites (Rochester was their western outpost). The other two of the "mystic seven" were the Oneida Community of John Humphrey Noyes near Utica and the Thomas Harris commune at Brocton on the shores of Lake Erie near Dunkirk.

In addition to these instances, the Finger Lakes Region was the center of the anti-Masonic movement between 1826 and 1850. It was a hotbed of both the abolitionist and temperance movements, and, most notably, it was the center of the Women's Rights Movement in the United States. In order to understand why this agricultural lake country encountered such restlessness, it is necessary to look at the settlers of the region, where they came from, and the religious background that they brought with them.

Settlement in the Finger Lakes Region began in the late 1780s and was dominated by Yankees from New England. Other settlers came up the Susquehanna River from Pennsylvania. Many New Englanders had settled first in eastern New York counties, and then pulled up stakes and resettled in lake country. Few pioneers came from Boston or the fertile Connecticut River Valley; however, many came from the hill country of New Hampshire and Vermont and from other areas of Connecticut.

Many settlers from New England were Baptists, Congregationalists, and Methodists. Presbyterians and one branch of Congregationalists merged in 1801 in the Plan of Union. All major denominations, except Episcopalians, were revivalistic. Baptists and Methodists were more emotional and easier for common people to understand than Presbyterians. From 1815 to 1818, eighty revivals occurred in the Burned-over District.

In 1823, when the Erie Canal from Rochester to Albany was opened, the cost of shipping a barrel of flour between those cities dropped from $3.00 to $.75. The Canal's completion in 1825 brought significant economic changes to the region. Population growth was phenomenal in the 1820s: Albany grew by 96 percent, Buffalo by 314 percent, Rochester by 512 percent, Syracuse by 282 percent, and Utica by 183 percent.

An increase in religious revivals in 1826 was credited to the influence of Charles Grandison Finney, a truly motivational speaker. This increase in activity continued through 1837. Growth in church congregations came with the growth in population.

In 1831, Finney came to Rochester for a revival that was one of the largest until that time. The three Presbyterian churches did not get along, but they pulled together to bring Finney to Rochester. Church membership boomed. The next peak in revivalism came in 1837, a year of recession. Interest in the church always increased in bad times.

The Fox sisters were the most notable examples of Spiritualists in the Burned-over District. The region had more mediums in 1859 than any other area in the United States. Leah, the oldest Fox sister, lived in Rochester. Her spiritualist sisters, Margaret and Kate, stayed with her when they gave a demonstration in Corinthian Hall of their communications with the dead.

The unique religious fervor of the region burned itself out over the last half of the nineteenth century. However, some of the legacies of the Burned-over District survived into the twentieth century and beyond: the Mormon Church; several Adventist denominations, including the Seventh-Day Adventists; two species of Methodism, including the Free Methodists; and some Spiritualist groups. The American tradition was enriched by these legacies, which formed a pathway to modern ideas about religion.

## SONNET

*Could I a beauty-sketching pencil wield*

*With all the witchery and magic skill*

*Of Gilbert's fingers I'd a picture fill*

*With beauties of fair Rochester. What field*

*Of Art could purer fascination yield?*

*I'd paint the "Flower City" growing still*

*From early germ near "Indian Allan's mill."*

*The plant was set by men of whose faith revealed*

*The trend of civic progress to their view.*

*They had persistent faith to work and wait;*

*They nurtured well, aye, better than they knew—*

*A wildwood region by auspicious fate*

*From "Flour" to "Flower" and then ... grew—*

*The pride and glory of New York State.*

*Helen E. Lucas*

# CHAPTER 1

# REFORMERS / PIONEERS

## Nathaniel Rochester (1752-1831)

"All three settlements [Bath, Painted Post, and Geneva] were thriving villages by 1800, with bustling inns and provisioning shops, ready to accommodate migrating settlers and speculators while they negotiated for suitable plots. It was to these towns that [Nathaniel] Rochester, [William] Fitzhugh, and [Charles] Carroll, three gentlemen from Maryland, resorted in 1800 and again in 1803, when they journeyed north to seek promising investments. Like many others, they were prospecting visits, and each made deposits on sizable tracts up the valley, but before their return to Maryland from their second journey, a [Charles] Williamson agent in Geneva persuaded them to examine the mill site at the upper falls of the Genesee. After riding on horseback through the forest, they forded the river below the small falls and found the gristmill idle and the sawmill in ruins. Nevertheless, the situation appeared ideal for a mill town, and they agreed to purchase the 100-acre tract at $17.50 an acre."

Blake McKelvey,
*Rochester on the Genesee: Growth of a City*

Nathaniel Rochester, second oldest son of John and Hester Thrift Rochester, was born on February 21, 1752, in Westmoreland County, Virginia. At the age of sixteen, he was employed by James Monroe, a Scottish merchant, at Hillsborough, North Carolina. In 1773, Rochester joined a partnership with his employer and Col. John Hamilton that was dissolved two years later at the beginning of the Revolutionary War.

In 1775, Rochester was appointed a member of the Committee of Safety of Orange County, which collected money for the coming conflict, prevented the sale and consumption of British tea from East India, and procured arms and ammunition. Later that year, he attended the first Provincial Convention in North Carolina, which ordered the enlistment of four regiments of Continental troops and organized the minutemen and militia systems. He was appointed a justice of the peace, major of militia, and paymaster.

In February 1776, Rochester commanded two companies of infantry and one company of cavalry in a successful effort to prevent British General Alexander McDonald, who had raised a regiment of 1,000 Scottish settlers in North Carolina, from reaching the port of Wilmington and transporting them to New York. At the second Provincial Convention in 1776, Rochester was appointed Commissary General of Stores and Clothing for the North Carolina line of ten regiments, with the rank of colonel. Unfortunately, he became ill at Wilmington and left the army.

In 1777, Rochester was elected a member of the North Carolina Assembly, which appointed him lieutenant colonel of militia and Clerk of the Court of Orange County. Later that year, he was selected to establish and manage an arms factory at Hillsborough. He resigned from the Clerk's office and was appointed an auditor of public accounts for the State and a colonel of militia.

In 1778, Rochester went into business with Col. Thomas Hart, who was Henry Clay's father-in-law. Hart purchased a large estate in Hagerstown, Maryland; Rochester moved there to manage it. In 1784, Hart and Rochester purchased wheat, operated a large flour mill, and sold flour. They also owned and ran nail and rope factories. In 1792, the partnership was dissolved, and Hart and Rochester ran separate businesses.

Rochester married in 1788 and became a member of the Maryland Legislature two years later. From 1791 until 1797, he was Postmaster of Hagerstown, a position that he resigned to become a judge of the Washington County court. He was a judge for one year and subsequently was reappointed Postmaster and later County Sheriff for three years. In 1807, he became the first president of the Hagerstown Bank and in the following year was appointed an Elector of the President and Vice President of the United States when James Madison was elected President.

In September 1800, with his friends Major Charles Carroll and Colonel William Fitzhugh, Rochester visited the Genesee Country of western New York for the first time. Carroll and Fitzhugh purchased 12,000 acres of land; Rochester bought an adjoining 400 acres in addition to 155 acres at Dansville.

In 1803, Carroll, Fitzhugh, and Rochester returned to Genesee

Country and visited the abandoned mills of Ebenezer "Indian" Allan at the falls on the Genesee River. Allan had constructed a gristmill and a sawmill as part an agreement with the region's prior purchasers, Oliver Phelps and Nathaniel Gorham of the Phelps-Gorham Purchase, who had promised to build a gristmill and a sawmill for the Native Americans if they would sell them a twelve-by twenty-four-mile parcel of land along the Genesee River.

Allan was given 100 acres for building the mills, but he was not an individual who stayed with an endeavor for long. The Marylanders purchased the Indian Allan plot, which later became part of Rochesterville. Rochester also purchased an additional 200 acres adjacent to his original 400 acres.

Rochester saw the potential of the site immediately. His flour milling experience in Maryland spurred his vision. He viewed the site as the nucleus for a commercial center. During the nineteenth century, the Genesee region was the wheat-growing capital of the country, and Rochester became known as the "Flour City."

In May 1810, Rochester settled his manufacturing, mercantile, and sheriff's business in Maryland and moved to Dansville. He constructed a large paper mill and increased his property holdings to more than 700 acres. In 1814, he purchased a 445-acre farm in Bloomfield, Ontario County, and moved there. In 1816, he was appointed an Elector of the President and Vice President of the United States when James Monroe was elected President. While residing in Bloomfield, he was appointed a director of the Utica Bank branch at Canandaigua.

During the winter of 1817, Rochester went to Albany as an agent for petitioners for a new county to be split off from Ontario County. He was unsuccessful in this first attempt. In April 1818, he rented out his farm and moved to Rochester. In 1821, he was successful in his second attempt in getting a law passed to create the County of Monroe. He was appointed Clerk of the County and was elected a member of the State Assembly from Monroe County. In 1824, he became a commissioner of the Bank of Rochester and was elected president of the Bank later that year.

Construction of the Erie Canal from the Hudson River to Lake Erie put the Village of Rochester on the map. Nathaniel Rochester worked with the Canal Commission and the State Legislature to ensure that the Canal passed through Rochester. He had to deal with appeals of the citizens of Canandaigua to have the Canal routed through the "Grande Dame" of the Finger Lakes Region. When construction of the Canal started in 1817 at Rome, Rochester was a newly incorporated village with 800 inhabitants. The Canal reached Rochester in 1823 and was completed in 1825.

By 1825, Rochester was a boom town with a population of 5,000. Nathaniel Hawthorne captured the flourishing atmosphere when he wrote: "It is possible to look at [Rochester's] worn pavements and conceive how recently the forest leaves have been swept away.... The whole street, sidewalks and centre, was crowded with pedestrians, horsemen, stagecoaches, gigs, light wagons and heavy ox-teams, all hurrying, trotting, rattling, and rumbling, in a throng that passed continually, but never passed away."

The aqueduct over the Genesee River, with the longest stone bridge in the country, was considered an engineering marvel. It was 802 feet long and was supported by nine fifty-foot Roman arches. (It now supports the Broad Street bridge). In 1825, Nathaniel Rochester was one of the dignitaries who gathered to commemorate the joining of Lake Erie and the Atlantic Ocean. On October 27, 1825, the festivities began in Buffalo and continued with Governor DeWitt Clinton and his entourage traveling the entire 364-mile length of his "ditch" to Albany and then on to New York City. On November 4, two casks of Lake Erie water were poured into the Atlantic Ocean in a "wedding of the waters" ceremony.

Nathaniel Rochester died in 1831, three years before the Village of Rochester with a population of 12,000 was incorporated as a city. Nevertheless, Rochester lived to see his village experience explosive growth and to realize that his vision in selecting Rochester as a flour milling site was justified. Ultimately, twenty-one flour mills along the Genesee River ground 500,000 barrels of flour each year. Rochester was the country's flour milling center from the mid- to the late-1800s, when wheat-growing and milling shifted to the Midwest with its large, flat, open spaces.

## Susan B. Anthony (1820-1906)

"Cautious, careful people, always casting about to preserve their reputation and social standing, never can bring about a reform. Those who are really in earnest must be willing to be anything or nothing in the world's estimation, and publicly and privately, in season and out, avow their sympathy with despised and persecuted ideas and their advocates, and bear the consequences."

Susan B. Anthony

In 1848, Susan B. Anthony's father, Daniel Anthony, moved from Massachusetts to Rochester, where he became a successful farmer and insurance salesman. Two weeks after the first Women's Rights Convention on July 19 and 20, 1848, in Seneca Falls, which was organized by Elizabeth Cady Stanton and Lucretia Mott, another convention was held in Rochester.

Anthony was working in Canajoharie as girls' headmistress of Canajoharie Academy and did not attend the convention. Her father, mother, and sister did; they signed petitions in support of the resolutions. When Anthony heard that they had attended the convention and agreed with the sentiments, she wrote that, in her opinion, they were getting ahead of the times.

Within two years, Anthony was not only informed on the subject of women's rights, but she had discussed the subject with the abolitionists Frederick Douglass and William Lloyd Garrison who were convinced that the women's rights cause should be advanced. Anthony's interest in the movement was sparked by meeting Elizabeth Cady Stanton in Seneca Falls after an antislavery meeting at which Garrison and the English abolitionist, George Thompson, spoke. It was the beginning of a friendship and a working relationship that lasted over a half century. Anthony's attention to detail and organizational skills were a perfect match with Cady Stanton's strengths as a philosopher and policymaker.

Initially, Anthony supported three causes. Her personal priorities were first, temperance; second, abolition; and third, women's rights. Cady Stanton supported all liberal causes of the time, but concentrated upon women's rights and, in particular, women's right to vote.

Susan B. Anthony House, Madison Street

Anthony was made painfully aware of the role of women at a Sons of Temperance convention in Albany. She thought that she was a member of the convention until she attempted to make a motion and was told by the chairman: "Sisters were invited here not to speak, but to listen and learn." That incident motivated her to organize the Women's State Temperance Society in 1852 in Rochester. Cady Stanton was elected president of the society, and Anthony was elected secretary—a pattern that was repeated over the years.

Anthony attended her first Women's Rights Convention in 1852; it was the third National Women's Rights Convention. Cady Stanton did not attend because she was at home awaiting the birth of her fifth child. However, she sent a letter to be read by Anthony at the convention. Two thousand delegates attended, including Lucretia Mott, James Mott, and Lucy Stone from New England, another of the movement's leaders.

The working relationship between Anthony and Cady Stanton was displayed by their respective roles in preparing for a speech that Cady Stanton gave to the New York State Legislature in February 1854. She addressed the right of women to earn and keep their own wages and their right to own property in their own names.

Cady Stanton was willing to give the speech; however, with her large, young family, she did not have time to prepare it. She sent a plea for help to Anthony, and an agreement was reached. Susan and a lawyer friend sympathetic to their cause would do the necessary research of the discriminating laws and would assemble the information, if Cady Stanton would prepare and present the speech.

The speech at Albany was well-received. Cady Stanton provided specific examples of ways in which women were discriminated against and means by which the law could be changed to address the discrimination. Anthony was well-prepared; she obtained 6,000 signatures on petitions for women's property and wage reform as well as 4,000 signatures on a petition in support of women's right to vote. Changes to women's property and wage reform would not come for another six years in New York. Nevertheless, Anthony and Cady Stanton knew that they had contributed significantly to this reform.

Cady Stanton described her perception of their working relationship:

Statue of Frederick Douglass and Susan B. Anthony at Tea, Madison St.

> In thought and sympathy we were one, and in the
> division of labor we exactly complemented each
> other. In writing, we did better work together than
> either of us could have done alone. I am the better
> writer, she the better critic. She supplied the facts
> and statistics, I the philosophy and rhetoric, and
> together we have made arguments that have stood
> unshaken through the storms of thirty long years....
> Our speeches may be considered the united prod-
> uct of two brains.

Anthony visited Seneca Falls frequently to take care of the Stanton children so that Cady Stanton could prepare a speech or present one. The children loved "Aunt Susan," even though she was a stricter disciplinarian than their mother.

Anthony and Cady Stanton differed on priorities during the Civil War. Cady Stanton wanted to concentrate on antislavery issues, and Anthony wanted to support both women's rights and abolitionism. Cady Stanton won, but she admitted later that Anthony had been right because the War delayed for four years activity to force women's rights reforms.

An example of Anthony's quick thinking was her exchange of words with Horace Greeley, editor of the New York *Tribune*. Greeley asked, "Miss Anthony, you are aware that the ballot and the bullet go together. If you vote, are you also prepared to fight?" Susan replied, "Certainly, Mr. Greeley, just as you fought the last war—at the point of a goose-quill."

As stated in the Fifteenth Amendment to the Constitution adopted in 1870, "The right of citizens of the United States to vote shall not be denied ... on account of race, color, or previous condition of servitude." Suffragettes wanted the phrase "or sex" in the Fifteenth Amendment. However, the phrase was not there, so women began to test the interpretation of their rights as citizens. Anthony was not the first woman to test this interpretation of the Fourteenth and Fifteenth Amendments, but she certainly received more newspaper coverage than any other woman.

On November 1, 1872, Anthony and her sisters Guelma, Hannah, and Mary decided to register to vote. The election judges told them that, according to New York State law, they would not be permitted to register. Anthony quoted to them from the Amendments to the Constitution and insisted that she, as a citizen, had a right to vote. They were permitted to register. Anthony and her sisters voted in the general election on November 5. She received wide newspaper coverage, including articles in the Chicago *Tribune* and the New York *Times*. She realized that she might have broken the law and might be liable for a $500 fine. On November 18, a U.S. Marshal came to Anthony's home and arrested her.

Anthony and her sisters were arraigned and their bond set at $500. Her sisters posted the $500 bail, but Anthony refused to pay it. Her lawyer, Henry Selden, who did not want to see his client go to jail, paid her bail. Unfortunately, by doing so, he had inadvertently prevented her from appealing to higher courts—potentially as far as the Supreme Court. Posting bail indicated that she was not contesting the lawfulness of her arrest. Anthony made many speeches describing what was happening to her, including speeches in Monroe County, where her case was to be tried. Because of this, the trial was moved to Ontario County, south of Rochester.

On June 17, 1873, Anthony's trial began in Canandaigua, county seat of Ontario County. Judge Ward Hunt, an inexperienced judge who had recently been appointed to the bench, was selected to try her case. Selden conducted a skillful defense, pointing out that Anthony sincerely believed that she had been given the right to vote by the Fourteenth and Fifteenth Amendments. Judge Hunt refused to let Anthony speak in her own defense.

Judge Hunt stated that it did not matter what Anthony's beliefs were; she had broken the law. He took a note from his pocket, turned toward the jury, and read from it. It concluded with the statement, "If I am right in this, the result must be a verdict ... of guilty, and I therefore direct that you find a verdict of guilty." An incensed Selden reminded the judge that he did not have the right to instruct the jury in that way and demanded that the jury be asked for their verdict. Judge Hunt ignored Selden, instructed the court clerk to record the verdict, and dismissed the jury.

This poor example of justice was widely covered by the press. People who disagreed with Anthony's voting sided with her because of this unfair treatment in the courtroom. Judge Hunt's actions were politically motivated. His mentor was Roscoe Conkling, U.S. Senator from New York and a professed foe of the Women's Rights Movement. Selden requested a new trial on the basis that Anthony had been denied a fair trial by jury. Judge Hunt denied the request and stated her sentence—a $100 fine. Anthony responded, "I shall never pay a dollar of your unjust penalty." Ultimately, the fine was dropped.

In 1880, Anthony and Cady Stanton began their monumental project, *A History of Woman Suffrage*. Cady Stanton wrote most of the first two volumes; Anthony verified the facts and assembled the material. Anthony had a major role in preparing the third volume because Cady Stanton was in England visiting her daughter. The last two volumes, edited by Ida Husted Harper, trace the history of the movement through 1920. Harper was also Anthony's biographer; her *Life and Work of Susan B. Anthony* was published in 1898.

Anthony never retired from her lifelong efforts to promote women's rights. The International Woman Suffrage Alliance was formed in 1904, and Anthony, at the age of eighty-four, was recognized as its leader. At their convention in 1906, she commanded the delegates: "The fight must not stop. You must see that it does not stop." At a dinner in her honor in Washington, D. C., she concluded her comments by stating, "Failure is impossible." Susan B. Anthony died in 1906. She was buried in the Anthony family plot in Mt. Hope Cemetery.

In 1920, the Nineteenth Amendment to the Constitution was ratified. It included the statement: "The right of citizens of the United States to vote shall not be denied or abridged by the United States or by any state on account of sex." It was called the "Susan B. Anthony Amendment." Anthony was right. Failure was impossible. In 1976, she was honored further when the United States government minted the Susan B. Anthony dollar.

Statue of Frederick Douglass, Highland Park

## *Frederick Douglass (1818-1895)*

"It rekindled a few expiring embers of freedom and revived within me a sense of my own manhood. It recalled the departed self-confidence and inspired me again with a sense of determination to be free.... He can only understand the deep satisfaction which I experienced, who has himself repelled by force the bloody arm of slavery. I felt as I never felt before. It was a glorious resurrection, from the tomb of slavery to the heart of freedom. My long-crushed spirit rose, cowardice departed, bold defiance took its place, and I now resolved that, however long I might remain a slave in form, the day had passed forever when I could be a slave in fact."

Frederick Douglass, after winning a fight with an overseer

Frederick Bailey was born in February 1818 in Talbot County on the Eastern Shore of Maryland; he was not sure of the actual date of his birth. His mother, Harriet Bailey, was a slave and his father, whom he never met, was a white man. His master was Captain Aaron Anthony. In March 1826, Frederick was sent to live with a member of Anthony's family, Hugh Auld, in Baltimore. Initially, Auld's wife, Sophia, was kind to Frederick and helped him learn to read and write; she did so willingly until her husband heard what she was doing. Then the lessons stopped, and Sophia was no longer friendly to him. However, living in Baltimore was a good experience for Frederick; he had many opportunities to learn.

Thomas Auld, Frederick's legal owner, brought him back to rural slavery in 1833. Frederick did not like Auld or his wife, Rowena. He was not completely obedient so Auld hired him out to Edward Covey, who had a reputation as a "slave breaker." Frederick endured six months of flogging and mistreatment, and then turned on Covey in a two-hour fight that Frederick won. After that, Covey did not bother him, but Frederick was even more committed to obtaining his freedom. In his spare time, he gave his fellow slaves reading lessons.

In April 1836, Frederick and five other slaves made plans to escape. Unfortunately, one of them told authorities of their plans, and they were jailed in Easton. Instead of selling Frederick, Thomas Auld sent him back to Hugh and Sophia in Baltimore.

Frederick became an experienced caulker in a boatyard, where slaves competed with poor white immigrants for jobs. He was severely beaten because he was perceived to have taken a job from a white immigrant.

Frederick continued his self-education with membership in the East Baltimore Mental Improvement Society, a debating club. He met Anna Murray, a freed slave, at one of their meetings. They became engaged in 1838, saved their money, and made plans for escape to the North. An argument with Hugh Auld motivated Douglass to board a northbound train and escape. The conductor asked to see his free slave papers, which he did not have; Frederick showed him seamen's papers instead. Despite some tense moments when he saw two local men who could identify him as a slave, he arrived in Philadelphia safely and continued on to New York City.

Frederick stayed with David Ruggles, publisher of the anti-slavery quarterly, *The Mirror of Slavery*. He sent for Anna Murray, and they were married on September 15, 1838. Ruggles, who was active in the Underground Railroad, suggested to Frederick and Anna that they move farther north.

They went to New Bedford, Massachusetts, where Frederick hoped to find work as a caulker in a shipyard. They lived with Nathan Johnson and his wife. Johnson suggested that since Frederick was an escaped slave who might be pursued, he should change his name. Johnson had just finished reading Sir Walter Scott's *Lady of the Lake*; he suggested the surname of "Douglass," based on the name of the Scottish lord and hero. Frederick Bailey became Frederick Douglass.

When Douglass looked for work as a caulker, he found that prejudice existed in the North as well as the South. White caulkers did not want to work with African Americans. He was forced to take odd jobs as a common laborer. Anna helped by doing domestic work. One day he found a copy of William Lloyd Garrison's antislavery newspaper, *The Liberator*, and it changed his life. Garrison was a strong-willed abolitionist who had helped to found the New England Anti-Slavery Society.

Douglass attended the annual meeting of the New England Anti-Slavery Society in New Bedford on August 9, 1841, and a meeting the next day on the Island of Nantucket. Called upon to speak, Douglass was nervous as he described his life as a slave;

however, he was well-received and was asked to become a full-time lecturer for the organization. He reluctantly accepted a three-month assignment and stayed for four years, improving his speech delivery techniques and becoming a popular lecturer.

The life of an abolitionist was not easy. Douglass had to learn to overcome hecklers. On September 15, 1843, thugs attacked him in Pendleton, Indiana. He escaped with a broken wrist and bruises. Abolitionist newspaper editor Elijah Lovejoy was killed in Alton, Illinois, while defending his press from an angry mob. Garrison was dragged through the streets of Boston with a rope around his waist and almost lost his life.

During the winter and early spring of 1844-45, Douglass took time out from the lecture circuit and wrote his autobiography, *The Narrative of the Life of Frederick Douglass, an American Slave.* In August 1845, he went on a successful lecture tour of England, Ireland, and Scotland.

One month after his return to the U.S., Anna and Ellen Richardson of Newcastle, England, raised money and negotiated with American agents to buy Douglass's freedom from Thomas Auld for $711.66. The deed of manumission was filed at the Baltimore Chattel Records Office on December 13, 1846, and Douglass was a free man.

Douglass went on another lecture tour of England in 1847. Upon his return to America, he proceeded with plans to publish an antislavery newspaper. His British friends raised $2,000 to help him get started. He was surprised when Garrison advised against it. Garrison, who did not want competition for his *Liberator,* said that there were already too many newspapers of that type.

Douglass started his newspaper in spite of Garrison's counsel. He knew that he would have to choose a base far from Garrison's in New England. Douglass chose Rochester, a booming city of 30,000 on the Erie Canal where he had been well-received in 1842 and 1847. The leading abolitionist of central New York, Gerrit Smith, supported him and gave him the deed to land in Rochester. Douglass moved his family there on November 1, 1847.

On December 3, 1847, the first edition of his newspaper, *North Star*, was published. He named the paper, "*North Star,*" for the celestial guide that the slaves used when escaping from the South to freedom. His printing office was located on the third floor of the

Talman Building, East Main street,
Home of Frederick Douglass's *North Star*

Talman Building on East Main Street. In 1851, *North Star* merged with the *Liberty Party Paper* financed by Gerrit Smith; the resulting paper was called *Frederick Douglass's Paper*. In 1858, he began publishing *Douglass's Monthly* for British readers. The weekly ran until 1860; he stopped printing the monthly in 1863.

Douglass also supported the Women's Rights Movement. On July 14, 1848, his *North Star* carried this announcement: "A convention to discuss the Social, Civil, and Religious Condition and Rights of Women will be held in the Wesleyan Chapel at Seneca Falls, New York, the 19th and 20th of July instant." The masthead that Douglass used for *North Star* was: "RIGHT IS OF NO SEX—TRUTH IS OF NO COLOR."

Douglass was not only a famous abolitionist speaker and editor but also a Rochester stationmaster on the Underground Railroad. He helped hundreds of slaves escape, and none of the fugitives under his care were ever captured; however, they had many close calls.

On one occasion, Douglass was advised by the law partner of the U.S. Commissioner that papers were being prepared for the arrest of three escaped slaves from Maryland. One of the fugitives was hiding at Asa Anthony's farm west of Rochester, a second was housed at the old Quaker settlement in Farmington, and the third was at Douglass's home. Douglass and his friends moved quickly, and before arrests could be made the men boarded a ship at the Port of Rochester and were on their way across Lake Ontario to safety in Canada.

On another occasion, three fugitives stayed in Rochester for several months. While waiting for passage to Canada, they attended antislavery meetings in Corinthian Hall. Douglass was advised that their master was in town with a warrant for their arrest. The men were moved around the city for three days while the U.S. Marshal searched for them. Finally, in the middle of the night, they were given Quaker bonnets and heavy veils, driven to the Port of Rochester in a closed carriage, and placed aboard a ship for passage to Canada.

Three other fugitives housed by Douglass were pursued more aggressively than the first two groups because they had killed one slavecatcher and wounded another in Christiana, Pennsylvania, while resisting capture. A large reward was offered for their arrest, and many law officers were searching for them. Douglass's English friend, Julia Griffiths, arranged for their passage to Canada on a British ship that was moored in the Genesee River. The men were disguised in women's clothing, and Douglass personally drove them to the dock in his carriage. They arrived just as the ship was about to leave the pier. Reverend Parker, one of the fugitives, gave Douglass the pistol that had killed the slavecatcher as a souvenir.

Douglass frequently used the African Methodist Episcopal Zion Church at the corner of Spring and Favor Streets as an Underground Railroad station. Slaves were hidden in the basement and in the pews while arrangements were made to transport them to freedom. Harriet Tubman, the "Moses of her people," was one of many with whom Douglass worked in helping escaped slaves.

In January 1871, President Grant appointed Douglass to a commission to Santo Domingo (Dominican Republic). Douglass moved to Washington, D.C., because he thought that more federal appointments would be forthcoming. In 1877, President Rutherford Hayes assigned him as U.S. Marshal for the District of Columbia. He served in that position until 1881, when President James Garfield appointed him Recorder of Deeds for the District of Columbia. He held that office until 1886.

Douglass's wife, Anna, died in August 1882. In January 1884, he married Helen Pitts, his secretary in the Office of the Recorder of Deeds. The mixed marriage caused controversy, but Helen said, "Love came to me and I was not afraid to marry the man I loved because of his color." Douglass's response to critics was that his first wife "was the color of my mother, and the second, the color of my father."

In September 1889, President Benjamin Harrison appointed Douglass Minister-Resident and Consul-General to the Republic of Haiti. He resigned that office in July 1891. Douglass, one of the strongest antislavery voices of his time, died of a heart attack in Washington, D.C., on February 20, 1895. He and his family were buried in Mt. Hope Cemetery in Rochester.

## *Amy Post (1802-1889)*

"They [Amy and Isaac Post] were not more amiable than brave, for they never seemed to ask, 'What will the world say?' but walked straight forward in what seemed to them the line of duty, please or offend whomever it might. Many a poor slave found shelter under their roof when such shelter was hard to find elsewhere, and I mention them here in the warmth and fullness of earnest gratitude."
    Frederick Douglass, *The Life and Times of Frederick Douglass*

Amy Kirby, who was born in Jericho, Long Island, in 1802 to Jacob and Mary Kirby, inherited from her parents a dislike for oppression and persecution. She married Isaac Post in 1828 and moved with him to Rochester in 1836. Amy and Isaac Post were active in the Society of Friends (Quakers) and were leaders of the Hicksite faction. She was active in the early temperance and antislavery movements in Rochester. The couple were followers of abolitionist William Lloyd Garrison. The Posts, who lived on North Plymouth Avenue (called Sophia Street at the time), were among the most active Rochesterians providing support to African Americans from 1836 until the signing of the Emancipation Proclamation in 1863.

   Amy Post spent considerable time away from home to work for "the world's people." She held bazaars and fairs to raise money for the antislavery cause. Quakers considered this a violation of their doctrine. They thought that Friend Amy Post should be spending more time at home with her family and less on antislavery activities. A committee visited her to remind her of her duties to her family. Eventually, Amy and Isaac Post left the Friends to pursue their perceived obligation to the world's people.

   The Posts hosted many visitors active in the abolitionist movement, including William Lloyd Garrison. Their home was considered the "central depot" of the Underground Railroad in Rochester. Many escaped slaves stayed there until they could be transported to Charlotte where they boarded ships for passage to Canada, particularly after 1850 when a harsher Fugitive Slave Law was enacted.

   The Posts helped an estimated 1,200 slaves escape at a time when one who aided fugitives could be fined $1,000 and imprisoned for at least a year. Amy Post visited Canada to see how the estimated 40,000 escaped slaves there were doing. Many knew her personally, and most of them were familiar with her name.

When Frederick Douglass visited Rochester as a lecturer for the American Anti-Slavery Society in 1842, he was entertained by the Posts. Douglass's friendship with Amy Post continued until her death in 1889.

Amy Post took the initiative in organizing the second Women's Rights Convention held at the Unitarian Church in Rochester two weeks after the first Women's Rights Convention in Seneca Falls in July 1848. Abigail Bush was elected chair of the convention, which was attended by Elizabeth Cady Stanton and Lucretia Mott, who had relatives in the area. Frederick Douglass and Daniel Anthony, Susan B. Anthony's father, were active participants in the discussions. Later, Amy Post convinced Susan B. Anthony to become active in the Women's Rights Movement.

Amy and Isaac Post became interested in Spiritualism. Leah Fox Fish, the oldest Fox sister, brought her sister, Kate, who claimed to have communicated with the dead, to Rochester to speak at Corinthian Hall. The Posts wanted to communicate with their departed friends. The annual convention of Spiritualists frequently met in Rochester, and Amy and Isaac Post served on the welcoming committee.

After Isaac's death in 1872, Amy Post became the "grand old champion of all liberal causes." The observation of her eightieth birthday established a precedent in honoring Rochester's reformist grand dames. Her birthday celebration was followed by honoring Susan B. Anthony on her seventieth birthday and Mary T. Gannett on her seventy-fifth birthday.

## *Antoinette Brown Blackwell (1825-1921)*

"I told her [reformer and best friend Lucy Stone] of my intention to become a minister. Her protest was most emphatic. She said, 'You will never be allowed to do this. You will never be allowed to stand in a public pulpit nor to preach in a church, and certainly you can never be ordained.' It was a long talk, but we were no nearer to an agreement at the end than at the beginning. My final answer could only be, 'I am going to do it.'"          Antoinette Louisa Brown

Antoinette Louisa Brown, seventh of ten children of Joseph and Abigail Morse Brown, was born in Henrietta in May 1825. She became the first ordained woman minister in the United States. Antoinette indicated her interest in religion early when she prayed spontaneously to conclude a family prayer meeting at the age of eight. The following year she asked about joining the village Congregationalist Church at a time when doing so at that age was rare.

The small Henrietta church was a member of the liberal branch of the Congregationalist Church that emphasized God's mercy and forgiveness in addition to human goodness and initiative. The orthodox branch of the Church believed that humans were morally corrupt, sinful, and dependent upon an all-powerful God, who would condemn them to hell if they did not obey His word.

Brown decided in her teens that she wanted to become a minister. No woman had been ordained as a minister; however, in the 1820s, a Methodist woman had attempted to preach in New York State but gave in to public opposition. Quakers, who considered all members ministers, permitted women to speak at worship services, but they were not considered leaders of the church community.

Brown was active in her Henrietta church and spoke frequently at prayer meetings, where any church member was permitted to speak. She decided to attend the Oberlin Collegiate Institute in Ohio, where her brother, William, studied theology. Oberlin was the first U.S. college to admit women to take college courses with men. In the spring of 1846, she began her studies there.

Oberlin had been founded in 1833 by ministers from New England and New York. By the time that Brown arrived, the

College had developed its own ideology, a combination of liberal religion, practical training, and the politics of reform. The spiritual leader of the Oberlin community was Professor of Theology Charles Grandison Finney, who had impressed Brown's parents at revival meetings in Rochester during the winter of 1831. He was a captivating speaker who advocated the dual responsibility of an individual's commitment to God and his or her working toward a better society. He suggested that this dual responsibility should be implemented by applying one's intellect and education to save individual souls and to improve society. He was Brown's mentor.

At Oberlin, Brown met Lucy Stone, who later became the New England leader of the Women's Rights Movement. Stone was older than her classmates and was paying her own way through college because her father, who was against higher education for women, refused to give her financial assistance. Stone was a follower of the radical abolitionist, William Lloyd Garrison; she enrolled at Oberlin specifically to learn public speaking skills to use in advocating women's rights and the abolition of slavery.

Women students at Oberlin discovered early that the College had no intention of training them as public speakers. They learned how to write, but they were "excused" from participation in discussions and debates. Oberlin President Asa Mahan advocated that women should be taught how to speak as well as how to write, but he was outvoted by the faculty. The policy was apparently based on the words of St. Paul: "Let a woman learn in silence with all submissiveness."

In the winter of 1846-47, during Oberlin's lengthy vacation, Brown taught at a large private academy in Rochester, Michigan. The experience verified what she already knew: "God never made me for a school teacher." However, the headmaster encouraged Brown to give her first public speech. She spoke in the village church and was pleased with the response: "It was fairly well received by the students and by the community."

Brown and Stone became close friends and confidants despite their differences of opinion. Stone was more radical on the subject of abolition; she left the Congregationalist Church because it approved of slavery and opposed women speaking in public. Brown was disappointed that her closest friend did not agree with her goal to become an ordained minister.

Brown completed her undergraduate studies at Oberlin in the summer of 1847. She returned home to Henrietta and practiced her public speaking: "I go out into the barn and make the walls echo with my voice occasionally, but the church stands on the green in such a way that I have too many auditors when I attempt to practice there. The barn is a good large one, however, and the sounds ring out merrily, or did before father filled it full of hay."

Brown returned to Oberlin in the fall to study theology. She felt that she was called to this vocation, and she was motivated to use her intellect, her ability as a public speaker, and her interest in public reform. However, although Oberlin was committed to providing women with a general education, the only profession that it prepared them for was teaching. In the Theology Department, women were permitted to sit in on classes if their goal was self-improvement.

Brown's classmate in her theology courses, Lettice Smith, shared her semi-official status in the department. However, everyone knew that Smith was going to marry her classmate, Thomas Holmes, and become a minister's wife. Smith, who was a serious student of theology, did not have much self-confidence and never responded in class. She did not provide the sounding board off which to bounce ideas that Stone did. However, Stone had graduated and had left Oberlin the previous spring.

Initially, Professor Finney did not call on the women to respond in class, and Brown was offended by this. When she questioned him on it, he said that any woman could respond in class if she wished to. In his view, "Though he did not think she was generally called upon to preach or speak in public because the circumstances did not demand it, still there was nothing right or wrong in the thing itself and that sometimes she was specially called to speak."

Brown and Smith were assigned to write essays on the passages in the Bible stating that women should not preach: "Let your women keep silence in the churches, for it is not permitted unto them to speak.... Let the women learn in silence with all subjection. I suffer not a woman to teach, nor to usurp authority over the man, but to be in silence." Brown found confirmation of her choice of a profession in the words of the prophet Joel: "And it shall come to pass in the last days, saith God, I will pour out my spirit upon all flesh; and your sons and daughters shall prophesy."

41

In her essay, Brown observed that St. Paul's suggestion that women should learn in silence had been misinterpreted. She suggested that St. Paul only intended to caution against "excesses, irregularities, and unwarranted liberties" in public worship. Her essay was selected for publication in the *Oberlin Quarterly Review*.

During the last year of their studies, Oberlin theology students were allowed to preach in area churches but not to perform the sacraments. Brown said, "They were willing to have me preach, but not to themselves endorse this as a principle.... They decided, after much discussion, that I must preach, if I chose to do so, on my own responsibility." Although she was not given official recognition, Brown spoke in small churches nearby, usually on the popular subject of temperance.

Upon completion of her theology studies, Brown chose not to be ordained at Oberlin. Not only did she think that it would be "a delicate thing" with Oberlin's difference of opinion on women ministers, but also she preferred the usual path of ordination by a local parish that wanted her as a pastor. She cited "an instinctive desire to be ordained in my own church and a belief that I could one day in the future be ordained by my own denomination which was then the Orthodox Congregationalist."

Neither Brown nor Smith participated in the graduation exercises. In later years, Brown observed: "We were not supposed to graduate, as at that time to have regularly graduated women from a theological school would have been an endorsement of their probable future careers." Their names did not appear in the roll of the Theological Department class of 1850 until 1908.

Brown attended the first "National" Women's Rights Convention in Worcester, Massachusetts, where she spoke to disprove the Biblical argument that women should not speak in public. She met Lucretia Mott and Elizabeth Cady Stanton, who had organized the Seneca Falls Convention two years earlier. Brown was introduced to many men and women active in social reform. She maintained her contacts with them, but she thought that her calling would probably not be best served by working with organized groups.

Brown decided to earn her living as a public speaker, as her friend, Lucy Stone, was doing. Before radio and television, the lecture circuit, or lyceum, was an important means of informing and entertaining people. Women speakers were usually paid less than men. Brown told lyceum organizers: "My terms, from principle, are never less that the best prices received by the gentlemen of the particular association where I speak." She found the work satisfying, and she consistently received favorable reviews in the local newspapers where she spoke.

Liberal ministers such as William Henry Channing and Samuel J. May invited Brown to preach in their churches. Her oldest brother, William, who had initially opposed her desire to preach, invited her to speak in his church in Andover, Massachusetts. She decided that the time had come to pursue her calling, and she began actively to seek a church in need of a pastor.

During one of her speaking tours across New York State, Brown visited South Butler in Wayne County. The small Congregationalist church listened to her speak and invited her to become their pastor at an annual salary of $300. In the late spring of 1853, she moved to South Butler and began to give two sermons every Sunday, one prepared and the other extemporaneous.

Brown's responsibilities included pastoral duties, such as visiting the sick, and she felt suited to her role as minister. She commented: "My little parish was a miniature world in good and evil. To get humanity condensed into so small a compass that you can study each individual member opens a new chapter of experience. It makes one thoughtful and rolls upon the spirit a burden of deep responsibility."

Brown's friend, Lucy Stone, met Henry Blackwell, brother of pioneer doctor Elizabeth Blackwell, at an abolitionist meeting. Henry fell in love with Stone and began to court her. Stone met Henry's older brother, Samuel, and suggested that he visit Brown while on his travels. The Blackwell brothers were business partners in Cincinnati. Samuel called on Brown while en route to Boston. Samuel "enjoyed the visit exceedingly." Brown observed: "He stayed perhaps a half a day and had a pleasant visit.... He was not handsome." She was preoccupied with church duties.

Brown's congregation was pleased with her work, and the governing body decided to proceed with her ordination. She already administered the sacraments, but the ceremony would provide public recognition of her ministry. Reverend Luther Lee, a minister from nearby Syracuse whom Brown knew from abolitionist meetings, agreed to preach the ordination sermon.

Reverend Lee based his sermon on the text: "There is neither male nor female; for ye are all one in Christ Jesus." He said, "In the Church, of which Christ is the only head, males and females possess equal rights and privileges; here there is no difference.... I cannot see how the test can be explained so as to exclude females from any right, office, work, privilege, or immunity which males enjoy, hold or perform."

Reverend Lee concluded by saying: "All we are here to do, and all we expect to do, is, in due form, and by a solemn and impressive service, to subscribe our testimony to the fact that in our belief, our sister in Christ, Antoinette L. Brown, is one of the ministers of the New Covenant, authorized, qualified, and called of God to preach the Gospel of His Son Jesus Christ."

During the winter of 1854, Brown's duties weighed heavily upon her. Her role was a difficult one, and her responsibilities began to cause her emotional strain. A minister's functions were many and varied. He or she was expected to be tolerant and understanding, but, at other times, authoritative and judgmental. It was difficult for Brown to be a "father" figure. Her role would have been easier if she had the support of her friends and associates. However, Susan B. Anthony, Elizabeth Cady Stanton, and Lucy Stone all disapproved of her church affiliation. They did not perceive Brown's ministerial duties as a contribution to advocating change in women's status.

As noted by Elizabeth Cazden in *Antoinette Brown Blackwell: A Biography,* Brown felt isolated:

> It was practically ten years after my ordination before any other woman known to the public was ordained. It was therefore doubly hard for me—a young woman still in her twenties—to adapt myself to the rather curious relationship I must sustain either to home conditions or to those of a pastorate. Personally this was more of an emotional strain than the enduring of any opposition that ever came to me as a public speaker or teacher.

This isolation began to affect her in a very serious way. Brown began to question her faith, particularly the emphasis on being condemned to eternal damnation unless saved by a stern God, as espoused by some members of her congregation. She was motivated more by Charles Grandison Finney's teachings that stressed human goodness and striving to approach moral perfection. In July 1854, overcome by mental conflict and nervous exhaustion, she returned home to rest.

Samuel Blackwell helped Brown find herself during this difficult time. Brown had stayed with the Blackwell family when she had been in Cincinnati on the lecture circuit. Blackwell's five sisters were all achievers: Elizabeth and Emily became doctors, Ellen and Marian were active in the Women's Rights Movement and other reform efforts, and Anna, who had lived at the transcendentalist commune at Brook Farm, was a newspaper reporter in Paris. He was used to activist women.

At the end of 1854, Stone agreed to marry Henry Blackwell if he would agree to devote his efforts to women's rights. Perhaps motivated by his brother's action, Samuel proposed to Brown at about the same time. Brown hesitated, but she considered some of the women that she knew—Lucretia Mott was an example—who had children, husbands, and homes, in addition to careers.

Later, Brown observed: "When the early faith seemed wholly lost and the new and stronger belief not yet obtained, there seemed no good reason for not accepting the love and help of a good man and the woman's appreciation of all else that this implied." After their marriage, she was known as "Reverend Antoinette L. B. Blackwell."

In January 1855, Brown wrote to Horace Greeley of the New York *Tribune* to inquire if he would help her to hire a hall in New York in which to preach on Sundays, an activity that he and Charles Dana had suggested three years previously. He encouraged her with her "experiment" and suggested that she visit the City's slums and institutions and write articles for the *Tribune* about her experiences.

The Blackwells moved to New Jersey, where Samuel found a job as a bookkeeper to support the family as the children began to arrive. During the winter and spring of 1859-60, Brown Blackwell rented a hall in New York and preached every Sunday. She was able to balance family and preaching duties; unfortunately, due to finances, the preaching venture was not long-lived.

In the late 1860s, Brown Blackwell devoted herself to writing. Her first large published work was *Studies in General Science*, a collection of essays. In 1875, her second work, *The Sexes Throughout Nature*, a compilation of essays first published in periodicals, was published. In 1876, came *The Physical Basis of Immortality*, a synthesis of her philosophy. The *Philosophy of Individuality, or the One and the Many*, was released in 1893. Her last two books, *The Making of the Universe* and *The Social Side of Mind and Action* were published in 1914 and 1915.

Brown Blackwell was drawn to the Unitarian Church, which Samuel Blackwell and three of his sisters had joined. In the spring of 1878, she joined the Unitarian Fellowship. In the fall of that year, the Committee on Fellowship of the American Unitarian Association acknowledged her as a minister.

In 1879, Oberlin College recognized Brown Blackwell's status by awarding her an "honorary" Master of Arts degree, the one that she had earned during three years of study in the Theological Department. One change from her status thirty years previously was that she no longer stood alone as a woman minister. By 1880, almost 200 women were recognized as ministers, and many held full-time pastoral jobs.

In addition to her participation in the Women's Rights Movement, Brown Blackwell was also active in the Association for the Advancement of Women and the American Association for the Advancement of Science. Although she had not had the responsibility of a parish for decades, she considered herself a "minister emeritus" during her later years.

In June 1908, Brown Blackwell was invited to Oberlin College to receive an honorary Doctor of Divinity degree. In introducing her to Oberlin President Henry Churchill King at the commencement ceremony, Dr. Charles Wager spoke to the audience:

> It is appropriate for the institution that was the first to provide for higher education of women to honor, at its seventy-fifth anniversary, a woman who has eminently justified that daring innovation, a woman who was one of the first two in America to complete a course in divinity, who as preacher, as pastor, as writer, as the champion of more than one

good cause, has in the past conferred honor upon her Alma Mater, and who today confers upon it no less honor by an old age as lovely as it is venerable.

Brown Blackwell's health began to fail during the spring and summer of 1921; she was at peace with herself. She was ready for death and looked upon it as a reunion with Samuel and her other loved ones. In late November 1921, at the age of ninety-seven, Reverend Antoinette L. B. Blackwell, the first woman minister, died in her sleep.

Sibley, Lindsay, and Curr Building, East Main Street

# CHAPTER 2

# ORGANIZERS / VISIONARIES

## Hiram Sibley (1807-1888)

"That Rochester, New York, before any other city in the United States, nourished and stimulated the magnetic telegraph in the days of its neglected infancy, saving it from failure and complete disaster, is a fact unknown save to the students of telegraphy. The story of Rochester's early interest in the inventions of Morse, House, and Bain, but particularly that of Professor Morse, is told in the names alone of her citizens [including Hiram Sibley, Jonathan Child, Samuel Selden, Henry Selden, and Alvah Strong] who became identified with the enterprise, and who have done much to make it what it is."

Jane Marsh Parker,
"How Men of Rochester Saved the Telegraph"

Hiram Sibley's first involvement with telegraphy occurred by coincidence. Jane Marsh Parker quotes Sibley in "How Men of Rochester Saved the Telegraph":

> No. I did not go to Washington on purpose to help Morse [get his appropriation].... I went to Washington to see [President] Harrison inaugurated. I don't remember that I was interested in magnetic telegraph particularly until a lady who was staying at the hotel came to me and urged my assisting Professor Morse in getting a favorable hearing before the Committee [for an appropriation], which she felt would turn a cold shoulder to him.... She succeeded in interesting me in Morse, and I started out to find the Chairman of the Committee, and to do my best for him.

In 1843, a bill was passed appropriating $40,000 to Morse for testing the feasibility of his invention.

On May 24, 1844, Morse sent the first telegraph message—"What Hath God Wrought"—from the Supreme Court chamber in Washington, D.C, to assistant Alfred Vail at the Baltimore Railroad Station. Henry Clay and Dolly Madison were among the onlookers. Private enterprise had to fund further development of the telegraph because the Postmaster General of the United States considered it a "toy." The next phase was to extend telegraph lines to Philadelphia and New York.

Later, when Albany newspaperman Henry O'Reilly acquired the option to develop intercity telegraph lines, he surveyed Rochester banks looking for backing for several independent telegraph lines. Individually, the lines did not generate a profit, and several attempts to consolidate them had failed until Hiram Sibley, Samuel Selden, and Henry Ward, Rochester stockholders in the O'Reilly-Morse lines, organized a new company, the Mississippi Valley Printing Telegraph Company. It built a line to the Midwest and absorbed thirteen other telegraph companies north of the Ohio River.

By 1851, fifty telegraph companies were in operation using the Morse patents. Too many companies had competing telegraph lines over parallel routes. Because these lines were not connected, delivery of telegrams was often delayed. Sibley proposed combining the short, unprofitable lines west of Buffalo into one network; then he purchased many of them.

The main difficulty for the newly formed company was competition from the Buffalo and Milwaukee line and others in the Midwest controlled by Ezra Cornell, the benefactor of Cornell University. Sibley and his partners formed an alliance with Cornell and other telegraph men to establish a consolidated system.

On April 4, 1856, the Western Union Telegraph Company was formed. Cornell, a director and the largest stockholder, proposed the name for the new company "because it represented the union of the lines in what was then the West." However, he played no active role in running the Company, which provided uniform telegraph rates and standards of service.

During the Civil War, a national telegraph network was urgently needed to tie the West with the rest of the country. However, even President Lincoln questioned the practicality of running telegraph lines across the country because of hostile

Indians and the lack of trees on the Great Plains from which to make telegraph poles. It was left to Sibley and private enterprise to construct the transcontinental telegraph system.

A 1,400-mile telegraph line between St. Joseph, Missouri, and Sacramento, California, was built. The western and the eastern construction joined at Salt Lake City on October 24, 1861. The first message was sent to President Lincoln by the Chief Justice of California. Completion of this line ended the operation of the pony express that had run between St. Joseph, Missouri, and the West Coast.

In his later years, Hiram Sibley became a philanthropist. In 1872, he donated money to construct a joint library and museum of science for the University of Rochester. In 1874, Sibley returned from a trip to Europe with "fifty-four fine paintings" that became the nucleus of paintings for the new Academy of Art. Subsequently, Sibley financed the construction of the Sibley Block on Main Street by selling some of his stock in Western Union.

## *Seth Green (1817-1888)*

"Seth Green's name had spread far and wide, from coast to coast, and throughout the world. A Westerner visiting in Rochester asked a *Post Express* reporter, one day, whom he considered the best-known Rochesterian. The reporter mentioned several names, but the stranger answered: 'No, your best-known man is Seth Green. Why, he is a thousand times more famed out of Rochester, I judge, than in it. The newspapers in other parts of the country have something about him every week or two, but I see no extracts of the same sort from the Rochester papers.'"  Sylvia R. Black,
"Seth Green, Father of Fish Culture." *Rochester History*

Seth Green was born on March 19, 1817, on a pioneer farm at the corner of Culver Road and Empire Boulevard. His father, Adonijah Green, had moved to Rochester from New England. The Green family lived in Carthage on the east side of the Genesee River at the lower falls when Seth was a young boy. Adonijah, who had become tired of farming, opened a tavern at Carthage Landing, a principal dock on the River.

Young Green left school after completing the fifth or sixth grade. Seneca Indians taught him about the behavior of fish and how to catch them. He fished using bent pins for fishhooks. He was an observant young man with the ability to focus on a subject. He studied the habits of fish, such as seasonal behavior and time of spawning, as well as the condition of the water and wind. The financial panic of 1837 affected Carthage and began its downturn. Kelsey's Landing across the River became a more active dock than Carthage Landing. Twenty-year-old Green realized that he was going to have to support himself.

Green fished in the Genesee River as far as the lower falls. He caught salmon in scoop nets, fifteen-to-twenty-pound catfish on nightlines, and 150-pound sturgeon that came up the River in April and May using a hook and line or a spear. He sold his catches to sailing vessels that docked along the River. One captain invited him to go to Canada in his ship. From 1837 to 1840, Green went to Grafton, Ontario, to fish for salmon entering Keeler's Creek from Lake Ontario.

In Canada, Green observed female salmon depositing fertilized eggs in their prepared nests. The operation was wasteful; the male salmon ate as many of the deposited eggs as he could find. Green considered hatching fish artificially, thus preventing considerable waste. Although Green had not heard about artificial propagation of fish, he experimented with propagation techniques in the Genesee River. He knew that his methods were more efficient than nature's. Although artificial propagation of fish had been done for centuries in China, France, and Prussia, Green was the American pioneer.

By 1857, Green was one of the best-known fisherman and one of the largest distributors of fish in New York State. His average daily catch ranged from 1,000 to 6,000 pounds. He employed 100 men who caught and sold fish; he opened a fish market on Front Street in Rochester.

Beginning in 1864, Green propagated hundreds of thousands of trout fry in his private hatchery on property along Spring Creek south of Rochester, where he had purchased exclusive fishing rights. He knew that he could sell brook trout for $1.00 a pound in the markets of Rochester and Buffalo. He used the dry impregnation method in which no water was added to the milt from the male and the eggs, and he achieved a hatch rate of ninety-seven percent. He found out later that the Frenchmen achieved only a twenty-five percent hatch rate using the wet impregnation method.

In 1855, Green was appointed one of the first three commissioners of the New York State Fish Commission when it was created by Governor John Hoffman. The other two commissioners were Horatio Seymour of Utica, who had served two terms as governor of New York State, and Robert B. Roosevelt, an uncle of Theodore Roosevelt. Green and Roosevelt collaborated on a book, *Fish Hatching and Fish Catching.*

In 1857, fish commissioners of Connecticut, Massachusetts, Vermont, and New Hampshire invited Green to help them propagate shad on the Connecticut River. Attempts dating back to 1848 had failed. He, too, failed in his early efforts. Trout hatched in cold water, forty to forty-five degrees, but shad needed warm water, seventy-five degrees, and a steady flow of water over the fertilized eggs. At one point he was extremely discouraged, but he persevered and succeeded in hatching shad.

In 1870, Green sold his private hatchery to New York State,

resigned his position as a commissioner, and became the first State Superintendent of Fish Culture, a position that he held for the rest of his life. One of his early tasks was restocking the Hudson River. Next, he turned his attention to restocking the Potomac River with bass, catfish, herring, perch, and sturgeon. Eventually, he helped to restock the Susquehanna, Delaware, Rappahannock, James, and York Rivers, principally with shad.

The New York State Fish Hatchery on spring-fed Caledonia Creek in Caledonia, established in 1870, was the first of its kind in the United States. Green began the State program with 80,000 eggs from thirteen lake trout from Lake Ontario and with whitefish eggs from the St. Clair River near Detroit. Trout hatch in 160 to 165 days; whitefish hatch in 140 to 145 days. He also propagated salmon and shad.

Green developed the means of transporting fingerlings around the country when he was asked to help restock a river. Replenishing the water en route was a key factor in transporting fish successfully. His work with fish was described in New York's newspapers; overnight he became a national figure. Trout ponds were established in many locations around the country.

In 1871, Green transported 12,000 shad fry to California at the request of the State's fish commissioners. His efforts to propagate them were successful, even though shad were not native to California waters. In 1873, a California fish commissioner notified the U.S. Fish Commission that he had purchased the first shad caught on the West Coast.

In 1882, Green contracted typhoid pneumonia, from which he never fully recovered. In January 1888, he injured his back when the carriage in which he was riding overturned. He was confined to his home and died in August that year. The Isaak Walton league placed a bronze plaque at the State Fish Hatchery at Caledonia commemorating him as the father of fish culture and as a "world famous pioneer in conservation." By 1974, the New York State Department of Environmental Conservation stocked 7.4 million trout and salmon from sixteen state hatcheries. Trout were stocked along 4,400 miles of 1,100 streams and in 700 lakes and ponds.

## *Daniel Powers (1818-1897)*

"The name of Powers has been synonymous with the growth and development of Rochester along various lines. Daniel W. Powers was the first builder of the modern business structure which is now a typical feature in every progressive city, and for many years was an outstanding figure in the financial life of this city.... In addition to the Powers Block he erected the Powers Hotel, which ... is scarcely equaled in the State outside of New York City. Mr. Powers became reckoned as one of the most distinguished and prominent citizens of Rochester. His labors were of the utmost benefit to the City along various lines of progress. He was one of the founders of the present park system and was a member of the commission which directed construction of the city hall.... He was charitable and benevolent, giving freely of his means to ameliorate hard conditions of life for others, and in all of his benefactions was entirely free from ostentation or display." Lockwood R. Doty,
*History of the Genesee Country*

Daniel Powers was born in Batavia on June 14, 1818, to Asahel and Elizabeth Powell Powers. As a young man, he worked on his uncle's farm but decided that he would make a better businessman than farmer. At the age of nineteen, he walked from Batavia to Rochester because he could not afford the fare.

Power applied for a position as salesman in the hardware store of Ebenezer Watts but was told that he was not big enough. He ensured Mr. Watts that not only was he able to do the work but that "I am the boy." He worked for Mr. Watts until March 1, 1850, when he opened an exchange business as a banker and broker with money that he had saved from his earnings. He was a success from the beginning because he was reliable and trustworthy.

In 1865, Powers began construction of the five-story, fireproof Powers building, with cast-iron facing, on State Street. After the Eagle Hotel on the corner of State Street and Buffalo Street (now Main Street), was damaged by fire in 1868, the Powers Hotel was built. The original Powers Block had a corner section faced with stone and a mansard roof, which served as a sixth floor, adjoined by two iron-faced wings with flat roofs.

Most Rochester businessmen doubted that Powers could fill the fifteen street-level store fronts and the 160 offices in the Powers Block. Not only were they filled, but the Powers Block motivated area businesses to improve and expand their buildings. In 1872, Powers added an attractive tower and a sixth-story mansard roof over both wings. Building downtown was popular until 1871, when the Great Chicago Fire caused insurers to increase their rates. The "fireproof" Powers Block was considered safe but, in the absence of a city water system, other downtown buildings were not. Later, buildings in the Powers Block were expanded to eight stories.

Powers became one of the most successful financiers in western New York; he was known throughout the State and in other parts of the country. He was a pillar of the community who was president of the board of trustees of Rochester City Hospital and the Home of the Friendless as well as a member of the board of trustees of the Industrial School. He attained the highest degree in Masonry and was a liberal supporter of Brick Presbyterian Church.

Powers was a patron of the arts and founder of the Powers Art Gallery, which was valued at over a million dollars. In 1875, the gallery opened, and its first catalog was printed.

James Delafield Trenor described the purpose of the gallery in the introduction to his publication, *A Descriptive Catalog of the Powers Art Gallery, Rochester, N.Y.:* "The Powers Art Gallery was established and has been maintained with a view to creating and fostering a love of art in its highest forms, among the inhabitants and as far beyond the city as its influence might eventually reach." Listed in the publication were 996 paintings and seventeen sculptures.

According to a brochure published in New York City in 1884, *Notes on the Powers Building and the Art Gallery of Rochester, N.Y.:*

> The Art Gallery was a growth from a small beginning. Mr. Powers first went abroad in 1875, where he engaged in the study and inspection among the famous galleries of the Continent, and made a number of purchases from well-known artists. At first his collection occupied four rooms; now it fills thirty, including the "Grand Salon"—thirty x ninety feet, besides the "Rotunda" and the halls;

and in the judgment of competent persons, has few
if any equals in the private galleries of the world....
Believing that this precious gem should have a
beautiful setting, his gallery is not a plain, somber,
bare-floored tunnel or series of dismal chambers,
but a suite of richly and artistically ornamented
and luxurious parlors.

Powers died in early December 1897. The Powers Art Gallery
was closed on December 11, 1897, and the entire collection was
sold at an auction in New York City. Daniel Powers was an honored
citizen of Rochester who was widely respected in the business
world. His efforts and philanthropy contributed significantly to the
development of Rochester.

## *Frank Gannett (1876-1957)*

"Frank Gannett's career parallels the last fifty years of American daily journalism [1900-1950]. He has been a newsboy, reporter, editor, business manager, and publisher. During those fifty years he has seen and had a part in the transformation of the newspaper that was, into the newspaper of today. He has fought venality and irresponsibility in the press that was. He has helped to shape the modern newspaper and to free it from evils of the past; and, like most publishers, he has much to say about freedom of the press."

Samuel T. Williamson, *Imprint of a Publisher*

Frank Ernest Gannett, third son of Charles and Maria Brooks Gannett, was born on September 15, 1876, on the family farm on Gannett Hill. The hill, the highest elevation in west-central New York, is 1,600 feet above adjacent Canandaigua Lake and 2,200 feet above sea level. The year after Gannett was born, the family moved to the Town of Atlanta, which was then called Blood's Depot. He was educated partly in the public schools and partly tutored at home.

At the age of nine, Gannett, future founder of the Gannett chain of newspapers, had his first job; not surprisingly, it was delivering papers—the Rochester *Democrat and Chronicle*. Tenant farming was difficult for Charles Gannett, who had served with General Custer during the Civil War and had ridden with General Philip Sheridan's cavalry through the Shenandoah Valley.

When Gannett was twelve, the family moved to a farm in nearby Wallace. Two years later, they moved again, to the Town of Bolivar. The family was poor; nevertheless, Gannett had a happy childhood.

Charles Gannett was the proprietor of the Clark House hotel in Bolivar, which thirty years previously had been one of the boom towns in the Bradford oil field. Since Bolivar was outside the circulation area of the Rochester *Democrat and Chronicle*, Gannett delivered newspapers for the Buffalo *News* and the Buffalo *Times*. He also wrote articles for the former, earning $1.00 for his first article.

The Gannett family moved across the State to Oneonta where

Charles Gannett became proprietor of the Wilson House hotel. Young Gannett continued his studies at Bolivar Academy, supporting himself by bartending at the Newton House, Bolivar's other hostelry. The speech that he delivered at his graduation ceremony in 1893 was entitled: "The Press and Public Opinion." He received high grades in more subjects than any other student in the New York State Regents' Examinations that year.

Gannett worked one more year in Bolivar to earn money to attend college. He took a correspondence course from Bryant and Stratton Business School in bookkeeping, a subject not offered in high school. He won a $200 a year Cornell University scholarship that was based on his high standing in a competitive examination. In the fall of 1894, at the age of eighteen, he went to Ithaca to begin his studies.

Gannett's scholarship paid his tuition, and he supported himself with four jobs: waiting on tables in a student boarding house, operating a laundry route, collecting and delivering for a pants presser, and ushering in Sage Memorial Chapel. He was strongly influenced by hearing many of the finest theologians of the day who spoke in Sage Chapel. Eventually, he became head usher at the nonsectarian chapel. He also participated in military drill with the Cadet Corps, which was compulsory since Cornell was a land-grant institution. Later, Gannett observed: "There was no leisure in any of my college years."

In the spring of his freshman year, Gannett was elected class representative on the board of editors of the *Cornell Sun*, the University's daily newspaper. An editor's annual share of the *Sun's* profits was $200, which allowed him to drop his job of waiting on tables. His assignment as reporter for the *Sun* was covering Cornell President Jacob Schurman's office. Gannett's ability to take shorthand was rewarded one day when Andrew Carnegie spoke to the student body without using a prepared text. The student reporter published every word of Carnegie's speech.

Gannett used the advice that his mother had given him: "Make the most of opportunity and spend less than you earn." He also listened to Andrew Carnegie: "Put all of your eggs in one basket, where you can watch them." This financial advice was counter to the popular saying, but Gannett followed it; his single basket was the newspaper business.

Gannett majored in liberal arts; the first two years consisted of required courses. Electives that he chose during his last two years at Cornell included criminal law, economics, and the psychology of salesmanship. During summers, he sold the medical compendium, *The Cottage Physician*, in rural areas. He won a sales award his first summer and trained other salesmen during his second summer.

Gannett left the *Cornell Sun* during his junior year to work for the Ithaca *Journal* at higher pay. He was given a list of names of individuals who were not to be mentioned in the *Journal,* principally because they did not buy advertising. He disagreed with the business office dictating to the editorial department, a practice that he did not follow in the newspapers that he owned later. Soon his byline appeared in newspapers in Boston, Buffalo, Chicago, New York, Philadelphia, and Syracuse, and he was able to drop his laundry route and his job for the pants presser. Sportswriting was one of his specialities.

In June 1898, Gannett graduated from Cornell University with a Bachelor of Arts degree. He had eighty dollars in his pocket when he enrolled at Cornell; he graduated with savings of $1,000 and joined the news staff of the Syracuse *Herald*. His motto was "to make myself more useful." He thought that he could do so by returning to Cornell to take graduate courses in economics, history, and literature and to earn a Master of Arts degree. He moved back to Ithaca but became so involved in reporting that he did not enroll for the courses.

Gannett's plans were changed by a telegram from Washington, D.C., from Cornell's President Jacob Schurman. Schurman had been appointed by President McKinley as chairman of a commission to determine how to govern the Philippine Islands, which had become a protectorate of the United States after the Spanish-American War. Gannett could not turn down the opportunity to be present where news was being made, to travel, and to earn $3,000 a year plus travel expenses as Schurman's secretary.

Schurman and Gannett arrived in the Philippines during the Aguinaldo uprising. Insurgents surrounded Manila, which was still in the control of the U.S. Army and its Philippine allies. Gannett was already an industrious, organized person. Schurman, who scheduled his own day in detail and then scrupulously followed it, was a model for the young secretary. Gannett became so efficient in carrying out his duties that he was given the nickname "Can do." Early in 1900, when the Schurman Commission finished its work in the Philippines, Gannett took three months to return to the United States via Singapore and the Suez Canal.

Schurman cabled Gannett in London, advising him that a second commission to the Philippines was to be chaired by William Howard Taft. Schurman had recommended Gannett to Taft as his secretary, and Taft offered him the position. Gannett visited Schurman in Ithaca and was advised to go into the newspaper business as planned and not to take the offered position. Gannett joined the Ithaca *Daily News* as city editor.

Two significant changes were occurring at this time in the newspaper business: ethics were improving and new production techniques were being implemented. Newspapers were becoming less sensational and less involved with political party influence. Halftone engravings, high-speed presses, and mechanical typesetters were being used increasingly.

Gannett had been successful in the news side of the business, and he wanted to gain experience in the management of a newspaper. He became business manager of the Ithaca *Daily News*, in charge of running the paper. He was appalled by accounting methods that prevented him from knowing whether he was operating at a profit or a loss. He instituted modern newspaper accounting techniques that were copied by many other newspapers. These techniques were used by the twenty-one newspapers that he later owned and controlled.

Eventually, Gannett became disenchanted with the dependence of the *Daily News* upon political advertising. He joined Frank Leslie's *Illustrated Weekly* magazine in New York as a feature editor. It was good experience for him, but he wanted to return to the newspaper business.

Gannett's return resulted from a chance meeting in the Langwell Hotel in Elmira, where he had lunch between trains while traveling to Ithaca. The Langwell Hotel proprietor knew of Gannett's reputation; he also knew that young Elmira newspaperman Erwin Davenport was looking for a partner to own and run the Elmira *Gazette*.

The half-interest in the *Gazette* that Gannett wanted to buy was owned by David B. Hill, who had been mayor of Elmira, governor of New York, and U.S. Senator. He visited Hill and was asked to stay for three days, probably so that Hill could evaluate him. They talked politics for the entire time, and, finally, Gannett brought the subject around to the business at hand.

Hill offered fifty percent interest to Gannett for the same price that Davenport had paid the year before. Gannett borrowed $2,000 from the Bank of Ithaca and $5,000 from the Bank of Bolivar to add to his savings of $3,000. Hill accepted his note for the remaining $10,000, and Gannett was part-owner of his first newspaper.

Gannett was responsible for the editorials and the news; Davenport managed the business side, including advertising and circulation. The *Gazette's* production equipment was antiquated, but they managed to keep it running. Elmira's morning newspaper was the *Advertiser*, and the *Star* was the other afternoon newspaper. The Elmira market could not support two afternoon newspapers. Owners of the *Star* proposed a merger with the *Gazette*; Gannett accepted.

Although the *Star* was three times the size of the *Gazette*, Gannett proposed that the shares be split fifty-fifty; the two owners of the *Gazette* and the two owners of the *Star* each received twenty-five percent ownership of the merged *Star-Gazette*. The elder statesman of the *Star* became the president, Davenport continued as business manager, and Gannett and the other *Star* partner shared the editorial and news duties. Gannett worked fourteen-hour days Monday through Saturday and part-time on Sundays.

Gannett's first opportunity to expand was an offer to buy the Ithaca *Journal*. Two estates had inherited the *Journal* when its owner passed away, and neither had any interest in running a newspaper. Gannett obtained a loan to buy the Ithaca newspaper. Gannett did not move to Ithaca to manage the *Journal*; he stayed in Elmira.

Gannett supported Woodrow Wilson for President in 1912 as did the Elmira *Star-Gazette*. However, he did not impose his views on the Ithaca *Journal*, which favored the candidacy of William Howard Taft.

The *Star-Gazette* was financially successful, but it did not generate enough income to support the four families of the quarter-owners. They considered buying the Akron *Beacon-Journal*, but Charles Knight decided not to sell. The *Beacon-Journal* became the foundation of the newspaper chain of Charles Knight's son, John S. Knight, who expanded into Chicago, Detroit, and Miami in his early ventures. Gannett and his partners investigated the Rochester newspaper market. The City had five newspapers that were backward in their presentation of the news and lacked modern production facilities.

Rochester had two morning newspapers and three afternoon newspapers, the *Post-Express,* the *Times,* and the *Union and Advertiser.* The partners decided to buy the *Times* and the *Union and Advertiser* and merge them into the *Times-Union;* however, they needed $250,000 that they did not have. They borrowed $100,000 from Elmira banks, and one of Gannett's partners asked for a loan from a friend, John N. Willys. Willys, chairman of the Willys-Overland Motorcar Company, had started his business career in Elmira. He did not give them a loan, but stock certificates in the Fisk Rubber Company instead. The partners used the stock as collateral for a $100,000 bank loan.

Gannett and Davenport moved to Rochester to manage the new acquisitions. Again, Davenport was the business manager, and Gannett was responsible for the news and editorials. In the middle of World War I, it was a risky venture. Newsprint was in short supply, and large orders from major city newspapers were crowding out orders from smaller papers. However, Gannett had a good relationship with the paper mills. He obtained sufficient newsprint not only for his own newspapers, but also for the weekly newspapers in the area as a favor to them.

Printing legal notices for the County was a plum of newspaper publishing. George W. Aldridge, Republican political boss of Monroe County visited Gannett and offered him a contract for printing the County's legal notices, which was worth $50,000 a year. Unfortunately, there were strings attached. Gannett surprised Aldridge by turning down the offer; the young newspaperman wanted to run newspapers that were independent.

Gannett had moved to Rochester in 1918 with a few letters of introduction to area notables. One letter of introduction from an Elmira friend was to Mrs. William E. Werner, whose late husband had been a judge of the New York State Court of Appeals. Gannett was captivated by the youngest Werner daughter, Caroline, who was seventeen years younger than he was. The family was surprised by Caroline's interest in a man who had just turned forty and owed large debts due to his newspaper commitments. They were married on March 25, 1920.

In 1920, the partners made their third acquisition by buying Utica's two afternoon papers, the *Herald-Dispatch* and the *Observer*, which they merged into the *Observer-Dispatch*. Initially, they had problems with the new Utica newspaper because none of the partners moved to Utica to manage it. Eventually it became profitable, largely due to the efforts of Prentice Bailey, the son of the *Observer's* editor.

In 1922, the Rochester *Times-Union*, which had become a profitable enterprise, was faced with its largest challenge: William Randolph Hearst started an afternoon newspaper, the Rochester *Journal*, in direct competition with the *Times-Union*. The *Journal* used all of the big city newspaper promotion techniques and gave away a Ford automobile a day for thirty days in order to gain circulation. Instead of competing by using Hearst's promotion schemes, Gannett concentrated on making improvements to the *Times-Union*. Hearst offered to buy out any of Gannett's partners who were interested in selling.

Gannett's partners were not nearly as aggressive in expanding as he was, and Davenport was suffering with stomach ulcers. The partners had an agreement to sell their shares to the other partners before selling to an outside party. Gannett realized that the only way to fight Hearst was to buy out his partners and pursue the business aggressively.

The 1920s were the time of Gannett's most rapid expansion. His venture into radio was not as successful as his newspaper business. He entered the field too soon and got out too early.

Gannett met George Eastman soon after moving to Rochester and worked well with him. Gannett said, "It was a great experience to have known George Eastman as I knew him." When Gannett's rival, the Rochester *Democrat and Chronicle*, planned to establish a radio station to compete with the one owned by the *Times-Union*, Eastman suggested that they join forces and establish one good station instead of two mediocre ones. The radio station was installed in the Eastman School of Music to broadcast quality music programs.

Gannett expanded his newspaper chain not by establishing new newspapers, but by buying existing papers and improving them. Frank Tripp, his trouble-shooter from Elmira, was a valuable asset. They did not always agree on issues, but they respected each other's judgment.

Over a forty-year period, Gannett acquired twenty-seven newspapers, ten of which he consolidated into five. He sold one newspaper, the Winston-Salem *Sentinel* (his only southern paper), and practically gave one away, the Brooklyn *Eagle*, which was not profitable.

Gannett placed heavy emphasis on the value of good auditors, both prior to the purchase and during the early ownership of an acquisition. He ensured that his papers were free from political influence or other interests. His principal goal was to be financially sound. In his opinion, "No newspaper is really free which is not financially strong. A newspaper editor who is constantly harassed by bill collectors can never produce a great newspaper.... One of the things that has influenced me most in building up a group of newspapers has been the desire to give them financial strength and independence."

During President Roosevelt's second term, Gannett formed the National Committee to Uphold Constitutional Government to fight the President Roosevelt's scheme to pack the Supreme Court with additional justices who supported his interests. Gannett served with Republicans on this committee and by 1938 was ready to switch his affiliation from the Democratic Party.

Gannett became a candidate for the Republican nomination for President in 1940. His rivals for the nomination at the Republican National Convention in Philadelphia were Dewey, Taft, Vandenberg, and Willkie. William W. Wadsworth, Jr., of Geneseo, gave the speech nominating Gannett at the convention. On the first ballot, Dewey received 360 votes, Taft received 129, Willkie 105, and Gannett 33. Willkie won the nomination on the sixth ballot and lost dramatically to President Roosevelt.

The young man from Blood's Depot had come a long way. He did it by being hard-working, honest, and self-reliant. From his early days delivering newspapers, to working his way through Cornell, to applying for loans to buy and expand his business, Gannett displayed perseverance and a sense of responsibility. He was willing to take risks and to trust his partners and key managers.

Gannett is an outstanding example of a self-made individual.

## *Al Neuharth (1924-    )*

"The most satisfying victories are those where the odds against your winning are the greatest. But long odds don't necessarily make the job more difficult. In fact, the more that people tell you that it can't be done, the more likely that you have a winner. That usually means that you know something that they don't know. Or that your idea is so different or so daring that they can't comprehend it. If your sights are clearly set on a goal, the fact that others say it can't be done shouldn't slow you down. It should spur you on."                         Al Neuharth, *Confessions of an S. O. B.*

Al Neuharth, the younger of two sons of Daniel and Christina Neuharth, was born in Eureka, South Dakota, in 1924. Daniel farmed eighty acres until he injured his leg in a farm accident, developed tuberculosis, and died in 1926. Christina took in laundry and sewing and waited on tables to support the family. Her motto was: "Do a little bit more tomorrow than you did today, a little better next year than you did this year."

At the age of eleven, Neuharth delivered the Minneapolis *Tribune* and, at thirteen, worked after school in the composing room of the Alpena *Journal*. In 1942, he graduated from high school and enlisted in the U.S. Army in early World War II. He won a bronze star as a combat infantryman, and by the end of the War he had earned sergeant's stripes.

In 1946, Neuharth returned home to enroll at the University of South Dakota on the G. I. Bill. He announced sports events for the college radio station before shifting his interest to the college newspaper, the *Volante*, and becoming its editor. In 1950, he was elected to Phi Beta Kappa. After graduation, he became a reporter for the Associated Press.

In 1952, with $50,000 from the sale of shares in the venture, Neuharth and a friend started *SoDak Sports*, a statewide sports weekly modeled on the national *Sporting News*. Within a year, circulation had increased to 18,000, but sales of advertising space were sluggish. Their few advertisers began to shift to television commercials.

In 1954, Neuharth and his partner tried unsuccessfully to sell their weekly. Finally, they declared bankruptcy; their creditors received less than thirty-five cents on the dollar. Neuharth looked upon it as a learning experience. No plan had been prepared for projected sales revenue, expected advertising income, or anticipated profit and loss. Lack of a business plan was their worst mistake, one that Neuharth would not make again.

Neuharth accepted a job as a reporter for the Miami *Herald*. He wrote a series of articles about mail order scams and was at the right place at the right time on some fast-breaking stories. His career took off, and he was given an assignment with the *Herald's* Washington bureau. In 1959, he was promoted to assistant managing editor of the *Herald* and was chosen to open its Brevard County, Florida, bureau to cover news from the Cape Canaveral Space Center.

The following year, Neuharth was appointed assistant to the executive editor of the Detroit *Free Press*. He worked in both news and business operations; his performance was noticed both inside and outside of Knight Newspapers. In 1963, he accepted a position with Gannett Newspapers as general manager of its Rochester newspapers: the *Democrat and Chronicle* and the *Times-Union*. He was considered heir apparent to Paul Miller, chief executive officer of Gannett Newspapers.

Neuharth suggested to Miller that Gannett start a daily newspaper in Brevard County serving the Cape Canaveral area. Miller had tried unsuccessfully to buy a small Florida daily as a nucleus for expansion; he was receptive to Neuharth's suggestion even though it was counter to the national trend of fewer daily newspapers. Neuharth bought the Cocoa *Tribune* for $1.9 million, but, instead of upgrading it, he started a new paper, *Today: Florida's Space Age Newspaper*, with a new format. He supplemented the small staff with "loaners" from other Gannett newspapers.

Neuharth avoided two mistakes that he had made in starting *SoDak Sports*. First, he authorized preparation of a comprehensive business plan; second, he ensured that he had sufficient funds to pay for the start-up. Neuharth was a hands-on manager. He was on-site in Cocoa functioning as managing editor. He organized the new paper into three sections: News, Business, and Sports. The comics section was printed in color, a *Today* innovation. *Today* was profitable in twenty-eight months, due mainly to the innovation and determination of Neuharth.

In 1973, Neuharth became chief executive officer of Gannett Newspapers. He was appointed chairman when Paul Miller retired in 1978. Neuharth had considered the concept of a national newspaper for ten years; finally, he proceeded with the idea for both professional and personal reasons. He knew that the profession of newspaper journalism could do a better job than it was doing, and he needed new worlds to conquer.

Improvements in satellite communications helped to make the idea achievable. Neuharth's intention was apparent in stating his goal: "We'll reinvent the newspaper." He intended to create a newspaper so captivating that it would attract millions of readers, including many who currently did not read a newspaper. He also wanted to innovate the design and content of the new paper to "pull the rest of the industry into the twenty-first century, albeit kicking and screaming."

By late 1979, Gannett had newspapers across the United States, including many in major city markets. In areas where Gannett did not own a printing plant, it could make contract printing arrangements. Neuharth considered three start-up possibilities that could use this network to Gannett's advantage:

- a national sports daily, similar to the *Sporting News* and *Sports Illustrated*
- a daily and/or Sunday supplement for the Gannett community newspapers with national news and advertising
- a national general-interest daily newspaper

Neuharth asked for opinions from three key Gannett managers: John Quinn, chief news executive; Jack Heselden, president of the newspaper division; and Douglas McCorkindale, chief financial and legal officer. At the year-end board of directors' meeting, Neuharth announced that he was going to set aside $1 million in 1980 to "study what's new in newspapers and television. And especially whether we can harness the satellite to deliver more news to more people in more ways."

The research and development effort was called Project NN for "National Newspaper" but Neuharth promoted the idea outside of Gannett that it stood for "New Newspapers." Project NN soon became known outside of the company as "Neuharth's Nonsense."

The project team that assembled in Florida included a newsman with an excellent record in news research, a research and marketing specialist, an expert in satellite communications technology, and a circulation specialist. Neuharth chose Vince Spezzano, the veteran publisher of *Today* in Florida, as coordinator of the team. The average age of the team's members, excluding Spezzano, was thirty.

Neuharth courted the board of directors' support for his project and kept them informed. In October 1980, the Project NN status report was presented to the board, and an additional $3.5 million was budgeted for planning and prototypes in 1981. In August 1981, the protypes were reviewed by the board as well as research conducted by Lou Harris and Associates and the Simmons Market Research Bureau. In December 1981, the board of directors voted to launch *USA Today* by a unanimous 12-0 vote, even though the Gannett financial organization counseled against going ahead.

The next phase was called GANSAT, Gannett Satellite Information Network. Team members were a supervisor of business planning, a planning editor responsible for prototype development, a finance director, and a director of circulation. Neuharth personally worked on the news product and circulation planning; he continued to be a hands-on manager. John Quinn, Gannett's chief news executive, worked virtually full-time with the planning editor on prototype plans.

The team decided that *USA Today* must be different from other newspapers, both in appearance and in content. Early goals were to have four highly organized sections, an emphasis on color, easy-to-read stories, frequent use of charts and graphics, news from all fifty states, and a concentration on sports, TV, and weather. Neuharth used "intrapreneurship" on *USA Today* by obtaining "loaners" from the other Gannett papers. Loaners were away from their parent newspapers for an average of four months and were not replaced. Young newspaper journalists were provided with a broadening experience as well as an introduction to new concepts and technology.

On September 15, 1982, *USA Today* was launched at a party in Washington, D.C., attended by President and Mrs. Ronald Reagan, Speaker of the House "Tip" O'Neill, and Senate Majority Leader Howard Baker. Red, white, and blue *USA Today* banners waved from the 60-foot-wide by 140-foot-long tent erected on the

National Mall. The 800 guests included cabinet members, Representatives, Senators, publishers, and executives. The party on the Mall was followed by dinner at *USA Today* headquarters across the Potomac River in Virginia, where food from every state was served.

By 1983, circulation of *USA Today* exceeded one million, which surpassed all other newspapers except the *Wall Street Journal*, the New York *Daily News*, and the Los Angeles *Times*. Attracting advertisers was difficult because the only official circulation statistics were those provided by the Audit Bureau of Circulations (ABC), and they would not review circulation until after the first year of operation. Neuharth commissioned a circulation survey by the public accounting firm of Price Waterhouse, who verified that circulation had surpassed one million. However, Madison Avenue did not consider the results official. Finally, in late June 1984, ABC verified that annual circulation was 1.28 million.

In August 1984, Neuharth estimated that *USA Today's* losses would be $124 million in 1984, $81 million in 1985, and $25 million in 1986, but that the venture would break even in 1987. He also estimated that the cumulative losses since start-up would approach $400 million before taxes by the end of 1987. That evaluation of *USA Today's* finances was "as close as we ever came to folding the tent." Advertising increased notably after Cathleen Black was brought in from *New York* magazine as president of *USA Today* and assigned the responsibility for advertising.

Losses continued at $10 million a month during 1984. Neuharth realized that serious steps would have to be taken to save the paper. On Sunday, November 11, 1984, he held a meeting of *USA Today's* management committee at his Florida home. He told the committee that current business conditions could not continue; they had alternatives of quitting or making a concerted effort to implement crucial changes.

As noted by Peter S. Prichard in *The Making of McPaper,* Neuharth stated that they must reduce their losses by substituting management for money, by taking the following steps:
- "We must produce and present even more news, with fewer people, in less space, at lower cost.
- We must sell and present even more advertising, at higher rates, with fewer people, at lower cost.

- We must produce and print more newspapers, with
  even better quality, with fewer people, at lower cost.
- We must circulate and sell even more newspapers,
  at higher prices, with fewer people, at lower cost...."

Neuharth directed a reduction of payroll costs by five percent by the end of 1985 and required that new hires have his or Gannett President John Curley's approval. Also, he set a goal for losses of under $75 million in 1985.

*USA Today* was not considered a serious newspaper by many members of the journalism community, to whom it was "McPaper." *USA Today* staffers heard the name, "McPaper," and commented that many papers were stealing their McNuggets. Chief news executive John Quinn quipped that if *USA Today* ever won a Pulitzer Prize, it would probably be for "the best investigative paragraph." In *The Making of McPaper*, Peter Prichard quoted Quinn's speech to the National Press Foundation, in which Quinn predicted headlines about the end of the world:

In the *Wall Street Journal*, the headline would read:
**STOCK EXCHANGE HALTS TRADING AS WORLD ENDS**

In the New York *Times:*
**END OF WORLD HITS THIRD WORLD HARDEST**

In the Washington *Post:*
**WORLD ENDS; MAY EFFECT ELECTIONS, SOURCES SAY**

In *USA Today*, Quinn said the end-of-world headline would be:
**WE'RE GONE ... STATE-BY-STATE DEMISE ON 6A, FINAL SCORES ON 8C**

Earnings from Gannett's other newspapers were paying the bills for *USA Today*. By mid-1985, the "Nation's Newspaper" began to turn the corner financially. Gannett reported a twenty percent earnings increase compared to the first half of 1984. Cathy Black had increased advertising revenue 106 percent compared to the previous year. Price was increased from thirty-five cents to fifty cents when the size of the paper was increased to sixty pages. However, losses were still staggering: $102 million in 1985, followed by $70 million in 1986.

In May 1986, Neuharth stepped down as CEO of Gannett but retained the title of chairman. He recalled his difficult transition with Paul Miller and wanted to ensure that his succession by President John Curley was orderly. He said that he intended to stay on as chairman until 1989 when he would be sixty-five.

In July 1986, Simmons Market Research conducted a survey noting that *USA Today* had 4,792,000 readers per day, the most readers of any U.S. daily. The *Wall Street Journal's* paid circulation was still much higher, but each *USA Today* was read by three readers while the *Journal* was read by only two readers, on the average. Increases in *USA Today's* advertising followed those in readership.

On June 15, 1987, Curley sent a telegram to Neuharth, who was on a business trip: "McPaper has made it. *USA Today* broke into the black with a profit of $1,093,756 for the month of May, six months ahead of schedule." The Nation's Newspaper had become profitable faster than many other media new ventures: *Sports Illustrated* required ten years to move into the black; *Newsweek* nine years; and *Money* magazine eight years.

Neuharth's vision and pure strength of will brought a daily national newspaper into existence when many said it could not be done. He was a driven achiever who truly believed that you should "do a little bit more tomorrow than you did today, a little better next year than you did this year."

Wilder Building, Corner of Main and Exchange Streets

# CHAPTER 3

# COMPOSERS / AUTHORS / EDUCATORS

## Alec Wilder (1907-1980)

"Alec Wilder's music is a unique blend of American musical traditions—among them jazz and the American popular song—and basic 'classical' European forms and techniques. As such, it fiercely resists all labeling. Although it pained Alec that his music was not more widely accepted by either jazz or classical performers, undeterred he wrote a great deal of music of remarkable originality in many forms: sonatas, suites, concertos, operas, ballets, art songs, woodwind quartets, brass quintets, jazz suites—and hundreds of popular songs.

Many times his music wasn't jazz enough for the 'jazzers,' or 'highbrow,' 'classical,' or 'avant-garde' enough for the classical establishment. In essence, Wilder's music was so unique in its originality that it didn't fit in any of the preordained musical slots and stylistic pigeon-holes. His music was never out of vogue because, in effect, it was never in vogue; its non-stereotypical specialness virtually precluding widespread acceptance."       Gunther Schuller,
Loonis McGlohon, and Robert Levy, "A Short Biography"

Alec Wilder's grandfather, Samuel Wilder, made the family fortune in banking and real estate in Rochester. He was the principal owner of Corinthian Hall, where the Swedish nightingale, Jenny Lind, gave her first Rochester performance. Alec's father, George, Samuel's second son, was also a successful Rochester banker. Alec's mother was Lillian Chew Wilder, daughter of Alexander Lafayette and Sarah Prouty Chew of Geneva, New York. The Marquis de Lafayette was Alexander Chew's godfather. The Prouty-Chew house in Geneva is now the Geneva Historical Society Museum.

Alec Wilder was born on February 16, 1907. He had an older brother, George, and an older sister, Helen, with whom he was close. Helen introduced him to music by singing the music of Jerome Kern to him. When Wilder was three years old, his father died. By the time he was a teenager, he knew that he did not want to be a banker like his grandfather and his father: "I wanted no part of it ... for my family was virtually littered with bankers, nor was I inclined to be friendly with the sons and daughters of the conventional families of my family's world."

The Wilder family moved frequently. Wilder attended three private schools: Saint Paul's in Garden City, Long Island, Lawrenceville in New Jersey, and the Collegiate School in Manhattan where they lived from 1921 until 1924. His first visit to the theater was to see *Shuffle Along,* Eubie Blake's all-black show.

In his late teens, Wilder toured Europe and became interested by music in Venice and Florence. He composed his first piano piece while in Italy and wrote to a friend:

> Something keeps shouting at me to look deeper and deeper into music. I've heard no music but that of countless people singing in the streets. Yet, I've started buying stacks of music, in fact I've even rented a piano. I don't know about music, don't play worth a damn nor read well, but ever since you took me to that concert at Carnegie Hall and I heard "L'Apres-Midi d'un Faune" I've got the bug. I've even written a piece of music that's not just a tune. I don't think it's good, but it is something which I wrote. And it's the first one.

When Wilder returned to New York, he wrote some popular tunes and then, at the suggestion of his friend, tried a cantata based on one of Kipling's poems.

In 1926, Wilder returned to Rochester for the first time since his family had moved to Garden City during World War I. He had decided on a career in music; however, he did not enroll at the Eastman School of Music. Instead, he took private lessons from two faculty members. He studied counterpoint with Herbert Inch, who later won the Prix de Rome, and composition with Edward Royce, son of Harvard University logician Josiah Royce.

Wilder was impressed with the Eastman School; he noted: "It's the wild, free, searching, roaring world of young people who know what they want ... and my God, how they love music." He met french horn player John Barrows, oboist Mitch Miller, violist Joe Schiff, and tenor Frank Baker. Wilder was becoming immersed in music: "Music, its sounds, rhythms, patterns and unverbal implications, directions and secret affirmations had always fascinated me. The more I heard, the more I learned, the more dedicated I became in to trying to speak its language."

Wilder's favorite composer was Bach. He was also influenced by Moussorgsky, Debussy, and Ravel. Although Howard Hanson was the director of the Eastman School at the time, he and Wilder were too dissimilar to become close. Hanson composed large works in the romantic tradition. His favorite composers were Beethoven, Handel, and Scriabin. Hanson was an autocratic leader; Wilder had little respect for authority. Nevertheless, Hanson said of Wilder's compositions, "His music—intimate, appealing, and very well done—had great charm."

In 1928, Wilder composed eight songs for voice and orchestra based on poems by James Stephens and the song *Annabelle Lee,* using text from Edgar Allan Poe. The following year, he composed one of his first works for orchestra, *Symphonic Piece.* Also, in his student days, he composed popular songs with a particular singer in mind, e.g. Mildred Bailey, Ethel Waters, and Bing Crosby. "Mildred wound up singing some, Ethel Waters none, and, at the end of his career, Crosby a few."

During his time at the Eastman School, Wilder wrote the revue *Haywire.* Fellow Eastman student Mitch Miller commented: "He was a very complicated man. I forced him to face his own talent. I got him to write *Haywire.*" Although two other students wrote some of the lyrics and one or two of the musical numbers were interpolated, it was loaded with his wit and essentially was a Wilder show.

While in Rochester, Wilder became close with his mentor and father figure, James Sibley Watson, Jr., grandson of Western Union co-founder Hiram Sibley. According to Desmond Stone in *Alec Wilder in Spite of Himself,* Watson was "a true renaissance figure: physician, major influence in American literature in the 1920s, translator of French poetry [such as Rimbaud], pioneer in radiology and in amateur filmmaking, artist, flyer, expert marksman, inventor, millionaire philanthropist." He was also part owner of *Dial* magazine.

In association with Melville Webber, Watson produced two American cinematic landmarks: *The Fall of the House of Usher* in 1929 and *Lot in Sodom* in 1932. In the opinion of James Card, previously film archivist at the Eastman House, "Watson produced avant-garde films long before there were avant-garde films." Watson provided Wilder with an introduction to filmmaking and film scoring.

Another of Wilder's close friends in Rochester was photographer Louis Ouzer. Later, Ouzer was known for his portraits of Marian Anderson, Louis Armstrong, Vladimir Horowitz, Isaac Stern, and other musicians who performed at the Eastman Theatre. He also used his talent in photography to document social change. He was particularly sympathetic to the cause of civil rights for African Americans.

In 1930, Wilder had his first success in writing popular songs: "All the King's Men" written with Eddie Brandt for *Three's a Crowd,* a Broadway revue starring Fred Allen, Libby Holman, and Clifton Webb. By the mid-1930s, Wilder's friends from the Eastman School, Mitch Miller and John Barrows, had moved from Rochester. By this time, Wilder had spent (and given away) his inheritance except for a small quarterly allowance from a family trust fund.

Wilder returned to New York City and lived at the Algonquin Hotel, which would be his home for four decades. As noted by biographer Desmond Stone, in later years Wilder observed:

> I have been coming here since I was a child, and there are still people on the staff who have been here as long as I have. They take care of me. They send out my laundry without my having to fill out a laundry slip, they hang a few suits for me when I'm away, they forward my mail, and they shepherded me through my drinking days.... I got into a cab to go uptown to a restaurant, and when I got there I simply couldn't move. I told the driver to take me back to the Algonquin, and whoever was on the door sized up the situation immediately. A

bellman appeared, and he and the doorman made one of those four-handed seats, got me onto it, and whisked me up to my room.

An anecdote about Wilder's drinking relates that on one occasion while in his cups at the Algonquin's Blue Bar, he asked Benny Goodman to step outside and take his glasses off. Wilder did not remember the incident the next morning. It is unlikely. One of Wilder's friends described him as a "great walk-away artist."

Wilder was influenced by the music of Harold Arlen, Jerome Kern, and Vincent Youmans. Wilder's friend, Mitch Miller, obtained a position for him as staff arranger for the *Ford Hour* on radio, but Wilder could not tolerate the lack of freedom that he encountered. Miller also encouraged Wilder to write the woodwind octets that were recorded by the Alec Wilder Octet and introduced him to people in musical circles.

In 1939, Wilder met William Engvick, who became one of his lyricists. Their first collaboration was in revising *Ladies and Gents,* on which Engvick had worked previously. Their collaboration "City Night" from that musical became the theme song of the Jack Jenney Orchestra.

Wilder met Frank Sinatra when the young singer performed at the Paramount Theater in New York in the 1940s. In 1945, Mitch Miller talked with Sinatra about performing some of Wilder's orchestral pieces. Sinatra, who had not conducted before, recorded a suite of six numbers mixing classical music, jazz, and pop, *Frank Sinatra Conducts the Music of Alec Wilder,* for Columbia Records. Sinatra observed that Wilder's music "helped my own musical conceptions to reach a higher plane than would have been possible without him."

During the 1940s, Wilder composed many of his best-known popular songs, including "Who Can I Turn To" (1940); "It's So Peaceful in the Country" (1941), which he wrote for Mildred Bailey; "I'll Be Around" (1942); "While We're Young" (1943); "Trouble Is a Man" (1944); and "Where Is the One" (1948).

Wilder had the highest regard for cabaret singer Mabel Mercer, whom he considered "the guardian of the tenuous dreams created by the writers of songs." Wilder wrote many songs for her, including "Did You Ever Cross Over to Snedden's?," "Goodbye, John," and "Is It Always Like This?" Mercer and Wilder were friends for forty years.

Wilder had successes but never the big one. His lyricist, William Engvick, identified the problem: "Wilder's unusual and, for the time, difficult arrangements and his oddly shaped, understated and unpredictable melodies caused much antagonism (as they still do) and his progress was difficult. This was complicated by a totally uncommercial dignity and a trenchant wit which left his antagonists sneering, unaware that they were bleeding internally."

Wilder hurt himself by refusing to promote his own works. At times, he was stubborn; he lost the opportunity to write the score for *Peter Pan* for Mary Martin because he did not want to work with Martin's lyricist. He turned down a man who called him to ask if he would do the score for a ballet because "I didn't like the sound of his voice." The ballet was *Fancy Free,* which established Leonard Bernstein's stage reputation. Wilder described his view of this behavior: "I blame no one but myself for the minimal success I have known. I have had to pay this price for keeping myself whole."

In the late 1940s, Wilder wrote his first opera, *The Impossible Forest.* Dancer Gene Kelly had recommended that Wilder compose the music. The libretto was written by Marshall Barer, who wrote *Once Upon a Mattress* with Mary Rodgers. Scenery and costume designer Lemuel Ayers, who had done *Kiss Me Kate,* was signed up, and Jerome Robbins was interested in staging the opera and doing the choreography. Henry Fonda considered starring in it. Unfortunately, sufficient funding could not be raised.

Wilder composed a second opera, *The Wind Blows Free,* with playwright and lyricist Arnold Sundgaard that suffered the same fate, insufficient funding. In Sundgaard's opinion, "The songs worked fine, but not the play itself." Two of Wilder's songs survived on their own. He went back to writing popular songs, some of which, such as "While We're Young,*"* were sung by Peggy Lee.

Wilder and Engvick were invited to Hollywood by Twentieth Century Fox to write the songs for *Daddy Long Legs.* After writing fifteen songs, they were told that the script was not ready and that they would have to wait until it was. Even though he would be retained on salary, Wilder decided to return to New York. Fox sold the rights to the movie and when *Daddy Long Legs* was finally filmed with Fred Astaire and Leslie Caron, the music of Johnny Mercer (who later wrote lyrics for Wilder) was used instead. The original songs remained out of the public domain.

Wilder developed a friendship with Judy Holliday. Her reputation had been made when she was asked, on short notice, to fill in for Jean Arthur, who had become ill while starring in Rochesterian Garson Kanin's hit comedy, *Born Yesterday.* In 1958, Holliday made a record album for Columbia Records, *Trouble Is a Man.* She chose songs by Berlin, Bernstein, Wilder, and others. She opened the album with the title song by Wilder. It was thought that Wilder had an idolized love for Holliday, whose personality he considered a "sometime, someplace woman, girl, female."

With the introduction of rock and roll in the 1950s and 1960s, interest in popular music waned. Wilder's old friend from the Eastman School, John Barrows, turned him toward concert music and introduced him to many musicians. Wilder's first efforts were two sonatas for horn and piano and *Suite for French Horn and Piano.* He composed for instruments that had been ignored by composers over the years, including the tuba, marimba, guitar, baritone saxophone, and harp.

In 1959, Wilder wrote *Sonata No. 1 for Tuba and Piano.* Only two solos had been written for tuba previously, one by Vaughan Williams and the other by Hindemith. Next he composed *Effie Suite* for tuba, about the experiences of an elephant named "Effie." These were followed by *Sonata for Bass Trombone and Piano, Concerto for Oboe, String Orchestra, and Percussion, Jazz Suite for Four Horns, Concerto No. 1 for Horn and Chamber Orchestra,* and *Suite No. 1 for Horn, Tuba, and Piano.*

Wilder also wrote many children's pieces, some by himself and some with Engvick or Sundgaard. In 1954, Wilder wrote, with lyrics by Marshall Barer, *A Child's Introduction to the Orchestra.* which Mitch Miller conducted with the Golden Symphony and the Sandpiper Chorus. In 1965, *Lullabies and Night Songs,* an illustrated collection of children's songs by Wilder and Engvick, was published by Harper & Row.

Wilder teamed with his third lyricist, Loonis McGlohon, on *Land of Oz,* an outdoor version of *The Wizard of Oz* staged on top of Beech Mountain in western North Carolina. It was the first of many successful collaborations with McGlohon. One of the finest was "Blackberry Winter." McGlohon was a composer as well as a lyricist. As a pianist, he had accompanied Eileen Farrell, Judy Garland, Maxine Sullivan, and Maxine VerPlanck. Buffalo native Harold Arlen gave them permission to use "Over the Rainbow" for *Land of Oz,* and Wilder composed many new numbers.

In 1968, Wilder began to work on *American Popular Song: The Great Innovators, 1900-1950,* edited by James Maher, who also wrote the Introduction. The book, a distillation of a half-century of of popular songwriting, was published by Oxford University Press in 1972 to critical acclaim. None of Wilder's works are included in the book, but 800 others are examined. In 1973, the book won the Deems Taylor ASCAP Award and a National Book Award nomination.

When Maher visited Wilder in Manhattan to begin their collaboration, Wilder invited him up to his room at the Algonquin Hotel. Maher, who assumed that he was being invited to a suite of rooms, observed: "This was the suite of Alec Wilder! No books, no records—no room, for that matter. There was a second chair, a side chair, but I couldn't see it because there was an opened suitcase on it. Tobacco, some shirts, a bobble bird, ... a jar of special honey, some airmail writing pads, and similar odds and ends lay on top of the dresser." Nevertheless, as soon as he and Maher began to discuss the book, Wilder knew that he had found the organized collaborator that he needed.

It was important to Wilder that he could be packed and out of his room in twenty minutes. One of his pastimes was riding the railroad—not to any particular destination. Biographer Desmond Stone quotes Wilder:

> Years ago, I'd check out when I had a little money
> and get on a train, and I'd stay on trains for weeks
> at a time. I'd travel the main trunks, and I'd trans-
> fer and take all the spurs. I loved sitting in a junc-
> tion in the back of the beyond on a hot day and
> reading a long novel and listening to the chatter
> between the baggage man and the conductor. I
> loved talking with the engineer when he oiled his
> engine. Can you imagine nattering with a man
> fueling a jet?

Wilder's persona evolved into that of a rumpled professor of English Literature. In 1974, Whitney Balliett described Wilder in his *New Yorker* profile, "The President of the Derriére-garde":

> Wilder is is a tall man with a big head and small feet. He was wearing a sports jacket, gray slacks, and loafers, and they had a resigned look of functional clothes. He has a long, handsome face and receding gray hair that flows out the back of his head, giving the impression that he is in constant motion. His eyebrows are heavy and curved, and when he has finished making a point—often punctuated by his slamming his fist down on the nearest piece of furniture—they shoot up and the corners of his mouth shoot down.
>
> He has piercing, deep-set eyes cushioned by dark, doomsday pouches—diamonds resting on velvet. His face is heavily wrinkled—not with the soft, oh-I-am-growing-old lines but with strong, heavy weather ones. He has a loud baritone voice, and he talks rapidly. When he is agitated, his words roll like cannonballs around the room. He laughs a lot and he swears a lot, in an old-fashioned, Mark Twain manner, and when he is seated, he leans forward, like a figurehead breasting a flood tide. A small, serene mustache marks the eye of the hurricane.

On one occasion, a visitor to the Algonquin Hotel asked the doorman if he had seen Wilder. The doorman replied that you don't see Mr. Wilder, you hear him.

In 1975, Wilder was commissioned by the New York State Arts Council to compose an orchestral piece. *Entertainment No. 6* was first performed in 1977 by the Rochester Philharmonic Orchestra. That year and the following year, he completed many more instrumental compositions, including *Brass Quintet No. 6, Concerto for Flute and Chamber Orchestra, Sextet for Marimba and Wind Quintet, Suite for Flute and Marimba, Woodwind Quintet No. 13,*

*Brass Quintet No. 7, Suite for Flute and Strings, Suite for Horn and Tuba,* and *Suite for Trumpet and Marimba.* Interest in these pieces was narrow, but they pleased the musicians for whom they were written.

By 1978, Wilder knew that his health was slipping. In November that year in Gainesville, Florida, the life-long smoker had a cancerous lung removed. He recovered slowly, but eventually he began to compose again. Two of his last collaborations with McGlohon were "A Long Night" and "South to a Warmer Place," which subsequently were recorded by Sinatra. By December 1980, Wilder was short of breath and hallucinating.

Wilder's friend Louis Ouzer told another Rochester friend, lawyer and jazz program host Thomas Hampson, about their mutual friend's condition. Hampson flew to Gainesville to find that Wilder's condition was deteriorating rapidly. Hampson updated his friend's will and was appointed executor. Wilder died early in the morning of December 24.

Wilder was buried in St. Agnes Cemetery in Avon, New York, near the plot where his friend, Father Henry Atwell, previously pastor of St. Agnes Church, had been buried. Wilder had requested that there be no funeral, no religious service, and no notice in the newspapers of his death.

Hampson notified friends that he had arranged for a modest gravestone and a short burial ceremony: "I intend to honor Alec's request that there be no religious service, but a number of his friends said that they wanted to be present, and I certainly think that they should be permitted to do so."

Mitch Miller and long-term friend jazz pianist Marian McPartland, for whom Wilder had written a dozen pieces, were among those who attended the burial ceremony. Loomis McGlohon paid tribute to his collaborator: "Letters from strangers never went unanswered, even when they came from, in your words, people who lived in old soldiers' homes who thought that you were Thornton's brother.... You were a soft touch, Alec. As long as people believed in something, you couldn't say no." The ceremony was concluded by a trumpet playing "It's So Peaceful in the Country" and by old friend Louis Ouzer blowing a string of bubbles, something that Wilder and his friends, including Marian McPartland, had enjoyed doing, over the grave.

Wilder's own observation on his music was: "My life's work is accepted in large measure only by the old and the young. The middle-aged self-proclaimed musical elite dismiss it as traditional, and therefore suspect." In 1983, Alec Wilder was inducted into the Songwriters' Hall of Fame, and, in 1991, the Alec Wilder Reading Room in the Sibley Music Library was dedicated at the Eastman School of Music.

## *Howard Hanson (1896-1981)*

"Howard Hanson ... typifies, as clearly as any living composer, what might be classed as a conservative modernist. For which reason, he may be more popular with a coming generation than in his own."                                      Critic Fullerton Waldo

Howard Hanson, noted composer, director, and music educator, was director of the Eastman School of Music of the University of Rochester from 1924 to 1964. Over those forty years, he developed the Eastman School into one of the top university schools of music in the Western Hemisphere. In 1964, he founded the Institute of American Music at the School to popularize American compositions and to promote twentieth-century musical styles.

Hanson's compositions of the 1920s were described as "dissonant, avant-garde experimentations." His similar compositions of the 1930s were described as "solid, conservative" works. He was the recipient of thirty-six honorary degrees and was considered the greatest proponent of American music in the second quarter of the twentieth century.

Hanson was born on October 28, 1896, in Wahoo, Nebraska, to Swedish immigrant parents. His mother was his first music teacher. After receiving a diploma from Luther College in Wahoo at the age of fifteen, he studied with composer Percy Goetschius at the Institute of Musical Art in New York City. In 1916, he received a B.A. degree from Northwestern University, where he was an instructor. He studied piano and cello but concentrated on studies in composition.

At the age of twenty, Hanson accepted a full-time position as teacher of music theory and composition at the College of the Pacific in California. In 1919, he was appointed Dean of the College of Fine Arts at the College. While in California, he composed a number of chamber and orchestral works including his first work to receive national attention, *The California Forest Play.*

In 1921, Hanson was awarded the first Prix de Rome ever given by the American Academy in Rome for two of his works, *The California Forest Play* and *Before the Dawn,* a symphonic poem. He studied orchestration in Rome for three years with composer

Ottorino Respighi, who had been a student of Rimsky-Korsakov. This experience had a profound influence on his compositions, which were praised for their "full, rich" orchestration at the time and in later years.

Hanson, considered a neo-Romantic composer, was influenced in his early compositions by the lyrical and harmonic styles of Sibelius and Grieg as well as by the structural unity of Handel. He was fascinated by the Gregorian chant. Eastman School professor Ruth Watanabe observed: "The result is music of rhythmic vitality and tonal richness, touched with gaiety and humor—in his own view, specifically American in spirit."

In 1924, Hanson made his American debut as conductor with the New York Symphonic Orchestra. At the invitation of Walter Damrosch, he conducted the première of his symphonic poem, *North and West.* On numerous occasions, Serge Koussevitsky invited him to direct the Boston Symphony Orchestra, for which Hanson wrote the *Elegy* and the *Second Symphony.* Koussevitsky was a staunch supporter of Hanson's music. He repeatedly programmed Hanson's *Symphony No. 3* until it finally received a favorable review. Hanson became a popular conductor in the United States and in Europe.

Hanson's conducting activities brought him to the attention of George Eastman, sponsor of the Eastman School of Music, which was looking for a director. Rush Rhees, president of the University of Rochester, offered the position to Hanson, who began his residency of fifty-seven years in Rochester in 1924. The following year, he began the American Composers Orchestral Concerts and made many changes at the Eastman School, as noted by James E. Perone in *Howard Hanson: A Bio-Bibliography,* including:
- making the curriculum more comprehensive
- hiring the best studio teachers that he could find
- improving the orchestras by establishing the Eastman-Rochester Symphony Orchestra, comprised of first chair players from the Rochester Philharmonic Orchestra and the top students from the Eastman School, and founding the Eastman Philharmonia, a select student ensemble

In 1934, the première of Hanson's opera *Merrymount, Opus 31,* was performed by the Metropolitan Opera. This early American opera based on an American story had an American librettist and an

American cast. Based on the success of this opera, Hanson was elected a member of the National Institute of Arts and Letters in 1935.

Hanson was an active conductor during the 1940s and 1950s and made many recordings with the Eastman-Rochester Symphony Orchestra. He conducted his own works plus those of American composers John Alden Carpenter, Charles Tomlinson Griffes, John Knowles Pain, Walter Piston, William Grant Still, and many others. He estimated that over 2,000 works by more than 500 composers were introduced during his forty-year tenure at the Eastman School.

During World War II, Hanson promoted American composers while suggesting that opportunities should be provided in the United States for displaced musicians and composers from Europe. He developed a strong faculty at the Eastman School by hiring both American and European musicians.

During the summer of 1945, Hanson met Margaret Elizabeth Nelson and immediately began to court her. He composed the *Serenade for Flute, Harp, and Strings, Opus 35* and dedicated it to her. They were married on July 24, 1946. Margaret was active socially and was well-known in Rochester. She received press coverage in her own light, not just the light generated by her husband. Later, she accompanied her husband to dinners at the White House during the administrations of Presidents Eisenhower, Kennedy, Johnson, and Nixon.

In 1944, Hanson was awarded the Pulitzer Prize for *Symphony No. 4,* which had received unanimous praise from the critics. The following year, he received the National Association for American Composers and Conductors citation "for the greatest contribution to American music." In 1946, he and Rochester radio station WHAM won the George Foster Peabody Award for outstanding entertainment programming.

From 1946 until 1963, Hanson was active in the United Nations Educational, Scientific, and Cultural Organization (UNESCO). In his opinion, his participation in UNESCO "supported his strong belief in the role of international cultural exchange to achieve world cooperation and associated world peace."

In 1955, Hanson made thirteen television films about the process of composing for a series produced by the Ford Foundation for the Advancement of Education. The success of this series led to additional television programs in 1956 and 1957. Between 1957 and 1963, he produced three record albums for *The Composer and His Orchestra* series.

The largest audience for a Hanson première, 23,000, heard his *Song of Democracy* at the National Education Association conference in 1957. That composition, accompanied by a Walt Whitman text, was also performed at the inauguration of President Richard Nixon in 1969.

In 1960, Hanson conducted the Los Angeles Philharmonic in a series of five broadcast concerts to 20,000 school children. In 1963, he returned to Los Angeles to conduct his *For the First Time*, which illustrates scenes of childhood, in eight concerts. He believed musical appreciation should begin to be developed in elementary school.

In 1961-62, Hanson led the Eastman Philharmonia on a tour to Paris, Cairo, Moscow, Vienna, and other cities. Audiences and reporters for the press were amazed at the professional caliber of the young musicians. They were also impressed by Hanson's conducting techniques. In Egypt, authorities prevented two members of the orchestra with French citizenship from entering the country. Hanson told the authorities that if the students were not allowed to perform, he would pack up the orchestra and travel to their next concert location. The French students performed.

Hanson's *Symphony No. 2* is the composition for which he is primarily remembered. His style was much more than just neoromantic. He advocated drawing upon not only the European tradition, but also African-American music, Native-American music, jazz, and American popular music. Among the many other awards that he received were the Alice M. Ditson Award and Phi Mu Alpha's Man of Music Award in 1953.

Many of Hanson's works have not found a permanent home in the concert hall. However, since the late 1980s, conductors Leonard Slatkin and Gerard Schwarz have been leading a revival of Hanson's music.

## Lewis Henry Morgan (1818- 1881)

"To say that Morgan was the most important scientist in nineteenth century America is an understatement. He belongs in that galaxy of brilliant New Yorkers which included DeWitt Clinton, [physicist] Joseph Henry, and [geologist and paleontologist] James Hall, who drew the attention of the whole world to New York State.... He has been claimed as the intellectual peer of Darwin, Herbert Spencer, and Edward Tyler."       William N. Fenton, Introduction,
*League of the Iroquois*

Lewis Henry Morgan was born in 1818 in Aurora, on the eastern shore of Cayuga Lake. After graduating from Union College in Schenectady, he organized the Gordian Knot, a club comprised of graduates of the Cayuga Academy in Aurora. He renamed it the Grand Order of the Iroquois, which he perceived as a replacement for the fading Iroquois Confederacy. He founded the Seneca chapter in Waterloo and the Cayuga chapter in Aurora. In 1844, Morgan and his club members initiated Abram La Fort, an Onondaga, into the Cayuga chapter to learn more about how the Iroquois were organized.

On a trip to Albany, Morgan met Ely Parker, a Seneca who was in town acting as an interpreter for three visiting Iroquois chiefs from the Tonawanda Reservation. Parker introduced him to the chiefs, including Jimmy Johnson, nephew of Red Jacket and grandson of medicine man Handsome Lake. Morgan was eager to learn more about the Iroquois chiefs and the organization of the Confederacy. Parker enrolled in the Cayuga Academy but moved to Washington after one year to work with Joseph Henry, the first Secretary of the Smithsonian Institution.

Late in 1844, Morgan moved to Rochester, where he was a successful corporation lawyer and State Legislator. Morgan, who was called the "Grand Tekarihogea," established a turtle clan of the Seneca Nation and considered himself an honorary "supreme chieftain of the Iroquois." He invited Henry Rowe Schoolcraft, a well-known geologist, explorer, and ethnologist, to speak at the annual meeting of the Grand Order of the Iroquois in Aurora. Schoolcraft's speech was a plea to Morgan to cease his "adolescent games" and begin a serious study of the Iroquois.

In September 1845, Morgan attended a meeting of the Grand Council of the Six Nations at Tonawanda at which new chiefs were elected. The Seneca, Onondagas, and Mohawks (the older brothers) sat on one side of the hall, and the Cayugas, Oneidas, and Tuscaroras (the younger brothers) sat on the opposite side. Jimmy Johnson spoke for three hours delivering his annual message of Handsome Lake. Morgan was fascinated even though he could not understand a word that was spoken. With the aid of an interpreter, Morgan documented Handsome Lake's teachings at this meeting.

Morgan's first field trip was followed by trips to the Buffalo Creek and Tonawanda Reservations in 1845 and 1846. He wrote a paper on the Iroquois government and a series of letters for the *American Review,* which were incorporated into his book, *League of the Ho-dé-no-sau-nee, or Iroquois,* in 1851.

In the Introduction to this book, William N. Fenton observed: "Lewis Henry Morgan published his *League of the Ho-dé-no-sau-nee, or Iroquois* ... [in] 1851, and his is still the best general book on this classic people. Morgan gave the world, in the oft-quoted words of Major J. Wesley Powell [of Mt. Morris], who founded the Bureau of American Ethnology, 'its first scientific account of an Indian tribe.' Since then so much has been written about the Iroquois that their combined ethnological and historical literature rivals that of any primitive people, being exceeded only by the Eskimo and Navaho."

In 1847, Governor John Young commissioned Morgan to gather artifacts for the Natural History Museum in Albany. Morgan acquired 478 items on three trips to the Tonawanda and Grand River Reservations in 1849-50. Unfortunately, all but seventy-one items were destroyed by a fire in the New York State capitol in 1911. In 1848-49, Morgan documented the teachings of Handsome Lake with the assistance of Jimmy Johnson.

In 1851, Morgan married Mary Elizabeth Steele and with her encouragement became a serious student of the Iroquois. Also that year, Francis Parkman published his multiple-volume history of the wars between the French and the British along with an account of their Indian allies. Parkman, who did not consider himself an ethnographer, had visited the Onondaga Nation in 1845. He had difficulty obtaining information from the Iroquois.

In his work, Morgan used Parkman's information in addition to that of other authors, including Cadwallader Colden. Between Parkman and Morgan, the story of the Iroquois began to emerge. By researching the Iroquois, Morgan became a founder of the discipline of anthropology. His contributions were recognized when he joined the American Association for the Advancement of Science in 1856.

## *Garson Kanin (1912-1999)*

"Rochester is America, proof of its basic character." Garson Kanin

Garson Kanin was an actor, author, director, dramatist, and screen-writer who wrote eighteen books, eight of which were adapted for stage productions. *Born Yesterday* (1946), *Do Re Mi* (1951), and *Tracy and Hepburn* (1972) were his most popular books. He also wrote eight screenplays, including four with Ruth Gordon: *A Double Life* (1947), *Adam's Rib* (1950), *Pat and Mike* (1952), and *The Marrying Kind* (1952), some of which starred Katherine Hepburn and Spencer Tracy.

In addition, Kanin wrote a new libretto for Johann Strauss's opera *Die Fledermaus* for the Metropolitan Opera Company. His short stories and articles appeared in many periodicals, including *Atlantic Monthly, Esquire, Ladies' Home Journal, Paris Match,* and the *Virginia Law Review.*

Kanin was born in Rochester on November 24, 1912, to David and Sadie Levine Kanin. He attended James Madison High School and, in 1932, began two years of study at the American Academy of Dramatic Arts in New York City. In 1933, he acted in his first of seven Broadway plays and performed in several other productions. From 1935 to 1937, he assisted noted director George Abbott in directing three Broadway plays before he began directing his own.

Kanin served in World War II, initially with the Signal Corps Training Film Section in Ft. Monmouth, New Jersey. He directed four films for the Offices of War Information and Emergency Manpower. In 1945, with Carol Reed, he directed the War Department's official film of the War in Europe. He and Reed received an Academy Award and citations from the New York Film Critics' Circle and the National Board of Review. He was promoted to captain for his last tour of duty, which was with the Office of Strategic Services in the European Theater of Operations.

The 1946 play adapted from his novel, *Born Yesterday,* is prob-ably the work for which Kanin is best remembered. The social theme of the play concerns the responsibility of the individual to display personal integrity and to stand up for the rights of everyone, regardless of wealth. The "hilarious" play was about sleazy politics

in Washington, D.C., after World War II. It involved influence peddling, strong industrial lobbies, and men of power and wealth looking out for their own selfish interests. *Born Yesterday* and its char-
acters, Harry Brock and Billie Dawn, became classics of modern
American theater. The play closed in 1950 after 1,642 perfor-
mances. The movie *Born Yesterday* starred Judy Holliday and
William Holden.

In 1960, the adaptation of Kanin's novel, *Do, Re, Mi,* with
music by Jule Styne and lyrics by Betty Comden and Adolph
Green, opened on Broadway. It was the entertaining story of four
small-time crooks attempting to enter the racket that controlled
juke boxes. The lead, Hubie Cram, was played by Phil Silvers, who
sang and danced to a successful run. Critic Walter Kerr said, "It's
fun. Silly fun, loud fun, fast fun, old-fashioned fun, inconsequential
fun, grand fun.... As entertainment ... it's delectable."

Kanin's 1962 play, *A Gift of Time,* was adapted from Lael
Tucker Wertenbaler's *Death of a Man* about her husband's struggle
with cancer. It was one of the few serious dramas undertaken by
Kanin. Henry Fonda and Olivia DeHavilland starred in the production. It was a successful play and received good reviews, such as
critic Howard Taubman's comments that it "affirms the values of
life even as it looks steadily at death."

Garson Kanin had a notable, successful career. In addition to
awards mentioned previously, he also received awards from the
Screen Directors' Guild, Writers' Guild, Academy of Motion
Picture Arts and Sciences, Jewish Theatrical Guild, and many other
organizations.

## Rush Rhees (1860-1939)

"It meant everything to him to have behind him one of the most progressive and public-spirited cities in the country. He had at the right hand one of the country's most generous givers, one who was abundantly able to provide help without stint. He was very fortunate, too, in being at the head of an institution in a city and a section which the General Education Board felt to be strategically located for medical education. But though these elements in the situation were essential, yet Rhees was the great leader who could marshal them all to achieve the amazing result."

> Dr. Edward Parsons, "The Fairy Story of Rush Rhees,"
> *Amherst Graduates' Quarterly*

Dr. Rush Rhees, third president of the University of Rochester, presided over the institution during a thirty-five-year period in which enrollment increased eight fold, the highly regarded Schools of Music and of Medicine and Dentistry were established, and the River Campus was built, adding a second campus to the original location in the Prince Street area. He also led the University in becoming not only a highly respected national university but also international university.

Rush Rhees was born in Chicago in 1860 to John Evans Rhees, a commission merchant, and Annie McCutchen Rhees. The Rhees family was descended from Welsh stock. The surname "Rhees" (rhymes with "cease") is a derivation of the Welsh name "Rhys." Dr. Benjamin Rush Rhees, named for Dr. Benjamin Rush, professor of the University of Pennsylvania Medical School and signer of the *Declaration of Independence,* was a great uncle of Rush Rhees. Rush became a popular first name for men in the Rhees family.

John Rhees moved his family to Williamsburg, Brooklyn, where in 1862 he died of tuberculosis. In 1867, his widow and three young children moved to Plainfield, New Jersey, to live with her father. In 1877, young Rhees graduated from Plainfield High School and spent the next two years in private study preparing to meet the entrance requirements to Amherst College, where he was admitted in 1879.

Rhees was a lifelong Amherst man. Not only did he attend the

College for four years, concentrating on the study of Greek, he taught mathematics there for two years and was an active alumnus and regular attendee of class reunions. He graduated fifth in his class and was elected to Phi Beta Kappa. His years between Amherst and becoming the third president of the University of Rochester were spent in religious vocations.

From 1885 to 1888, Rhees attended the Hartford Theological Seminary, a Congregationalist institution. After spending the summer following graduation studying at the University of Berlin, he was pastor of Middle Street Baptist church in Portsmouth, New Hampshire, for the next three years. From 1892 until 1900, he taught New Testament interpretation at the Newton Theological Institution in Massachusetts. In 1900, his first book, *The Life of Jesus of Nazareth,* was published. These fifteen years, between the ages of twenty-five and forty, were very formative ones for Rhees.

In 1897, Rhees met Harriet Chapin Seelye, daughter of President L. Clark Seelye of Smith College. Harriet was from an old New England family. Not only was her father a college president, her uncle was president of Amherst College. In March 1899, they became engaged and were married in July that year. When Rhees was offered the presidency of the University of Rochester, the newlyweds decided to accept it. Harriet was to become as close as it is possible to be the ideal wife of a college president.

The University of Rochester was fortunate to have had Martin Brewer Anderson (1850-1888) and David Jayne Hill (1889-1896) as its first two presidents. Acting presidents professors Samuel A. Lattimore and Henry F. Burton served ably from 1896 to 1899.

Although the University was founded as a Baptist college, by 1900 the majority of Baptists on the Board of Trustees were there by custom, not by charter. By that time, the college was not a denominational institution, and the only financial support received from the State Baptist organization was in the form of scholarships.

Members of the Board of Trustees of the University were not looking for a ministerial president; also, they realized it would be desirable to select a candidate with financial experience, which Rhees did not have. Rhees was the board's fourth choice; the first three were not available.

In 1898, Mrs. Joseph T. Alling, wife of a University trustee, visited a friend in Newton Centre, near the Newton Theological

Institution where Rhees taught. She and her friend attended a ladies night of the discussion group to which Rhees belonged and talked with him at length. Mrs. Alling's friend suggested that Rhees might be just the man that the University of Rochester was seeking.

Rhees was unable to attend the semicentennial commencement at the University of Rochester because his son, Morgan John Rhees, was born that day in Newton Centre. An announcement was made at the commencement that Amherst College had awarded him a LL.D. degree. Governor Theodore Roosevelt spoke at the dinner on "Promise and Performance": "Before making a promise think of what you are doing, of what you say you will do; and in the next place, do it." This advice certainly was timely for the incoming president of the University of Rochester.

Rhees was inaugurated as the third president of the University on October 11, 1900. His address was entitled: "The Modernizing of Liberal Culture." He concluded by saying, "As new demands arise and new resources are found, we pledge to you that we will meet the demands most eagerly and use the resources with the broadest wisdom we can attain." Over the next thirty-five years, he fulfilled that pledge and more.

In 1900, the University of Rochester had 200 students, seventeen teachers, four buildings on twenty-five acres in its original location on Prince Street, and little endowment. Rhees approached his tasks in a deliberate manner, which was his way. The students used to say: "You can't rush Rhees." He was confronted with three problems that needed attention: overcoming financial deficits, admitting women students, and hiring new faculty.

In seeking support from the Andrew Carnegie Foundation for the Advancement of Teaching, particularly for an academic pension system, the University had to adopt the following resolution: "Resolved, that no denominational test is imposed in the choice of trustees, officers, or teachers by the University of Rochester, or in admission of students, nor are distinctly denominational tenets or doctrines taught to the students."

Rochester, a technology based city, needed to provide technical education for employees of local industrial companies. Early in the twentieth century, the University of Rochester, essentially a liberal arts college, did not fill this need. A young man from Rochester who wanted to become an electrical engineer, mechanical engineer, or chemist had to go to Cornell University, Columbia University, or the Massachusetts Institute of Technology.

The Rochester Atheneum, founded in 1829, had lecture halls and library facilities. The Mechanics Institute, established in 1885 by Henry Lomb and his associates, provided industrial training. In 1891, the Atheneum and the Mechanics Institute joined into one organization, a nonprofit trade school for industrial education. This privately funded and managed institute with no connection to the public school system eventually evolved into the Rochester Institute of Technology in 1944.

Rhees perceived the need for technical education in Rochester. In 1903, he was elected to the board of directors of the Mechanics Institute. In his 1902-03 report to the trustees of the University of Rochester, he described pretechnical studies at the University that would permit students to enter third-year engineering classes at Cornell, Columbia, and M. I. T. These pretechnical studies included courses at the Mechanics Institute.

In 1905, Andrew Carnegie gave $100,000 to the University of Rochester for an Applied Science Building with the stipulation that the amount be matched by other donors. Also that year, the Eastman Laboratory for Physics and Biology was constructed on the campus.

In late 1908 and early 1909, the Rhees family toured Europe. This vacation permitted Rhees to visit universities at Cambridge, London, Manchester, and Oxford to get ideas relative to the future growth of his university. While in England, Dr. and Mrs. Rhees received an invitation to visit Andrew Carnegie at Skibo Castle in Scotland, where they met the heads of Aberdeen, Edinburgh, Glasgow, and St. Andrews Universities. From Scotland, they traveled to Germany to visit Göttingen University, where Rhees studied technical developments for two months. They also visited France and Italy.

Upon his return to Rochester in 1909, Rhees proceeded with plans to award degrees in chemistry and mechanical engineering but postponed instituting other technical curricula. He also made plans for establishing an Institute of Optics, which particularly suited the needs of Rochester's industries.

The first two presidents of the University of Rochester had been civic-minded individuals; the third was also. Rhees had been a member of Boston's Twentieth Century Club, where public questions were discussed. He was an active member of the Rochester Chamber of Commerce and of the City Club, which had goals similar to those of the Twentieth Century Club when it was founded in 1908. He also became a director of the Rochester Bureau of Municipal Research, founded by George Eastman.

Through these organizations, Rhees met businessmen involved in city planning such as George Eastman and James G. Cutler, who were outside of his usual contacts with University alumni and trustees. Joseph T. Alling is an example of one that he knew as a University trustee. As noted by John Rothwell Slater in *Rhees of Rochester*, Rhees observed:

> We are the fortunate possessors of one of the most beautiful sites for a city to be found in this or any other country.... individual taste and initiative have given us a city of beautiful homes ... We are now conscious that we have allowed ourselves to ignore too much the priceless possession which the city has in its river, to mention but one feature of natural beauty.... I am confident that all our citizens must welcome the fair dream ... of something worthier, lovelier, and more significant which the Rochester of tomorrow may hope to become....

Rhees was also active in social welfare, particularly the consolidation of many charitable organizations into one enterprise, the predecessor of the Community Chest and the United Way. Rhees was a trustee of the Reynolds Library, a privately funded facility that later merged with the Rochester Public Library. In 1911, the mayor appointed him to the Public Library Board.

In 1914, Rhees served as a member of the Constitutional Convention in Albany to streamline State bureaus, to reform civil service, and to improve the conservation of State lands. He served on three committees, including the civil service committee of which he was chairman. He had the opportunity to meet and work with individuals such as Elihu Root, Henry Stimson, Seth Low, Jacob Schurman, and Alfred E. Smith.

The effort to enroll women at the University of Rochester was begun in the 1870s by Lewis Henry Morgan, ethnologist, anthropologist, and friend of the Iroquois. When he died in 1881, he left his estate to the University to be used for the education of women. The will was contested, and the Morgan Fund did not become available to the University until 1909.

In 1890, Susan B. Anthony, Mary T. Gannett, Helen B. Montgomery, and others began to push for the admission of women to the University of Rochester. Shortly after Rhees's arrival in Rochester, the first thirty-three women were admitted to the University. The first dean of women, Annette Gardner Monro, was appointed on January 2, 1910.

Of several approaches to education for women, Rhees had always favored a "co-ordinate" College for Women in the University. The University would have two colleges, one for men and one for women. In his view, "In educational privileges and in dignity, they will be strictly co-ordinate. The organization of the two colleges will make it possible to provide more adequately and exactly for the needs and the interests of the men in their college and the women in theirs."

The year 1912 was a turning point for Rhees. Because of his solid reputation at the University of Rochester, Amherst College considered inviting him to succeed their retiring president. Amherst had a national reputation, a substantial endowment, good teaching salaries, supportive alumni, and established educational principles, all of which were still in the future for the University of Rochester. It was a difficult decision.

Rhees told the trustees that the two urgent necessities for the University of Rochester were:

1. Provision for some increase in the faculty, and
   for definite increase in the scale of salaries paid
   to professors and assistant professors
2. To take immediate steps to establish our work
   for women on a co-ordinate basis

He added that if these conditions were not met, "I feel it my duty to reply that if Amherst wants me, I will accept."

The Rochester community responded immediately to retain Rhees. George Eastman donated $500,000 on the condition that other donors match that amount. The General Education Fund pledged $200,000 to the endowment fund if $300,000 could be raised from other donors. Also, the trustees approved the establishment of a co-ordinate College for Women.

Rhees responded, "I can think of no task which life could present to us more fascinating and delightful than living amongst our friends in Rochester and carrying through to measurable realization our ideals in the work of building up this institution as an integral part of the life of the community, as well as a significant factor in the educational enterprises of the country."

First president Martin B. Anderson had given popular lectures on art history during his tenure at the University. In 1902, Dr. Elizabeth Denio was hired to teach art history. She was a graduate of Mt. Holyoke College with a Ph.D. from the University of Heidelberg and had taught art at Wellesley College for many years.

In 1912, Mrs. James Sibley Watson, daughter of Hiram Sibley, donated money to build a University art gallery in memory of her son, James S. Averell. She shared with President Rhees and others an interest in promoting interest in fine arts in Rochester. She was motivated by the efforts of Dr. Denio and local artist George Herdle, who became the first director of the Memorial Art Gallery.

Until 1900, when George Eastman donated money to build the Mechanics Institute on Plymouth Avenue, he had not contributed to educational causes. Just before that time, two women had visited him to solicit funds for admission of women to the University of Rochester. He rejected their request and said, "I am not interested in education." As she was leaving, one of the women turned to him and predicted, "Mr. Eastman, you may not be interested in education now, but you are going to be."

Lord Kelvin visited Rochester in 1902 as the guest of George Eastman and was given a tour of the University of Rochester by President Rhees. This visit seemed to open Eastman's eyes to the value of education, particularly scientific education. Within a few days of the visit, Eastman pledged $10,000 to the University building fund.

In 1904, Rhees visited Eastman in an attempt to interest him in sponsoring the construction of a building for biology and physics. Eastman offered to contribute $5,000 to the building project. Rhees said, "I hoped that you might feel like giving us the whole building." Eastman said that he would think about it.

Later Eastman offered $60,000 and then increased that donation to $77,000 to cover the actual construction cost of the building. Eastman told Rhees, "But this is the last I shall do for the University. I am not interested in education." This was Rhees's only request for money from Eastman, who forgot about the incident. Eastman later said, "Dr. Rhees never asked me for a cent."

Early in the twentieth century, Rochester had a small orchestra, which was conducted by Hermann Dossenbach. In 1905, Hiram Sibley established the Sibley Music Library at the University of Rochester. The library consisted of choral and instrumental music scores as well as reference material on music history, biography, and theory, most of which had been imported from Europe. Dossenbach was sent to Germany in 1911-12 for extended studies in music sponsored by the Musical Council, particularly Mr. Sibley, Mrs. Watson, and Mr. Eastman. In 1911, local music teachers founded the Rochester Conservatory of Music to provide lessons in piano, violin, voice, and music theory.

Eastman had an organ installed in his mansion on East Avenue, and his musical Sunday evenings at the Eastman House, consisting of organ recitals and string quartets, were popular with his friends. In 1918, Eastman asked Rhees, "Why don't you have school of music?" Also that year, Eastman purchased the property and charter of the Institute of Musical Art and donated them to the University. In 1919, Eastman announced his intentions to fund the construction of a theater and to establish a quality school of music at the University.

Eastman described his motives:

> It is necessary for people to have an interest in life outside their occupations. Work, a great deal of work, is drudgery.... All sorts of sports, recreation, and diversions must be developed if we are to make full use of our leisure.... I am interested in music personally, and I am led thereby to want to share my pleasure with others. It is impossible to buy an appreciation of music. Yet without appreciation, without the presence of a large body of people who understand music and get enjoyment out

of it, any attempt to develop the musical resources of a city is doomed to failure. Because in Rochester we realize this, we have undertaken a scheme for building musical capacity on a large scale from childhood.

Rhees and Eastman jointly drafted the goals of Rochester's musical endeavor. Included in these goals were:

- To provide professional music education of the highest quality for students of sufficient talent to enable them to make music their career

- To organize a preparatory department for talented boys and girls, enabling them to have the best instruction in instrumental music at an early age when such training is of the highest importance

- To maintain a special course for teachers of public school music, including not only musical and pedagogical theory but instruction in piano, sight reading, conducting, and reasonable proficiency in two orchestral or band instruments

- To erect, under one roof with the School of Music, a large motion-picture theater, equipped with an organ, an orchestra pit, and a stage adequately equipped for opera as well as concerts; motion-picture programs accompanied by high-grade orchestral and organ music, such as already exists in New York, to serve the triple purpose of entertaining the public, educating musical taste, and earning profits to supplement the endowment of the School of Music. Since all profits would be used for educational purposes, not for private gain, there would be no commercial aspects.

Inscribed on the facade of the Eastman Theatre are the words: "For the Enrichment of Community Life."

The proposal for a medical school in Rochester did not originate with president Rhees. In 1920, the General Education Board decided that since Albany, Buffalo, and Syracuse all had medical schools, Rochester should also. The board's proposal was based not only on reasons of geography, but also because there already existed in Rochester a quality college, to which the Board had made large endowment grants.

Eastman donated $9 million for the construction of medical school buildings and an endowment, in addition to financing the Eastman Dental Dispensary. Two early concerns were financing construction of the hospital, which was not included in the support from Eastman, and choosing a dean for the new medical school.

Eastman approached the daughters of his late associate, Henry Alvah Strong, the first president of the Eastman Kodak Company. Mrs. Gertrude Strong Achilles and Mrs. Helen Strong Carter donated $1 million for a hospital that was to be a memorial to their father and mother. The need for a city hospital had been discussed in Rochester for years. The City decided to build the Rochester Municipal Hospital adjacent to Strong Memorial Hospital and the School of Medicine and Dentistry, which opened in 1925.

In selecting a dean, Rhees consulted with Dr. Abraham Flexner of the General Education Board and Dr. William Welch, dean of the Medical School at Johns Hopkins University, among others. Dr. Welch, a pathologist, suggested that the new dean should also be a pathologist, specifically, his previous assistant, Dr. George Whipple, director of the Hooper Foundation of the University of California. Dr. Whipple's specialty was the chemistry, pathology, and physiology of the blood and liver.

Rhees traveled to San Francisco to encourage Dr. Whipple to undertake this new responsibility. Letters had not been enough to motivate Dr. Whipple to move to Rochester. On the trip west, Rhees visited a number of medical centers, including the Mayo Clinic at Rochester, Minnesota. Whipple was an excellent choice; the University was fortunate that he accepted its offer. He and two others later won the Nobel Prize for Medicine in 1934 for work on the use of the liver to combat blood deficiencies.

In 1925, a campaign was undertaken to raise $10 million to build a separate College for Men along the Genesee River on the original site of the Oak Hill Golf Course. The College for Women would remain at the Prince Street location near the Memorial Art Gallery and the Cutler Union, which had been sponsored by James G. Cutler.

In 1930, seventy-year-old President Rhees submitted his resignation to he board of trustees; they did not accept it. Nor did they accept it later that year when the College for Men on the River Campus was completed and dedicated.

On March 14, 1932, the University of Rochester lost its foremost sponsor when, faced with a long-term debilitating illness, George Eastman took his own life. Rhees wrote of his friend and benefactor to the trustees:

> Our largest benefactor in gifts, he was still more our boldest leader in the adoption of the highest ambitions. And he rejoiced to see his gifts at work, aiding us in the pursuit of such ambitions. And now he tells his friends that his work is done. For him, as respects active participation, this is sadly true. For us who carry on what he has inspired, his work is only just begun. Only the future years will be able to measure the greatness of that continuing work.

Eastman gave most of his estate to the University of Rochester. This from the man who had said, "I am not interested in education," but who later said, "The progress of the world depends almost entirely upon education." In addition, Eastman's home on East Avenue, along with an endowment for its maintenance, was left to the University to be used as the president's residence. Dr. and Mrs. Rhees moved into the Eastman House and resided there for the last three years of his tenure as president.

In June 1933, Rhees renewed his request to the trustees to resign, and a search for his replacement was begun. In January 1935, he had his first angina attack, an early warning of heart problems. The trustees nominated Allan Valentine, Master of Pierson College at Yale University, as the new president. Dr. Valentine had been educated at Swarthmore College and Oxford University, where he had also been associated with Oxford Press. He was a respected scholar with many contacts in the academic world. On

November 15, 1935, Dr. Valentine was inaugurated as president of the University of Rochester.

Dr. Rush Rhees suffered a fatal heart attack on January 5, 1939. Mrs. Rhees was at his side as she had been all of their married life. His funeral service was conducted in the Henry A. Strong Auditorium on the River Campus. He was buried in Mt. Hope Cemetery.

# CHAPTER 4

# HUMANITARIANS / INDUSTRIALISTS

## George Eastman (1854-1932)

"Eastman was a stupendous factor in the education of the modern world. Of what he got in return for his great gifts to the human race, he gave generously for their good; fostering music, endowing learning, supporting science in its researches and teaching, seeking to promote health and lessen human ills, helping the lowest in their struggle toward the light, making his own city a center for the arts, and glorifying his own country in the eyes of the world."

New York *Times,* 1932

George Eastman, founder of the photographic industry, was born in Waterville, New York, on July 12, 1854. He was the third child and first son of George W. and Maria Kilbourn Eastman. In 1842, Eastman's father established a business school, Eastman's Commercial College, in Rochester. The school prospered in the thriving Erie Canal community, but George W. Eastman did not move his family from Waterville to Rochester until 1860.

George W. Eastman died in 1862, leaving the family in reduced economic circumstances. Maria Eastman took in boarders to supplement her income. Young Eastman's first employment was a part-time job with an insurance agency. He began his first full-time position as junior bookkeeper for the Rochester Savings Bank in 1874.

The first reference to photography in Eastman's diary was in 1869. His interest became serious during the summer of 1877, when he purchased $100 worth of "sundries and lenses" and arranged for a local photographer to teach him "the art of photography." Taking photographs in 1877 was a complex process requiring bulky equipment. Glass plates had to be exposed in the camera while wet, and development had to be completed before the emulsion dried. Eastman was bothered by the cumbersomeness of the process. He commented: "The bulk of the paraphernalia worried me. It seemed that one ought to be able to carry less than a pack-horse load."

Eastman's thinking was given focus when he read an article in the *British Journal of Photography* containing a formula for a sensitive gelatin emulsion for glass plates that could be used when dry. He spent long hours experimenting until he found a combination of gelatin and silver bromide that had the photographic qualities that he wanted. Initially, he experimented to support his hobby of photography; he soon realized the commercial potential of his effort and resigned his job at the bank to make and market dry photographic plates.

By June 1879, Eastman was manufacturing quality photographic plates and had designed and built equipment for coating them. He sailed to England, the center of the photographic industry, and obtained his first patent on July 22, 1879. On September 9, 1879, his patent attorney, George Selden, submitted an application for him to the U.S. Patent Office for "An Improved Process of Preparing Gelatin Dry Plates for Use in Photography and in Apparatus Therefor."

In April 1880, Eastman leased the third floor of a building on State Street in Rochester to produce dry plates in quantity. An early investor in the Eastman Dry Plate Company was Colonel Henry Alvah Strong, who, with his wife, boarded with Maria Eastman. Strong was a partner in Strong-Woodbury and Company, a thriving manufacturer of whips.

During the winter of 1879-80, Eastman formulated four business principles upon which to build his enterprise:
- Production in large quantities by machinery
- Low prices to increase the usefulness of the products
- Foreign as well as domestic distribution
- Extensive advertising as well as selling by demonstration

In 1881, a near-fatal catastrophe struck the business—photographers complained that Eastman dry plates were no longer sensitive and did not capture an image. Customers discovered something that had not been realized until then: passage of time lessened the sensitivity of the emulsion on the plate. The New York City distributor had placed the recently received plates on top of the older plates and had sold the new plates before using up the old. By the time the older plates were sold, they had lost their photographic sensitivity. At significant expense for a small company, Eastman recalled all of his plates and replaced them.

Then Eastman received a second staggering blow—he could no longer make a satisfactory emulsion. During many weeks of sleepless nights with his factory shut down, Eastman conducted 469 unsuccessful experiments to produce a usable emulsion. On March 11, 1882, Eastman and Strong sailed for England, where they discovered that the problem was due to a defective supply of gelatin received from a manufacturer. It was not a problem with the emulsion formula or Eastman's equipment.

On April 16, they returned to Rochester, conducted sixteen more unsuccessful experiments, and were successful on the seventeenth. Eastman learned two lessons from this experience: to test samples of material received and to control the supply, whenever practicable.

On October 1, 1882, the Eastman Dry Plate and Film Company was incorporated with $200,000 capital stock. Henry A. Strong was president, and Eastman was treasurer of the Company, which purchased the plant and stock of the Eastman Dry Plate Company.

Eastman searched for a material to replace the fragile, heavy glass as a support for the emulsion. He experimented with collodion, which was made from gun-cotton (nitro-cellulose) and nitric acid. On March 4, 1884, he filed his first patent application for photographic film. Then he designed a mechanism to hold film in the camera, a roll-holder in a wooden frame. On March 26, 1885, the first commercial film was manufactured by the new company.

An early setback to the company was a serious fire on February 10, 1888, that destroyed most of the interior of the State Street factory and shut it down for two months. Eastman was back in business by April, and by June he had his first camera on the market.

Eastman conceived of the name "Kodak" as a trademark for his products. He liked the letter K, the first letter of his mother's maiden name. On September 4, 1888, "Kodak" was registered as a trademark in the United States. The first camera was the "No. 1 Kodak." Eastman explained the origin of the word to the British Patent Office:

> This is not a foreign name or work; it was constructed by me to serve a definite purpose. It has the following merits as a trademark word:

First:     It is short.

Second:   It is not capable of mispronunciation.

Third:     It does not resemble anything in the art
           and cannot be associated with anything
           in the art except the "Kodak."

The small, inexpensive cameras sold well, and the Company expanded to meet market demand.

Eastman used Dr. Samuel Lattimore, head of the department of chemistry at the University of Rochester, as a consultant. The first chemist hired by Eastman was Henry Reichenbach, one of Dr. Lattimore's assistants. Eastman was too involved with the operation of the business to devote much time to experiments; however, he continued to work on mechanical developments, such as roller mechanisms. On December 10, 1889, a patent for manufacturing transparent nitro-cellulose photographic film was granted to Reichenbach. Joint patents were granted to Eastman and Reichenbach on March 22, 1892, and July 19, 1892.

The next challenge that Eastman faced was one that he least expected—employee disloyalty. Reichenbach and two other employees secretly formed a rival company using the filmmaking formulae and processes of Eastman's company. Eastman investigated the charges and found them to be true. He also found that they had made 39,400 feet of unusable film and had let 1,417 gallons of emulsion spoil. He discharged them.

On November 28, 1889, the Eastman Photographic Materials Company, Ltd., was incorporated in London to represent the Company in all areas of the world except the western hemisphere. In December 1889, the Eastman Company was incorporated in Rochester with $1 million capital to represent the firm in the western hemisphere. In August 1890, the Company purchased several farms in the Town of Greece that were to become Kodak Park, the world's largest film manufacturing complex.

On May 23, 1892, the name of the Eastman Company was changed to the Eastman Kodak Company, and the capitalization was increased to $5 million. Camera and film development continued as Kodak designed and made uncomplicated products that lived up to the slogan: "You press the button and we do the rest."

In 1912, Eastman established the Eastman Kodak Company

George Eastman House, East Avenue

111

Research Laboratories and brought Dr. Kenneth Mees from England to serve as its head. Mees and his chief assistant, S. E. Shepard, who were both graduates of the University of London, made significant contributions to the growth of the company. Motion pictures were introduced in the early 1920s, and Kodacolor film was announced in the late 1920s. Many significant film improvements followed, including Technicolor film, Kodachrome film, and the replacement of nitrate-based film with acetate-based product.

Eastman never married; he lived alone in his mansion on East Avenue. He was instrumental in founding the Eastman School of Music at the University of Rochester and building the Eastman Theatre. He gave over $60 million to educational institutions, including the University of Rochester, the Massachusetts Institute of Technology, Hampton Institute, and the Tuskegee Institute. He funded the Eastman Visiting Professorship at Oxford University and gave $5.5 million to establish dental clinics in Brussels, London, Paris, Rome, and Stockholm.

On March 14, 1932, George Eastman took his own life at his East Avenue home. He left a note that read: "To my friends. My work is done. Why wait? G. E." His death shocked the community. Karl K. Compton, president of the Massachusetts Institute of Technology, wrote in the April 15, 1932, issue of *Science* magazine:

> Consider for a moment the full significance of his last words. He had invented the modern photographic plate; he had invented the photographic film; he had made the Kodak a household object throughout the entire world; he had created a business; he had created a great research laboratory which had strikingly fulfilled his faith in it; he had selected certain fields of education, health, and art to which he had devoted his fortune for the benefit of the entire world; he had satisfied his distinctive desires for the excitement of exploration and big game hunting; he had no close relatives; the infirmities of old age had come upon him and were about to master him. He who had always been his own master remained so to the last.

## Henry Alvah Strong (1838-1919)

"Eastman's bedrock support in all of his industrial and financial dealings came from Henry Strong. Together, the former bank clerk and erstwhile whip manufacturer succeeded in the burgeoning photographic business where professionals with special technical knowledge came up short. Strong's way with people was a crucial element. Affable and approachable, the gregarious Strong was comfortable wherever people gathered—in a dignified lobby of a London hotel or strolling down Rochester's State Street hailing passers-by. Strong inspired immediate trust; he knew everyone and was universally liked. Consequently, he could get away with armtwisting, peddling Kodak stock to his adult Sunday school class, or enveloping a friend in an exuberant bear hug."

Elizabeth Brayer, *George Eastman: A Biography*

Henry Alvah Strong was born in Rochester on August 30, 1838, to Alvah and Catherine Hopkins Strong. He served in the Civil War for four years as a Navy paymaster. When he returned to Rochester, he worked with his uncle, Myron Strong, in manufacturing buggy whips. Eventually, he bought out his uncle's interest in the company and formed a partnership with Edmund Frost Woodbury until 1889. Their whip company was the second largest in the United States, employing 100 people and producing a million whips a year. Strong had money to invest, and he was willing to take risks.

In 1880, Strong formed a partnership, Strong and Eastman, with George Eastman. In December 1880, Strong invested $1,000 in the newly formed Eastman Dry Plate Company. Strong was the president; Eastman was the treasurer. Strong invested $1,000 in January 1881, $1,873 two months later, and by August had invested over $5,000.

The Company subsequently became the Eastman Kodak Company. Strong and Eastman worked well together. Strong said of Eastman: "I have great faith in that young man. He is doing wonders." In 1921, Strong's daughter Gertrude, looking back on Eastman's relationship with her father, observed: "You were more of a son to father than was Harry [her brother] or any of his sons-in-law."

113

Strong was called "Colonel Strong." Obviously, the Navy has no rank of colonel; people wondered about the origin of the "honorary" rank. Apparently it was given to Strong by Eastman, who always called him "colonel." Strong was a friendly big man. He radiated trust and was very approachable. He was a superb salesman. Strong and the somewhat reticent Eastman formed a great team. In a sense, they were opposites who complemented each other. Eastman was sixteen years younger than Strong, and he looked even younger. Strong provided the firm's needed maturity.

Tom Craig, who was responsible for many years for Eastman Kodak's ciné processing and repair department, compared the two men:

> You were charmed by Strong, but you depended on Eastman for the things that mattered. When you met Strong and Eastman together on State Street, Strong's hearty "hello" could be heard for blocks; Eastman didn't even see you. But if you had a [technical] problem, you wouldn't dream of approaching Strong. Eastman was the one who would give you a fair hearing, a decisive answer, and heartening advice.

Strong continued to invest and to take risks. He invested in Michigan and in the boomtown of Tacoma, Washington. He took many risks, including investments in a bank, a dry dock, and a foundry. The investments were not particularly successful, especially during the Panic of 1893. His investment in Traders Bank began to drag him down financially. His good friend Eastman bailed him out. Eastman counseled Strong to cut his losses.

Strong spent almost a year in the Pacific Northwest attending to his investments and recouping many of his losses. When he returned to Rochester, Eastman said, "It is a great relief ... to have him here." Strong, who had not been active in managing the company became much more involved than he had been previously. Eastman began to travel, establishing branches for distributing Eastman Kodak products in Europe and establishing a holding company in England. Strong managed the company in Rochester in Eastman's absence and forwarded detailed reports. He enjoyed being more actively involved with running the company.

In 1901, Strong retired as president of the New Jersey holding company for the Eastman Kodak Company. However, he continued as first vice president and treasurer of the holding company and president of the manufacturing company in Rochester until he died.

After retiring, Strong traveled around the country playing golf. John D. Rockefeller was his favorite golf partner. Strong played on courses from Atlanta to San Francisco, where he was in 1906 during the severe earthquake. He also played golf in Hawaii while visiting his daughter Helen, who had married George Carter, later the governor of the Hawaiian Islands. He lived up to the name that Eastman had given him, "Prince Henry."

Strong also served as president of Rochester Button Company and of the United States Voting Machine Company, as well as a director of the Alliance Bank, the Monroe County Savings Bank, and the Security Trust Company. In 1907, Strong funded the building of the Rochester Theological Seminary's Alvah Strong Hall, named for his father. Henry Alvah Strong died in 1919.

## *John Jacob Bausch (1830-1926) / Henry Lomb (1828-1908)*

"The Bausch and Lomb Optical Company is now one of the most important industrial establishments of our city and the largest and best equipped of its kind in America. Yet how significant was the beginning in 1853, when John Jacob Bausch and Henry Lomb made their start in the Reynolds Arcade on Main Street with a capital of sixty dollars.... The important factors were: the inventive genius of the elder Bausch in discovering and utilizing hard rubber as suitable material for spectacle frames, and in building and equipping machinery for the grinding of optical lenses. Added to these were the indefatigable industry, the firm resolve of producing the best that technical skill could bring forth, and the business foresight of the men who later succeeded to the business. These were some of the factors which helped to build up an industrial plant which carries the name of our fair city to the ends of the earth."
"The German People in Rochester," Rochester Historical Society

John Jacob Bausch, one of seven children, was born on July 25, 1830, in Würtemberg, Germany. His father, George Bausch, was a baker, and his mother, Annie Schmidt Bausch, was from a family of foresters. John Jacob's oldest brother was an apprentice in the optical trade. The family was poor and struggled to provide the apprentice with tools that cost 125 gulden ($46.25).

Young Bausch also became an apprentice in the optics trade. He learned to grind lenses and to make horn spectacles. However, these were poor economic times in Würtemberg and it was difficult to make a living in the optical business. Bausch moved to Bern, Switzerland, which offered opportunity for an optician. By working from dawn to dusk, he could produce six pairs of spectacles a day that sold for six cents a pair.

The region experienced crop failures, and the Revolution of 1848 caused social and economic disturbances. Many Europeans immigrated to America, and Bausch was one of them. After being at sea for forty-nine days, seeing New York was uplifting. However, Bausch soon found that New York was crowded with immigrants looking for work, and that he must move farther west to find a job. He traveled to Buffalo but could find no work there in the optical trade. His brother had trained him as a woodturner, and he was able to find short-term work in that trade. He borrowed five dollars and traveled to Rochester.

A small inheritance of less than $100 from his family allowed Bausch to set up an optician shop that was unsuccessful even when he took it on the road as a peddler. Eyecare was not a priority in those days, and he did not speak English well enough to educate the public. He was forced to return to woodturning to support himself. He earned enough money to marry and to rent a small house. Unfortunately, after seven weeks of marriage, his hand was drawn into a circular saw at work, and he lost two fingers. His entire savings was his previous week's wages, $7.50.

While Bausch was recuperating, a friend, Henry Lomb, visited him at home and brought $28.00 that he had collected at work. This was the beginning of a long-term friendship between two individuals who trusted each other completely, and who never quarreled. Also, Bausch's employer advanced him $50.00 upon which to live while he was out of work. He returned to work as a woodturner, but his heart was not in it. He was never again completely comfortable around a circular saw.

Bausch asked his brother in Germany to send him a stock of optical goods, which he promised to pay for in six months. He set up his optical store in the front of a shoemaker's shop in the Reynolds Arcade on Main Street (then Buffalo Street). During the winter, the shoemaker burned old shoes in a cast-iron stove for heat. Customers did not stay long. Bausch walked the streets looking for cracked windows because he knew how to put rivets in plate glass. He made fifty cents for each repair and averaged $4.00 a week with this sideline. The extra income was needed because of the birth of the first of the Bauschs' six children.

Bausch had no nest egg with which to expand the business. He turned again to Henry Lomb, a hardworking carpenter who earned four dollars a week. Bausch asked bachelor Lomb how much he had saved and was told that he had sixty-two dollars. Bausch said, "Lend it to me and when my business grows large enough so that it can support us both, you shall have half interest." No contract was drawn up; they trusted each other implicitly.

Lomb lived at the Bausch home and sold the optical products. By 1861, when Lomb enlisted to fight in the Civil War, Bausch owed Lomb $1,000. Lomb sent Bausch several dollars a month from his army pay.

One day Bausch was walking down the street in Rochester when he found a piece of hard rubber on the sidewalk. He realized that the material would make excellent eyeglass frames. Hard rubber frames were less costly than those made from horn and were better frames. A watchmaker was impressed with the hard rubber and asked to have watch cases made from it, establishing a new market. When Captain Henry Lomb returned home after serving with the 13th Regiment in the Civil War, he found that his partner had paid off their debts and had savings of $800.

Bausch & Lomb secured the exclusive right to use India rubber in optical products in 1868, the year in which the Optical Instrument Company was incorporated. Bausch managed manufacturing in Rochester; Lomb opened a marketing office on Broadway in New York City. Bausch & Lomb offered eyeglass frames in other shapes, e.g. initially oval in addition to round, and they manufactured a variety of styles and finishes as well as frames that were adjustable.

In 1865, because of delays in receiving shipments from European lens grinders, Bausch & Lomb began a lens grinding operation. The firm ground basic eyeglass lenses as well as the finest lenses required by opticians and scientists.

In 1875, Bausch & Lomb began to manufacture microscopes, and in 1890 the Company made an alliance with the Carl Zeiss Works of Jena, Germany. Zeiss granted the firm the exclusive right to manufacture its Anastigmat lenses in the United States, and, within several years, the Company was producing Zeiss stereo field glasses. Also, Bausch & Lomb acquired world-class instrument maker Saegmuller of Washington, which specialized in products such as gun sights used by the U.S. military and the armed forces of other countries.

Bausch & Lomb contributed heavily to the U.S. war effort in World War I. In early 1917, Bausch & Lomb produced 2,000 pounds of optical glass a month; the General Munitions Board required 2,000 pounds a day. By the end of that year, the Company was producing 40,000 pounds of quality optical glass a month. From April 1917 to November 1918, Bausch & Lomb produced 450,000 pounds of optical glass, seventy percent of the 650,000 pounds provided to the General Munitions Board by U.S. industry.

John Jacob Bausch's interests outside the firm included serving on the executive committee and as president of the Mechanics Savings Bank. He was a member of the Rochester Club.

Henry Lomb helped to establish the Public Health Association in Rochester and was active in the German-American Society. In 1885, he was instrumental in founding the Mechanics Institute, of which he was the driving force for twenty years. Lomb's cousin, Carl Lomb, vice president of Bausch and Lomb and vice president of Yawman and Erbe Manufacturing Company, became a principal leader of the Mechanics Institute for forty years after the death of his cousin, beginning with his election to the board of directors of the Institute in 1910.

## *Thomas J. Watson (1874-1956)*

"Watson was a durable bridge between the manual, agricultural small-town world of the nineteenth century and the congested, technologically sophisticated, urbanized world of the present. With persuasiveness adapted from the backwoods peddler, refined in time to emulate the savvy city drummer, with techniques developed in Billy Sunday camp meetings and along the Chatauqua lecture circuit, with a strait-laced code of personal conduct that in no way impinged on an insatiable desire for praise and commendation, and with a personal style that combined courtliness and conservative dress with a deadly, dedicated concentration on his work. Thomas Watson left the imprint of his resolute will on corporate life at IBM, and on a whole new breed of men fashioned in his image."

William Rodgers, *Think: A Biography of the Watsons and IBM*

Thomas John Watson, founder of the IBM Corporation, was born on February 17, 1874, in East Campbell, Steuben County. He was the first of five children of Thomas and Jane White Watson. Watson's father, who was in the lumber business, wanted his son to study law, but young Watson did not want to pursue that career. He applied for a temporary teaching certificate for three years and then enrolled at the Albany Teachers' College. However, one day of teaching changed his mind: "I can't go into a classroom with a bunch of children at nine o'clock in the morning and stay until four."

Watson enrolled at the Miller School of Commerce in Elmira. In May 1892, he completed the accounting and business courses there and accepted a position as a bookkeeper in Painted Post. He soon decided: "He couldn't sit on a high stool and keep books all my life." He certainly formed opinions quickly about what he did not want to do.

A neighbor of the Watson's, Willard Bronson, operated a hardware store and a consignment business. He acquired Estey organs, pianos, and sewing machines, and sold them on consignment around the countryside from a wagon. Watson went on the road selling for Bronson; it was the first of his many sales jobs.

Watson learned the importance of a good appearance and of

making a good first impression. He sold for Bronson for two years without a raise in salary and without many kind words from his boss. Bronson was astounded when Watson quit the job after two years. Only then did Bronson offer him a raise. He even offered to sell the business to Watson. Watson's father suggested that he seek opportunity outside the area; he thought that Buffalo might be a good place to look for a job.

Watson applied for a sales position with the National Cash Register Company. He met the manager of the Buffalo office, John J. Range, who was not interested in hiring him, but Watson persisted. Watson made no sales in the first two weeks, and Range made his disappointment clear. Watson absorbed Range's constructive criticism and, within a year, was one of the most successful National Cash Register salesmen in the East. By the time he was twenty-five, Watson was the top salesman in the Buffalo office.

John Henry Patterson, chief executive officer of the National Cash Register Company, made the cash register virtually indispensible to businessmen; then he monopolized its manufacture and distribution. Patterson was a successful manager because he combined paternalism with an emphasis on training. He realized that his salesmen responded to the fear of punishment and the promise of reward. Patterson knew just how hard he could push Watson. He became the prime shaper of Watson's life over the next eleven years.

In the summer of 1899, Patterson selected Watson to manage the Rochester office. Watson moved sales of the Rochester branch from near the bottom of all the Company's offices to sixth from the top within several months. He used some ruthless techniques to beat his main competitor, the Hallwood Company. His performance was followed closely by Hugh Chalmers, National Cash Register's general manager, and by Patterson. Watson lived in Rochester for four years.

The National Cash Register Company sold between eighty and ninety-five percent of new cash registers. However, Patterson wanted to take aggressive action to reduce the impact of sales of used cash registers. Patterson gave Watson $1 million to set up a company to front for the National Cash Register Company in driving out used cash register competition in the United States.

Watson established Watson's Cash Register and Second Hand

Exchange in Manhattan, undercut the prices of his main competitor, and bought the company out. He repeated this activity in Philadelphia and Chicago. He made the second-hand machine business a profitable unit of National Cash Register and was offered a position at Company headquarters in Dayton.

Eventually, Chalmers could no longer tolerate Patterson's dictatorial style and, as the number-two man in the Company, disagreed with some of Patterson's non-business decisions. Chalmers was fired, and Watson replaced him as general manager. Patterson went to Europe for two years, and, by the time he returned, Watson had doubled the sales volume (to 100,000 cash registers a year in 1910). The increase in sales was partly due to the redesign of the cash register by Charles (Boss) Kettering; he replaced the manual operation of the cash register with an electric motor. Kettering moved on to General Motors, where he designed the self-starter for automobiles.

The Company's monopolistic practices in the second-hand cash register business caught up with it. On February 22, 1913, Patterson, Watson, and twenty-eight other company managers were indicted on three counts of criminal conspiracy. They were placed on trial in Cincinnati for restraint of trade and maintaining a monopoly.

While awaiting trial, Watson met Jeanette Kittridge of Dayton, whose father was president of a railroad car manufacturing company. The Kittridges were neighbors and friends of Patterson, and Jeanette was Patterson's choice of a wife for Watson.

On February 13, 1913, Patterson, Watson, and the other managers were found guilty as charged. Patterson was released on $10,000 bail, and Watson was released on $5,000 bail. Watson wanted to postpone the wedding until the results of the appeal were known. Jeanette disagreed. She was as strong-willed as he was; together they made a powerful team. Shortly after their marriage, Watson was fired, just as Chalmers had been abruptly terminated earlier. Watson looked for another job.

Charles Flint had assembled a company called the Computing-Tabulating-Recording Company (CTR) by combining a computing scales company, the Tabulating Machine Company, and a time recorder company. CTR was unprofitable, and Flint was looking for a new manager. He offered the position to Watson; however,

Watson was not elected to the board of directors because of the pending appeal of the lawsuit. On March 13, 1915, the District Court verdict was set aside, and a new trial was granted. No new trial was conducted, and Watson was cleared of any wrongdoing. CTR promptly elected Watson president and general manager of the company.

Watson authorized the redesign of the Hollerith tabulating machine, and the Tabulating Machine Company became the star unit of CTR. From 1914 until 1920, CTR's gross income increased from $4 million to $14 million. In 1924, Watson renamed the company International Business Machines (IBM). Watson was appointed chief executive officer and, for the first time, was really in charge of the company.

Unlike many companies, IBM expanded during the Great Depression. By 1940, IBM was still small ($50 million sales per year), but it had become the largest company in the office equipment industry. World War II made IBM a large company. From 1939 to 1945, gross income increased from $40 million to $140 million. By 1949, the company was five times larger than it had been in 1939.

In 1952, Watson's son, Thomas Watson, Jr., became president of IBM and another son, Arthur, was appointed general manager of the IBM World Trade Corporation. From 1914 through 1953, assets grew by a multiple of 24 times, employees by 34 times, the data processing business by 316 times, and development expenditures by 500 times.

On May 8, 1956, Thomas Watson, Jr., became chief executive officer of the IBM Corporation. Just over a month later, on June 19, Thomas Watson, Sr., died of a heart attack.

## *Joseph C. Wilson (1909-1971)*

"The life of the businessman in this [twentieth] century is rich in the intellectual challenge imposed by dazzling technological and social change.... The best of them must have, on one hand, the resources of the artist whose penetrating perception allows him to master and interpret phenomena he does not fully comprehend; and yet, on the other, he must strive constantly for the facts the scientist wants and use his method with precision.... Businessmen, more than money changers, must work with human beings and, the most rigorous obligation of all, create in them a common will to do worthwhile work, to achieve together aims which add dignity to their lives and pride in the company of their associates."

Joseph C. Wilson, "Beauty in Management,"
*University of Rochester Review*

Joseph C. Wilson was born in Rochester on December 13, 1909, to Joseph R. and Katherine Upton Wilson. He attended Rochester public schools, including West High School, and graduated from the University of Rochester with honors in 1931. In 1933, after earning an MBA degree with distinction from the Graduate School of Business Administration of Harvard University, he joined the Haloid Company, a manufacturer of photographic chemicals and paper, as assistant to the sales manager.

Wilson's grandfather had founded Haloid in 1906, but he sold the majority interest six years later. Wilson's father, Joseph R. Wilson, who developed photographic emulsions, was one of the first employees of the Company. Joseph R. Wilson was elected secretary/treasurer of Haloid in 1933 and president in 1936. Sales of the Company's Record photocopy paper allowed Haloid to survive the Depression. In 1935, the Company sold stock to buy the Rectigraph Company, which produced a photocopier that used Haloid chemicals and paper. Among other applications, the Rectigraph Duplex Machine was frequently used in making copies of court records.

In 1936, Joseph C. Wilson married Marie Curran. They had six children. Wilson was a strong family man who was very close to his children. During his busy career, he always made time for them, including recreation, birthdays, and school events.

Wilson replaced his father as secretary of Haloid in 1936, was elected secretary/treasurer in 1938, and became president and general manager in 1946, when his father became chairman of the board. As the new president, Wilson knew that he faced serious competition in photocopying, so he asked Dr. John Dessauer, the research director, to search for new technology in which Haloid might invest. Wilson and Dessauer were fascinated by Chester Carlson's invention of electrophotography, which had the advantage of using plain paper to make copies from electrostatic images that formed on a metal plate.

Carlson's first successful copy had been made in October 1938, but he could not find a sponsor for further development of his invention until, in 1944, the Battelle Memorial Institute, a nonprofit research institution in Columbus, Ohio, agreed to develop his process further in return for control of his patents. In January 1947, Battelle granted limited rights to Haloid to commercialize electrophotography. In 1956, after being turned down by major corporations, Battelle granted compete control of Carlson's patents to Haloid for 50,000 shares of Haloid stock.

In effect, Wilson was betting his company's survival on the successful introduction of the technology called "xerography," from the Greek words for "dry" and "writing," to the market. He borrowed money and issued stock to pay development costs. Between 1947 and 1960, Haloid, spent $75 million on development, about twice the Company's earnings during that period.

The first operating model, manufactured in 1950, was overly complex. A trained operator had to step through thirty-nine operations on three machines to make a copy. It had to compete in the decade of the 1950s with desk-top machines such as the Kodak Verifax and the Minnesota Mining and Manufacturing Thermo-fax, which cost $300 to $400 and used wet chemicals or specially coated paper to make poor copies.

Wilson attempted to find a major corporation to help Haloid commercialize xerography, including Eastman Kodak and IBM, but they did not want to take the risk. IBM asked a consulting firm for a report on the demand for a desk-sized machine costing many times as much as the Verifax or the Thermo-fax. The consultant told IBM that the total demand was 5,000 machines.

In the early 1950s, Wilson asked Haloid's general counsel, Sol Linowitz, to erect a legal firewall around xerography patents not only in the United States but also in Europe and Asia where Wilson looked for partners, unfortunately with little success. Finally, the Rank Organization, a British producer of motion pictures, expressed interest in a joint venture, and the Rank-Xerox Company was formed in 1957. In 1962, the Fuji Film Company entered into a joint venture with Xerox. Haloid had become Haloid-Xerox in 1958 and the Xerox Corporation in 1961.

In 1960, Haloid-Xerox introduced the 914 copier, which was a resounding success. The machines were leased, not sold, and revenue was based on the number of copies made. Copy quality made the wet-chemical and special-coated-paper machines obsolescent. In the October 1966 issue of *Fortune* magazine, the Xerox 914 was called "probably the single most profitable product ever manufactured in the United States."

In 1966, Wilson was elected chairman of the board of the Xerox Corporation and began to delegate some of his responsibilities. In 1968, he turned over the responsibilities of CEO to Peter McColough. Wilson was a role model for the socially responsible executive; this move gave him more time to devote to community, State, and national interests. He was a heavy contributor of time and money to many educational and philanthropic organizations. He served on the board of trustees and was board president of the University of Rochester and the Rochester Community Chest. He led fundraising activities for both boards and served as president of the Rochester Chamber of Commerce.

Wilson's national stature increased when he joined the board of trustees of the Alfred P. Sloan Foundation, the Carnegie Endowment for International Peace, and the United Nations Association. He was a founder of the Business Committee for the Arts and served on numerous State and national commissions.

In 1946, when Wilson became president of Haloid, the company had sales of $7 million and net profits of $138,000. By 1970, Xerox had sales of $187.7 billion and earnings of $1.72 billion. However, profits were never Wilson's only goal. Wilson said, "To set high goals, to have almost unattainable aspirations, to imbue people with the belief that they can be achieved—these are as important as the balance sheet."

Joseph C. Wilson died of a heart attack on November 22, 1971. He collapsed in the New York apartment of Governor Nelson Rockefeller while attending a luncheon in his honor as the incoming president of the Governor's Club. W. Allen Wallis, president of the University of Rochester, observed: "He has given $20 million to the University, but his other contributions, what he has done for the University, far overshadow what he has given."

As noted by biographer Blake McKelvey in *Business as a Profession: The Career of Joseph C. Wilson, Founder of Xerox*, Wilson defined his personal philosophy, which was also the corporate philosophy of Xerox: "A philosophy which fully recognizes that ... we must shoulder some obligations of the community, nation, and man." One of his favorite quotations was by Matthew Arnold: "Hath man no second life? Pitch this one high!" Joseph C. Wilson led a life that deserves to be emulated.

Mt. Hope Cemetery Gatehouse, Mt. Hope Avenue

# CHAPTER 5

## ENGINEERS / ENTREPRENEURS

### Elisha Johnson (1786-1865)

"The location of our city as a frontier commercial depot, and our citizens being extensively engaged as a commercial people, enjoying rights secured to them by national treaties, demand of us high and honorable duties, in being obedient to the laws in matters involving our national faith, and in strict obedience to those principles of justice upon which depends the complexion of our national character. The reputation of our city for the intelligence, good sense, and honorable feeling of its citizens, and their regard to law, justice, and good order, should stimulate all to preserve unsullied her fame."                                                              Elisha Johnson

Elisha Johnson, who was educated at Williams College, was one of the early leading citizens of Rochester. The planner and practicing engineer became the City's fifth mayor. In 1817, he prepared the plan for the Village of Carthage, which overlooked the lower falls of the Genesee River. The main street, Ontario Street, connected with a new highway to Canandaigua and terminated in a public square. His plan included a road down to the mill properties at middle falls and a trestle to the docks to be built below the lower falls. He also planned the construction of a bridge over the Genesee River connecting west Ridge Road with east Ridge Road.

Johnson's goals were to build a mill town at the lower falls that would have access to commerce on Lake Ontario and to promote trade with settlements in the area. Obviously, the plan required access to traffic on the upper Genesee River. To facilitate his plan, Johnson bought most of Enos Stone's farm on the east bank of the upper falls. He laid out another settlement with a landing above the upper falls, a raceway on the east side, and another public square next to a street he called Court Street. Its northern boundary was Main Street, which connected with the old Pittsford Road. A new road to Pittsford originated at the public square.

Johnson planned to have Rochester and Carthage linked to his upper falls development. He obtained the permission of Nathaniel Rochester to build a dam to serve both Johnson's new raceway on the east side and the race that the three founders of the Flour City, Rochester, Fitzhugh, and Carroll, were building on the west side.

The growing city needed a public market. Wagons with grain, hay, and other produce had no place to stand while waiting for sales to customers. Johnson, who had just completed construction of the second bridge over Main Street, suggested that the public market building should be built at the northwest corner of the bridge, extending over the River up to the first pier. City trustees approved Johnson's plan.

Johnson was a member of the first board of trustees of the Franklin Institute, an organization formed to cultivate literature and science. In 1825, he became a member of a stock company formed to construct a railroad from the south end of Water Street to the Village of Carthage on the Genesee River. Johnson began its construction in 1829; it was completed in early 1831.

Three years later, Johnson was the surveyor, contractor, and chief engineer for the Tonawanda Railroad, which extended from Rochester to South Byron and to Attica in the late 1830s. He filed a patent on an invention for laying railroad tracks by driving spikes through flat iron bars into stringers placed on heavy blocks of wood. In 1835, he was granted the patent.

As Rochester grew, the need for a city water supply became evident, particularly for volunteer fire companies. Johnson drafted a proposal for a community waterworks. In January 1832, a fire consumed the wooden buildings along the north side of the Main Street bridge, including the public market building, causing an estimated $100,000 property damage.

Johnson's next project as a construction engineer was building a railroad from Rochester to Batavia. He completed the thirty-two-mile railroad's construction in May 1837 at a cost of $10,000 per mile. Two six-car trains operated daily, powered by wood-burning engines. The success of this railroad motivated financial backers to build a railroad to the east, from Rochester to Canandaigua, Geneva, and Auburn.

Johnson was president of the Village of Rochester from 1827 through 1829. In 1838, he became Rochester's fifth mayor. He

130

pushed for the improvement of streets and the construction of the Andrews Street bridge north of high falls. He prepared another plan for the construction of a public waterworks. Unfortunately, the City Council voted against proceeding with its construction.

During Johnson's tenure as mayor, Mt. Hope cemetery was established, based on plans prepared by a committee of which he was a member. He suggested the name for the first Victorian municipal cemetery in the United States. Also, Washington Square, which became Washington Square Park, was a gift from Johnson to the people of Rochester.

The New York State Legislature authorized construction of the Genesee Valley Canal on May 6, 1836. The proposed Canal would extend from Rochester to Hinsdale, outside of Olean, with a branch to Dansville. The bed of the Canal from Rochester to Sonyea, with a side-cut to Dansville, was relatively flat and few locks were required; however, the Canal's route from Nunda south was through rocky, rugged country, particularly in the "Deep Cut" near Oakland.

An attempt was made to dig a tunnel over 1,000 feet long through the palisade below the Middle Falls at Portage, which is now part of Letchworth State Park. Johnson directed the effort until it was stopped by landslides. The State halted construction of the Genesee Valley Canal until an alternate route could be found. Later, construction of the 125-mile canal continued through Fillmore, Houghton, Caneadea, Belfast, and Cuba to Olean.

Elisha Johnson had encountered two major disappointments: the City Council's failure to authorize the construction of a public waterworks and the State's termination of work on the Genesee Valley Canal. In 1839, he moved to Tennessee, where he retired on a plantation that had ore beds and an iron works. Historian Blake McKelvey considered Johnson "one of the city's ablest and most enterprising men."

## George B. Selden (1846-1922)

"Few of his [Selden's] devices were original, for he adapted an engine of the Brayton [two-cycle] type to road use by enclosing the crankcase and substituting a short for a long piston stroke. He incorporated a clutch to permit varied speeds, a foot brake, a muffler, front wheel drive, and other essential features that had not previously been brought together successfully for a road engine—not prior to the original application of 1879, that is, for by 1895 many others were working along these lines, and the first horseless carriages had actually made their appearance."      Blake McKelvey,
*Rochester: The Quest for Quality, 1890-1925*

George B. Selden was a member of an established Rochester family. His father, Henry Selden, a lawyer and later a judge, is remembered for representing Susan B. Anthony in her trial for voting in the general election of 1872. George B. Selden was a patent attorney known for his early patent for a "horseless" carriage powered by a gasoline combustion engine.

On June 15, 1903, papers creating the Ford Motor Company were filed in Lansing, Michigan. The company was confronted with a challenge just as it was gearing up for production. In 1877, George B. Selden, an inventor and lawyer from Rochester, New York, had built a gasoline combustion engine. Then he designed a carriage for the engine and obtained patent number 549,160 in 1895 for "the application of a compression gas engine to road or horseless carriage use." However, Selden did not build a car based on the design at that time.

Others were already manufacturing this type of vehicle, but they had not applied for a patent. In 1899, the Selden patents were purchased by the Columbia & Electric Vehicle Company of Hartford, which specialized in electric cars. The Association of Licensed Automobile Manufacturers (ALAM) was formed to prevent the Columbia & Electric Vehicle Company from charging a royalty for every car sold with a gasoline combustion engine. ALAM, which had gained control of most of Selden's patent rights, received a royalty of 1.25 % of the retail price of all cars using his patents. Twenty percent of the royalties went to Selden; eighty percent was used for research.

Henry Ford refused to pay royalties. The Ford Motor Company published a notice in Detroit newspapers: "To dealers, importers, agents, and users of our gasoline automobiles. We will protect you against any prosecution for alleged infringement of patents. The Selden patent does not cover any practicable machines. No practicable machines can be made from it and never have been."

On October 22, 1903, ALAM sued the Ford Motor Company and attempted to prevent Ford from exhibiting cars in the New York City automobile show, an important sales forum. Ford received unexpected support from John Wanamaker, the Philadelphia department store merchant. Wanamaker, who knew the manager of Madison Square Garden, arranged for Ford's presence at the auto show to help "fight the automobile trust." Unfortunately, Ford's display space was in the basement.

Finally, Selden used some of the royalties from ALAM to build a car, which was introduced to the public in front of the Seneca Hotel in Rochester in October 1908. In May 1909, Henry Ford and his lawyer went to court to address the problem of the Selden patent. They pointed out that others had built gasoline engines before Selden, and that the Selden engine was not the same engine used in Ford cars. In 1910, the Federal District Court of New York determined that the Selden patent was valid; Ford appealed the court's decision. On January 9, 1911, Judge Walter C. Noyes of the U.S. Circuit Court of Appeals decided in favor of Ford.

Ford was not to be restricted by the Selden patent because he did not use the Selden engine. Ford used the Otto four-cycle "instantaneous explosion" engine, a different design from Selden's "slow combustion" two-cycle engine. Ford was hailed in the press as "a magnificent individualist" and "a giant-killer."

Selden was a patent attorney, not an entrepreneur. He retired to pursue other patents after Ford won the appeal. If Selden had won the appeal, he might have become the Bill Gates of his day. George B. Selden died in 1922. His son estimated that his father had earned $360,000 from his automobile patent. In 1925, the Rochester Automobile Show in Exposition Park attracted over 37,000 people for a Silver Jubilee show honoring George B. Selden's early work on automobile design.

## *James Cunningham (1815-1886)*

"Cunningham was aware of the challenge to its kind of excellence and made efforts to catch up with Detroit, but in the nature of things it could not hope to succeed. The point is that what Cunningham [automobiles] represented: luxury, elegance, high style, was becoming outmoded, and the firm was not equipped materially or temperamentally to adjust to the new trend. A cheap, mass-produced Cunningham was unthinkable."                    Noel Hinrichs,
"The Pursuit of Excellence"


James Cunningham founded a company that was known primarily for the automobiles that it built from 1908 until 1936. However, the Cunningham Company began by making quality horse-drawn carriages, engaged in defense production in World Wars I and II, designed and built aircraft, and ultimately made cross bar switches for telephone companies and other customers. At one time, the company was Rochester's largest employer.

Cunningham was born in December 1815 in County Down, Ireland. After the death of his father when Cunningham was four, his mother moved with her five children to Cobourg, Ontario, where they ran a farm. Young Cunningham displayed an interest in woodworking at an early age and, for a short time, worked for a Cobourg carriage maker.

When Cunningham was eighteen, he moved to the United States to work briefly for an uncle who was an architect in New York City. Then he moved to Rochester, at that time a city of 10,000, which had impressed him when he traveled through it en route to New York City. Rochester had received its charter as a city that year; three-quarters of its population had been here less than five years. Most of its businessmen were merchants or flour millers.

Cunningham accepted a position with Hanford & Whitbeck, a Rochester carriage maker. In 1838, he joined with two partners to form Kerr, Cunningham & Company, which made small, light carriages (buggies), and one-horse-open sleighs, called "cutters." A depression that began that year caused the 1846 dissolution of the partnership, whose liabilities Cunningham assumed. Six years later, he formed his own carriage-making firm, which emphasized quality. Since much of the workmanship of that era was shoddy, Cunningham's products were popular.

In 1848, Cunningham's original carriage works on State Street burned down and was replaced by another on Canal Street, off West Main Street (then called Buffalo Street). His home was adjacent to the factory. By 1853, Cunningham had fifty employees and manufactured all components, including axles, springs, wheels, and accessories, such as lamps and folding steps for access to the carriage. Power tools, e.g. machine saws, came into use at this time; Cunningham designed many of his own.

The Panic of 1857 and the subsequent depression, due primarily to the collapse of the railroad boom, forced Cunningham into bankruptcy. Rufus Keeler, a former mayor of Rochester, was appointed receiver for the firm. When reorganization was completed in 1860, Keeler asked Cunningham to provide a job for his nephew, Rufus Dryer. Dryer would become Cunningham's son-in-law in 1875 and a partner in the firm that year.

By 1861, the company was again profitable and in a position to make wheels for artillery pieces and carriages for the Union Army during the Civil War. Following the War, Cunningham resumed carriage making. Cunningham's son, Joseph, who was born in 1843, became a partner in 1868. The name of the firm was changed to James Cunningham & Son.

By the 1880s, Cunningham had earned an enviable position in the manufacture of personal carriages, as well as ornate hearses and utilitarian ambulances. The firm manufactured more carriages in the United States than all other carriage makers combined. The company was incorporated in 1882 with James Cunningham as president, Joseph Cunningham as secretary, and Rufus Dryer as treasurer. In 1884, Cunningham was the largest industry in Rochester in terms of capitalization ($800,000) and plant size. The Kimball Tobacco factory had more employees, 1,000 compared with Cunningham's 550, but had a smaller factory. Bausch & Lomb had 200 employees at the time, and Eastman Kodak had forty.

The introduction of springs to improve suspension was an important advance in carriage manufacture. Rubber tires were not invented until 1886. Although Robert Thompson received patents for the pneumatic tire in the mid-1840s, "elastic belt" tires did not come into use until 1888, when John Dunlop designed hollow tires for tricycles and bicycles. Their use on automobiles on any scale began in 1898.

Carriage makers concentrated on making the body. Many materials were used: brass, iron, wood, glass, horsehair, leather, and wool. Carriages were made to last for the long term. Although the design evolved, no "model year" existed at the time. Elaborate woodcarving was an important facet of carriage making. At one time, 200 woodcarvers were employed by the firm. It was not rare to see beautiful, ornate carriages being raced down East Avenue.

James Cunningham died in 1886. He had always been a production man, and he knew most employees by name. One of the workers composed a tribute, which all employees signed, that was read at his funeral: "Himself a workman, he knew the wants of workingmen, he appreciated the difficulties and hardships to which they are exposed.... He came to be looked upon, especially by those in his employ, as a kind of loving father. They felt he was their friend. They could ask help of him as a brother. They regard his death as a personal bereavement."

Joseph Cunningham became president of the company and Rufus Dryer was vice president. Joseph, like his father, was a production man, and Dryer handled the finances of the business. Few developments in carriage making occurred during the 1880s except for the production of the tally-ho, an idea borrowed from England. The tally-ho used between London and Manchester was a four-in-hand, that is, a carriage drawn by four horses. Pictures of tally-hos appeared frequently on greeting cards.

As the turn of the century approached, the use of horse-drawn carriages was threatened by the introduction of the automobile, or "horseless carriage." Cunningham had considered producing automobiles in the late 1890s; in 1896, the firm had negotiated with the Duryea brothers to manufacture their automobiles, but nothing came of it. The firm's conversion from manufacturing carriages to making automobiles did not begin until 1908, the year before the next generation began running the company.

By 1900, 8,000 automobiles traveled the roads of the United States, most of which were powered by electricity or steam. An electric car could not travel very fast and a steam-engineer's license was required to operate a steamer, such as the Stanley Steamer. The scene was set for the gasoline engine to become the power plant of choice for automobiles. Of 1,000 automobile companies in existence at the turn of the century, only fifteen survived their first twenty-five years.

In 1909, Joseph Cunningham and Rufus Dryer retired. Augustine Cunningham, Joseph's older son, became president, and James Dryer, a graduate of M. I. T., became vice president of engineering. Harvard graduate Francis Cunningham, Joseph's younger son, became secretary and general manager. Eventually, the manufacture of automobiles superceded the making of carriages. The last Cunningham carriage was built in 1915; however, many of the techniques used in manufacturing of carriages were also used in making automobiles.

In 1908, the Cunningham Company entered the automobile business, beginning with the production of chassis and bodies for other manufacturers. Cunningham's first models had engines built by Buffalo or Continental and many components, including axles, radiators, and transmissions, purchased from other companies. Within two years, the firm produced all of these components itself. Its market was the "carriage trade" to whom it had sold carriages.

Cunningham cars were quality products and were not inexpensive; in the early years, price ranged from $3,000 to $ 5,000. Most of the metalwork and woodwork was done by hand, as it had been in making carriages. The company advised its customers not to have maintenance done by local garages but to call Cunningham, which would send out mechanics from the plant. From 1909 to 1912, the company manufactured bodies for other companies, such as Cadillac, Chalmers, Empire Electric, Peerless, and Velie.

In 1910, the first car completely manufactured by Cunningham, including the four-cylinder engine, was introduced. Later, the Model H had uncluttered, classic lines and the first V-8 engine in the United States. It had aluminum steps instead of running boards, a built-in air pump, a coil of hose for filling tires that was stored under the driver's seat, and a self-contained lubrication system. The company manufactured touring cars, coupes, runabouts, limousines, and landaulets.

In 1913, Cunningham cars were changed to left-hand drive, and, the following year, self-starters were added. During World War I, Cunningham manufactured ambulances for the U.S. military. The

Company also built windlasses used by the Army Signal Corps on observation balloons on the Western Front. The windlasses had a sturdy clutch, a large radiator, a planetary transmission, a drum with one mile of cable, and a V-8 engine mounted on a truck chassis.

On November 17, 1919, racecar driver Ralph DePalma set U.S. speed records at Sheepshead Bay, New York, in races of six, eight, and ten miles. Driving a stripped Cunningham roadster, his top speed was over ninety-eight miles per hour; his average speed was over ninety miles per hour. Later, he set a twenty-four-hour endurance record. These victories boosted sales of the roadster, which sold for $6,200.

By the early 1920s, a new class of buyers of Cunningham cars emerged: Hollywood actors, directors, and producers; wealthy Central- and South-American businessmen and politicians; Japanese executives; and Chinese warlords, one of whom ordered a custom car with a yellow body and green fenders.

Cunningham's hand manufacturing techniques were a striking contrast with assembly line methods employed by Detroit. Cunningham could not compete on cost, and it was not its intent to do so. However, Detroit had labor disputes, and Cunningham had satisfied employees whose names were known to senior management. By the early 1920s, the company had 800 employees, which included forty blacksmiths, and production continued to be limited, usually less than 350 cars annually.

The Cunningham automobile's interior woodwork was principally mahogany, maple, and Circassian walnut. Many materials, including leather, were used for the upholstery. Glass used in the cars was cut and polished at the plant. The exterior finish was fourteen or fifteen hand-polished coats of paint. The company drove the car 300 miles for final testing before turning it over to the buyer.

Cunningham automobiles built from 1926 to 1931 were considered "classics," the Rolls Royces of the United States. The firm was the first to install a radio in a car—a locally produced Stromberg-Carlson; the headlamps were produced by Bausch & Lomb.

Charles Lindbergh's solo cross-Atlantic flight heightened public interest in aviation. Looking ahead, Cunningham decided to go into the business of manufacturing airplanes, since many of its potential customers would again be its "carriage trade" customers. The design goal was to combine stability with speed.

The firm's first aircraft, the Cunningham-Hall airplane, was a biplane that had a large lower wing and a much smaller upper wing. Its maximum speed was 110 miles per hour. Because of slots in the lower wing, the craft could land at speeds as low as thirty miles per hour.

Cunningham-Hall also produced cargo aircraft and experimental airplanes for the U.S. Army and Navy. Its last aircraft was a low-wing all-metal plane produced in 1934 that had a cruising speed of 145 miles per hour and a maximum speed of 165 miles per hour. Cunningham left the aircraft manufacturing business in 1938 because of decreased demand due to the Great Depression, which also had dramatically affected the upscale automobile business. Buying habits changed, and conspicuous consumption, such as the purchase of expensive automobiles, decreased.

Detroit was making reliable cars at reasonable prices. A significant change was Detroit's emphasis on changing styles slightly each model year. Buyers were motivated to own the latest model car instead of a car like the Cunningham that was built for the long term. Cunningham stopped manufacturing automobiles in 1931.

Until 1936, the firm made bodies for other automobile companies, particularly a town car body for Ford and hearse bodies for Buick, Cadillac, Oldsmobile, and Packard. In 1936, Cunningham dropped out of the automobile manufacturing business completely. From the first Cunningham-assembled car in 1908 until the last in 1931, the firm had assembled approximately 5,600 cars, ambulances, and hearses.

During the 1930s, Cunningham manufactured products such as diving helmets and safety belts for aircraft. Leading up to World War II, the Company became increasingly involved in defense production. In the 1920s, a group of young Cavalry officers in the U.S. Army had become convinced that the next war would be mechanized and that maneuverability would be a vital factor, unlike the stationary trench warfare of World War I. George Patton and Levin Campbell were two of the officers advocating fast, maneuverable tanks.

In 1927, these officers obtained an appropriation for the production of experimental tanks and armored vehicles and negotiated a contract with Cunningham whose first tank was tested at the Aberdeen Proving Grounds in Maryland in March 1928. This nineton tank had a revolving turret with a thirty-seven mm cannon and a .30 caliber machine gun; it could travel at twenty-five miles per hour, three times as fast as previous tanks that had been designed to blast holes in a defense line.

By 1933, Cunningham had designed and produced a tank track with rubber treads that permitted faster speeds. In 1935, a tank equipped with these treads traveled across country at fifty miles per hour. Until appropriations ceased, the Company also produced experimental armored cars, cargo-carriers, half-tracks, and a weapons carrier with a seventy-five mm cannon. The Company was out of the defense business for five years.

Cunningham's first defense work for World War II was producing mounts for .30 and .50 caliber machine guns. The number of employees working on defense contracts increased from six in January 1940 to 360 in 1942 and to 800 the following year. The Company won the Army-Navy "E" (for efficiency) award, a selective award. Cunningham produced many items as a subcontractor to a prime contractor: airplane canopies, servo-motor gear boxes for controlling aircraft wing control surfaces like ailerons, aircraft gun turrets, and tail surfaces for bombers.

With the end of World War II in 1945, Cunningham was again without a product line. The Company began to produce equipment for gardens and farms: mowers, tillers, and small tractors. Within two years, over ninety other manufacturers had entered the field. Next, the firm produced plumbing fixtures for house-trailers. However, when these items began to be mass-produced, Cunningham looked for another product line and chose crossbar switches, electro-mechanical devices used in telephone switchboards.

Cunningham's crossbar switch was designed by Andrew Vincent who had left Stromberg-Carlson in 1946 and joined Cunningham in 1950. His design was unique because he did not merely build on existing designs. He studied the fundamentals of switching and designed a completely new switch that was extremely reliable and had a long life. Essentially, his design switched electrical data from low-level direct current signals to 100 megacycle signals at high speeds.

One of Cunningham's products was a crossbar switching control for the NASA Telemetry Center in Huntsville, Alabama. Full-scale production began in 1956. Other products included crossbar systems, that is, automated equipment that used a crossbar for its switching function, e.g. a system to read and record analog computer calculations.

By 1961, Cunningham, which had a need for more modern production facilities, moved to a twenty-acre site in Honeoye Falls, fifteen miles south of Rochester. There the Company built crossbar applications for manufacturers of automated machine tools, computers, printed circuits, transistors, and closed-circuit television monitors. The Company's crossbar designs were used by aircraft manufacturers, university laboratories, government laboratories, and by the space flight launching site at Cape Kennedy.

In 1968, Cunningham became a subsidiary of Gleason Works. The Company had evolved a long way from the carriage making begun by patriarch James Cunningham.

## Kate Gleason (1865-1933)

"Has my work been made harder because I am a woman? No. I have no hard knocks to report. Indeed, I think engineering must be different from any other profession in that regard. Engineers are as a class so successful, so progressive that they bear no grudges; feel no jealousies for any newcomers to their ranks, whether man or woman."                                                   Kate Gleason

Kate Gleason, businesswoman and housing developer, oldest child of William and Ellen McDermott Gleason, was born in Rochester on November 25, 1865. William Gleason, an Irish immigrant, opened a toolmaking shop in Rochester in the late 1860s. He was a supporter of opportunities for women and instructed his children, two sons and two daughters, in the principles of mechanical engineering. Ellen Gleason, an active suffragist and a friend of Susan B. Anthony, encouraged her daughters' interest in careers.

Kate Gleason always liked a challenge. As a young girl playing with boys in her neighborhood, she observed, "They didn't want me. But I earned my right. If we were jumping from the shed roof, I chose the highest spot; if we vaulted fences, I picked the tallest." Her half-brother, Thomas, died when Kate was eleven. Thomas had been his father's helper in the business. Young Kate, as the next oldest, was determined to help her father in the office of the toolmaking shop. During her high school years, Gleason worked as a bookkeeper in her father's business office.

In 1874, William Gleason designed an automatic machine for planing beveled gears, which transmit mechanical power around angles. Gleason's design transformed the business because gears that previously had to be cast or cut by hand could now be mass-produced without the previous imperfections. The success of this evolving design allowed Gleason Works to phase out the manufacture of hand machine tools by the late 1890s. As the demand of the automotive industry for beveled gear planers increased, Gleason Works dominated the gear-cutting machinery business.

In 1884, Kate Gleason enrolled at Cornell University but had to return to Gleason Works at the end of the year. She reenrolled in 1888, but again the demands of the business forced her to leave school. She rounded out her education with evening courses at the Mechanics Institute, predecessor of the Rochester Institute of Technology.

When Gleason went on the road to market Gleason Works products, she was the only woman salesperson calling on the male-dominated machine tool industry. She commented on her experience in making sales calls: "In those early days, I was a freak; I talked of gears when a woman was not supposed to know what a gear was. It did me much good. For no matter how much men disapproved of me, they were at least interested in seeing me, one distinct advantage I had over the ordinary salesman. I dealt wholly with men—no women were then running factories and foundries."

A humorous anecdote about a sales call made by Gleason to sell gear cutters to the Acme Machinery Company was told by manager A. H. Carpenter. Carpenter suspected that the young saleswoman calling upon him knew little about the products she was selling, so he called in Thompson, his gear expert, to test her knowledge.

As described by Fred Colvin in *60 Years with Men and Machines,* Carpenter discussed the interchange between Gleason and Thompson:

> "Well, young woman," Thompson began, "tell us what you can about your father's gear-cutting machines, in a general way, at least, and why you think they are better than the ones we are using at the present time—although I should perhaps warn you in advance that I am considered something of an expert, you know, on gears and gear-cutting machinery."

> "I am very glad to hear that, sir," said Kate demurely, "for it will make what I have to say much easier."

> "Let us get on then," replied Thompson. "What are the special features, if any, about the Gleason gear cutter?"

"Our machines, as you undoubtedly are aware, sir, are intended for making bevel gears only, although like all other gear-cutting machines, they are merely specially designed milling or shaping machines, which when used with a rotary cutter such as in our bevel-gear planer, fall into the milling-machine class—a feature that gives them greater speed of operation and a greater degree of accuracy than previously possible."

"As you know, the accuracy of the teeth depends upon the proper shaping of the teeth of the cutting tool, and the spacing on the accuracy of the indexing mechanism used, regardless of whether the gear teeth are being cut by a tool that follows a path established by a template, or by a cutter shaped to the space between the teeth, or by the relative motion of the cutter and gear. Now, on our spiral bevel gears...."

"Your what?" interrupted Thompson, somewhat bewildered by the rapid-fire delivery.

"Spiral bevel. You're familiar with them I'm sure?"

"Er ... oh, certainly, Miss Gleason—I've seen them around. I mean I've heard of them—in fact we've got quite a few spiral gears here at Acme. They sort of run together at an angle, don't they?"

"Ah, but those are not really spiral gears, you see. They are really spur gears with helical teeth, whereas true spiral bevel gears have spiral or curved teeth that are cut with a trepanning machine. And these machines are made only by Gleason Works. You see the difference, I presume?"

"Sure—I was just thinking of the other type—I mean when you said spiral, well, a spiral is a spiral, you know."

"Not necessarily," said Kate, with a sweet smile, "but let us go back to the theory of gears. If it were possible to have a modification of the spiral bevel in which the pinion is located below or above the center of the mating gears, what kind of gear action would you expect from that sort of arrangement?"

"Why, er ... what kind of gear action, you say? Well, now, let's see ... the pinion is where did you say?"

"The action of spiral bevel gears under this arrangement," ignoring Thompson's embarrassment, and sketching with her gloved finger tip a few mystifying circles in the air, "should more nearly approach that of a worm drive, the location of the pinion permitting its shaft to extend beyond the gear for support or other reasons. Such a gear arrangement exists only in theory of course, though a few designers are said to be working on the problem at the present time."

"Are they? That is to say, aren't they?" Thompson fumbled, beginning to wish Miss Gleason were back in Rochester.

"Yes. But I really wanted to talk about our gear-cutting machines. Now first let us consider a pair of miter gears, where the angle of intersection is forty-five degrees. If we ..."

"Excuse me, Miss Gleason," interrupted Thompson, mopping his brow with his handkerchief, "but if you don't mind I would like to continue this interesting discussion at another time. I

believe I have a slight touch of migraine coming
on." And he left the office hurriedly without having
given Kate an opportunity for placing an order for
Gleason gear cutters.

Gleason was given more credit for the design of the beveled
gear planer, her father's design, than she deserved. She always cor-
rected someone who gave her credit for its design instead of her
father. Henry Ford spoke highly of the beveled gear planer. He considered it "the most remarkable machine designed by a woman."
Her main talent was in promoting the business. From 1890 to 1913,
she was secretary/treasurer of Gleason Works and the company's
chief sales representative. She traveled extensively in the United
States and Europe.

In 1913, Gleason left the company due to a family disagree-
ment. Her first undertaking on her own was an appointment as
receiver of a bankrupt machine-tool business that was $140,000 in
debt. The shop's creditors thought they would be lucky if they
recovered ten percent of their debts. Within three years, Gleason
announced a $1 million profit, and creditors received 100% of their
debts.

In 1914, Gleason became the first woman elected to the
American Society of Mechanical Engineers. Two years later, she
was the first woman member of the Rochester Engineering Society.
Also that year, she was one of the first woman members of the
Rochester Chamber of Commerce.

In 1917, the president of the First National Bank of East
Rochester left to assist the war effort in France during World War I.
Gleason was unanimously elected by the board of directors to
replace him. She was one of the first woman bank presidents in the
United States and probably the first one not having family connections with the bank. When she resigned in 1920, the bank was considerably more prosperous than when she assumed the presidency.

In the 1920s, Gleason devoted her efforts to providing low-cost
housing for working-class families who had been paying inflated
wartime rents. She financed Conquest, a development of 100 six-
room, poured-concrete houses in East Rochester based on a standard house plan but orienting the homes differently to lessen the
appearance of a tract. The houses, which required a small down

payment, were loaded with extras. Gleason was the first woman member of the American Concrete Institute. She also began construction of a resort complex in Beaufort, South Carolina, intended as an artists' and writers' colony.

Kate Gleason died of pneumonia in Rochester on January 9, 1933, leaving $1.4 million to a long list of organizations and friends. Included in her behests was $100,000 to the City of Rochester for the establishment of a Local History Department in memory of her high school history teacher, Amelia Bretelle. Earlier, Gleason had made donations to the Rochester Institute of Technology (R. I. T.). In 1947, a women's dormitory was named in her honor. Those donations plus an additional donation in her will amounted to $613,750.

In 1998, the Gleason Foundation gave R. I. T. $10 million in Kate Gleason's name to upgrade engineering facilities and to expand educational opportunities for engineering students, particularly women. In recognition of this contribution, the R. I. T. College of Engineering was named the Kate Gleason College of Engineering.

Kate Gleason's motto was "I can do it if I will." She admitted: "I owe a great deal of my inspiration to Susan B. Anthony. She showed me that women could take an active part in outside affairs, and I shall always cherish the memory of our friendship." Susan B. Anthony gave her a copy of the first volume of *History of Woman Suffrage* with the inscription: "Kate Gleason—the ideal businesswoman of whom I dreamed fifty years ago—a worthy daughter of a noble father. May there by many more such in the years to come is the wish of—Yours affectionately, Susan B. Anthony, Rochester, N.Y., December 2, 1903."

Claire Ross published several quotations of Kate Gleason in "Kate Gleason of Rochester: America's pioneer Woman Machinist" in the September 1919 issue of *Pictorial Review:*

- I have always placed great faith in my fellow men, and I find that in response they give me their best.
- Of course, to have a thing done properly, you must be able to do it yourself; that's why I take each of my projects in turn so seriously. I have been accused of being single-tracked, but I find it pays in the end. I never put my goal too far ahead; it is better to concentrate on what you are doing and then, when

you have reached that end, try the next thing.

• The greatest fun I have in life is building-up, trying to create.

A capstone Kate Gleason quote is provided by Helen Christine Bennett in "Kate Gleason's Adventures in a Man's Job" in the October 1928 issue of *The American Magazine:* "A bold front, determination, and willingness to risk more than the crowd, plus some common sense and hard work, win out."

## *Chester Carlson (1906-1968)*

"Now, through the use of the copying machine, the twenty-five-page document can be reproduced in a matter of minutes, and one can have as many copies as one desires.... This is true in every profession, in every business, in government agencies, in colleges and hospitals and institutions of all sorts, wherever people communicate with written words or charts or pictures. That is why Chester F. Carlson's invention has so often been called one of the most significant of our age."  John H. Dessauer,
*My Years With Xerox: The Billions Nobody Wanted*

Chester Carlson began experimenting with a dry copy process in 1935, and, on October 22, 1938, he produced the first crude copy using his electrophotography process. Carlson, a patent attorney, filed a comprehensive patent in 1939. He spent five years looking for a sponsor to finance further development and commercialization of his new technology. During this period, he was turned down by the National Inventor's Council, the U.S. Army Signal Corps, and thirty-two companies, including A. B. Dick, Eastman Kodak, IBM, General Electric, and Remington-Rand (Univac). Carlson said that they all displayed "an enthusiastic lack of interest."

In 1944, he found a sponsor, the Battelle Memorial Institute of Columbus, Ohio. Battelle was to receive sixty percent of future proceeds in return for helping to develop the technology. Their scientists suggested using selenium instead of sulphur in the process and a different black toner powder. They, too, were unsuccessful in promoting the product. An Ohio State University professor renamed the process "xerography," from the Greek words "xeros," meaning dry, and "graphos," meaning writing.

Finally, John Dessauer of the Haloid Corporation saw an article about electrophotography in *Radio News*. Dessauer's boss, Joe Wilson, Jr., wanted to increase the $100,000 yearly earnings of the company and had asked him to read technical journals to look for new products and/or processes. Haloid Corporation purchased the patent and rights to Carlson's technology from Battelle. They produced a flat plate copier in 1949 that required 3-5 minutes per copy. Haloid spent more on research and development than it earned each year, but, by 1956, received forty percent of its sales from xerography. The name of the company was changed to Haloid-Xerox.

In 1959, IBM was asked to manufacture copiers for Haloid-Xerox. IBM commissioned Arthur D. Little, a consultant from Cambridge, Massachusetts, to do a study of the market potential. The study identified a total potential market of 5,000 units of sales for Haloid-Xerox's new 914 copier. IBM declined the offer to participate in xerography a second time, and Haloid-Xerox began to manufacture the model 914 copier. By 1968, they had produced 200,000 of them. The fallacy in the Arthur D. Little study was in basing their recommendations on an estimate of the number of copies made at the point of origin, using the original. Most copies are made at the point of receipt from copies made elsewhere.

Haloid-Xerox changed its name to the Xerox Corporation in 1961. By 1988, three billion copies were being made each day worldwide, and the business of making copies had become a $22 billion a year business. The technology that nobody wanted made millionaires out of many people and revolutionized the way in which we communicate with one another.

# CHAPTER 6

## SPORTSMEN / NOTABLES

### Walter Hagen (1892-1969)

"Walter Hagen made himself the leading player of golf and led his fellow professionals out of bondage. He won more than seventy-five championships and over a million dollars. He gave his victory medals and cups to friends as souvenirs and spent his winnings on their entertainment. He kept the Prince of Wales waiting on the first tee on one occasion and the Japanese ambassador on another. He introduced democracy into golf in the British Isles.... [Golfer] Chick Evans once said of him: "He's in golf to live—not to make a living."                              H. G. Salinger, Detroit *News,* 1947

Walter Hagen's parents, William and Louise Hagen, both of German descent, lived in Corbett's Glen in Brighton. Hagen was the second of five children and the only boy. William Hagen worked as a blacksmith in the railroad car shops in East Rochester.

Young Hagen could see the Country Club of Rochester by climbing a hill near Allen's Creek and looking across East Avenue. When he was just under eight years old, his father asked the master caddy at the Country Club for a job for his son. That was Hagen's introduction to golf, at ten cents an hour plus tips.

His first set of clubs was a mixture of clubs given to him by club members, one club at a time. He caddied for George Eastman of Eastman Kodak and for Walter and John Powers who owned the Powers Block of buildings in downtown Rochester, including the Powers Hotel.

In late spring of Hagen's seventh-grade year, he looked out of the window in the classroom and watched golfers on the course of the Country Club of Rochester. He envied their being outdoors while he was cooped up indoors. He made a sudden decision, and, when the teacher was not looking, climbed out of the window and walked over to the clubhouse to see if he could caddy for someone. He never returned to school.

As a caddy, Hagen was allowed to play the club course. He broke eighty by the time he was fifteen and was asked to be assistant to the club pro. Four years later, the pro at the County Club of Rochester left for a position in New England, and Hagen, only nineteen, was asked to succeed him. The following year, he asked for time off to play in the U.S. Open at Brookline and surprised himself and everyone else by tying for second.

During his teenage years, Hagen also had a strong interest in baseball. He played semi-pro ball with the Rochester Ramblers, a team that won the City championship three years in a row. He was invited to try out for the Philadelphia Phillies and seriously considered a career in baseball instead of golf.

Club member Ernest Willard, editor of the Rochester *Democrat and Chronicle,* heard of Hagen's interest in baseball and told him that Rochester was proud of him for his second-place finish in the U.S. Open at Brookline. Willard offered to pay his expenses to the National Open golf tournament in Chicago in 1914.

Hagen worked hard to prepare for that tournament at the Midlothian Country Club. He finished with a record-breaking 68 and won the Open championship. After that victory, he never considered a career in baseball again and began to study the game of golf seriously. In addition to giving lessons and making golf clubs at the Country Club of Rochester, he played in exhibitions and tournaments and endorsed products. His life changed dramatically.

In 1918, Hagen became the pro at the Oakland Hills Golf Club near Detroit, a city that was booming because of the automobile industry. It was the home of "new" wealth compared with "old" wealth at the Country Club of Rochester. The following year, Hagen won the U.S. Open at Brae Burn, near Boston. He needed proof that his win in Chicago five years previously had not been a fluke. About this time, Hagen became known as one of the best-dressed golfers.

Hagen traveled to England in 1920 to participate in his first British Open. Little was said in the British press about his win at Brae Burn the previous year. Most of his press coverage was about his golfing attire. He was a natty dresser compared with British golfers, who dressed in old tweeds. His first outing in Great Britain did not go well. Writing much later, in 1939, sportswriter Grantland Rice captured Hagen's experience at the event:

I always thought that Hagen's greatest crash in golf told a truer story of his nature than any of his successes. He left for England in 1920 to play in his first British Open at Deal. He went over as U.S. Open champion, a title he had won at Brae Burn the year before. He drew major headlines of the tournament. But in his first test he finished in fifty-third place [out of fifty-four]. He couldn't break eighty. He started with a big gallery and finished with his caddy and a lone scorer. But he finished without a complaint. Not only that, he walked up and posted his terrible 72-hole count in front of a big British crowd. As he gave in the figures he turned to this crowd with one remark, "I'll be back." He came back to win four British titles....

Hagen returned for the British Open in 1921 at St. Andrews. He did better than the previous year, but he did not win. However, he learned something about the game of golf: why a course has eighteen holes. Oldtimers at St. Andrews told the story of one of the charter members of the club board who liked a couple of nips from his flask prior to teeing off at each hole. His flask was just large enough to provide him with two good snorts at each tee for eighteen holes. This limited his range, and he was not willing (or able) to continue beyond the eighteenth hole.

In 1923, one of Hagen's Detroit friends arranged for him to star in a movie in Hollywood opposite Mae West. Filming began on *The Man Who Cheated* in the California mountains. The producers ran out of money, and it was never finished. However, he starred in another movie, *Green Grass Widow*. Norma Talmadge was supposed to star, but she could not play golf so she was replaced by Marge Beebe. Hagen decided that he was a better golfer than movie star, and he returned to his primary interest.

By the mid-1920s, Hagen was a well-known public figure whose activities on and off the course made news. In 1927, Bill Cunningham observed in the Detroit *News:*

The man who makes up his mind to do something and then goes after it with every ounce of power, blasting every barrier with an indomitable will to win, fighting where fighting is necessary, relaxing a bit where he can, gambling like a gasconade where gambling means victory, clamping the pressure on early and bearing down on the positive end—he is the fellow who picks up and goes places.... He has fashioned himself into a colorful personage, like a grand opera tenor, or a top movie-liner. He seldom moves without at least three trunks of clothes. His valet is in constant attendance. He drives only the fastest and flashiest cars.

Hagen became known as a serious competitor on the course who did not want to place second or lower. He became known as a player who welcomed a challenge. He was not bothered by having to come from behind to win. It was almost as if he welcomed the additional pressure. In 1925, Grantland Rice observed in *Colliers* magazine:

Golf is a game which can start a mental flurry in a second, but Hagen has won so many championships because in addition to fine physical skill ... he has built up a philosophy which Fate can't overthrow.... It takes an avalanche of accidents to make him sore. An earthquake would hardly leave him grouchy. He seems to be happiest when there's a hard battle ahead, and he must come from behind to win.

Hagen won the British Open in 1922, 1924, 1928, and 1929. By 1929, in addition to these victories, he had won two U.S. Opens and five American PGA tournaments, plus thirty-one other major tournaments. He was a big spender who spent every dollar that he earned.

In 1922, looking for an additional source of income, Hagen formed the Walter Hagen Golf Products Corporation in Longwood, Florida. He soon realized that because of the high humidity in that part of Florida, it was not the place to manufacture hickory-shafted clubs. The humidity caused the hickory to swell and when they were used in the southwestern states, the heads of the clubs loosened on the shafts. Also, when the shafts dried out, they produced slivers.

While he managed the business, Hagen lost money. He sold out to a manager who moved the venture to Detroit and turned it into a profitable business. Hagen's subsequent earnings from the business helped him live in the style to which he had become accustomed. In 1944, the company was sold to Wilson Sporting Goods Company and became Wilson's Walter Hagen Division.

In 1925, controversy existed as to whether Walter Hagen or Bobby Jones was the better golfer. Sports writers plotted to have a match between Jones the amateur and Hagen the professional. Jones had learned to play the game on the course of the club to which his moderately well-to-do father belonged; Hagen, the son of working-class, German immigrant parents, had learned golf as a caddy.

Hagen had won more major tournaments, but in National Open competition, Jones had finished ahead of Hagen five out of six times. They agreed to a seventy-two-hole home-and-home contest on consecutive Sundays. *Southern Golfer* magazine called it "The Battle of the Century." Hagen won the match decisively; unfortunately, no return match was played.

Hagen played in many countries, including ᵣ        ˢcotland, Ireland, Wales, France, Germany, Switzerl          ˡand, Australia, the Philippines, China, and Japa                ᵈ him). He played the game with many f         George Eastman, John D. Rockefeller, the Prince of Wales, and the Duke of of the U.S. Ryder Cup team for seven yₓ

One of the golfers of his era that Hage         was Gene Sarazin, with whom he played frequentlᵧ         arazin commented about his friend in *Thirty Years of Cha*        *ip Golf:* "Golf never had a showman like him. All the profess.onals who have a chance to go after the big money today should say a silent thanks to Walter Hagen each time they stretch a check between their fingers. It was Walter who made professional golf what it is."

Many fans of golf and sportswriters observed that Hagen was not only a good golfer, he was a personality. He had a huge following, some of whom considered him larger than life. In 1948, Herbert Warren captured this in *The Story of American Golf:*

> Whenever he entered a tournament, buoyant crowds ran out to find him, passing up the pace-makers so that they could watch Sir Walter.... On his tours back and forth across the country, Hagen would step, shining and unconcerned, from the limousine his chauffeur had moored near the first tee—always a little late for his matches.... He would stride erect down the fairway, his black hair gleaming above his weather-beaten face, and not until he had holed out on the last green did he relinquish, even for a moment, the attention of every person in the gallery.

Of all of the observations made about Walter Hagen, one of the most complimentary was made in 1953 by Harry Molter in *Famous American Athletes of Today:*

> The term *fabulous* is reserved for an even more select group. It is greatness grown into legend. It describes the astonishing and incredible. It exudes color, magnetic personality and the intangible something that attracts crowds and makes news both on and off the field. It is as much the manner of victory as the triumphs themselves.... In golf, men like Ben Hogan, Gene Sarazin and Sammy Snead wear the cloak of greatness. Bobby Jones rates as perhaps the most brilliant of them all. Walter Charles Hagen can be classed as fabulous.

## Cabell "Cab" Calloway (1907-1994)

"I don't know how it got started, really, the scat singing. I think one night in the Cotton Club I just forgot the words to a song and started to scat to keep the song going. It was in 1931. And it went over so big that I kept right on doing it. It became a style that people began to identify me with. I did it because people responded. And the people responded because it looked to them, I guess, like I was having such a good time just scatting it. It made them feel good. And it made me feel good 'cause that's all I've ever wanted, when you come right down to it—to have a house jumping like that, to see people really enjoying themselves, to entertain. Those are the things that have always made me happiest and given me the most satisfaction."      Cab Calloway, *Of Minnie the Moocher and Me*

Cab Calloway was a bandleader, actor, songwriter, and singer known as the "Dean of American Jazz." He started his shows with his theme song, "Minnie the Moocher":

> Now here's a story 'bout Minnie the Moocher
> She was a low-down hoochy coocher
> She was the roughest, toughest frail
> But Minnie had a heart as big as a whale.

Calloway would call out: "Hi-de-hi-de-hi-de-ho."
The band answered: "Hi-de-hi-de-hi-de-ho."
He would sing: "Wah-de-doo-de-way-de-ho."
The band responded: "Wah-de-doo-de-way-de-ho."
The audience joined in:"Wah-de-doo-de-way-de-ho."
Calloway would continue to call out scat phrases, and the audience responded until the place was jumping. He concluded each show, as he started, by singing "Minnie the Moocher."

Cabell Calloway III was born to Cabell Calloway II and Martha Reed Calloway on December 25, 1907, at 40 Cypress Street, which is between Mt. Hope and South Avenues in Rochester. His family later moved to 14 Sycamore Street, off Field Street, a house that has since been razed. Calloway's mother, who graduated from Morgan State College, was a teacher in the Rochester public school system.

His father, a lawyer educated at Lincoln University, was in the real estate business.

Due to a downturn in his business in 1918, Calloway's father moved the family to Baltimore, where he died two years later. Calloway described himself as "wild and independent" in his early teens. He skipped school frequently to hustle on the street, mainly by selling newspapers. He took the trolley to Pimlico Race Track, where he walked horses after races and helped to wash them down. His lifelong interest in horseracing began at Pimlico. In the evenings, he shined shoes at a stand near the Race Track. His earnings of twenty to thirty dollars a week helped to support the family.

Martha Calloway was unhappy about her son's skipping school and his life on the street and at the track. She decided to send him to the Industrial and Agricultural School in Downingtown, Pennsylvania, a church-supported boarding school run by a granduncle, pastor of a Philadelphia church. The 200 students cultivated the farm, learned a trade such as woodworking, and took academic courses, including history, mathematics, and reading. Calloway admitted that the school benefitted him; nevertheless, he left after a year and returned to Baltimore.

In junior high school, Calloway played baseball and basketball, his first experience with organized sports. He attended Frederick Douglass High School and continued to play baseball and basketball. In his senior year, he played professional basketball for the Baltimore Athenians.

At fourteen, Calloway began to take voice lessons and elocution and to sing in the choir at the church where his mother played the organ. In high school he continued voice lessons and studied basic musical theory. He played the drums, sang with a small group, and did vaudeville with his classmates. When he began singing and playing drums in clubs, he discovered that he could earn money for entertaining and making people happy. Baltimore was one of the centers of jazz at the time. Drummer Chick Webb was from Baltimore and was one of Calloway's inspirations. Calloway became known as the singing drummer, singing songs such as "Muddy Waters."

Calloway formed his own four-piece band and later joined Johnny Jones's Arabian Ten Orchestra, which played in the area.

Eubie Blake was another Baltimore musician. He moved to New York and starred in *Shuffle Along,* the same revue that Calloway's older sister, Blanche, joined when she moved to New York.

Blanche tried to discourage her brother from going into show business. She supported her mother in encouraging him to go to college. Blanche returned to Baltimore with the cast of *Plantation Days,* a popular musical revue about the Old South. Calloway begged his sister to get a part for him and to arrange for him to travel to Chicago with the cast. Blanche agreed to schedule an audition for him if he would enroll in college in Chicago.

Chicago at that time was a major jazz center. Among the musicians playing there were Eddie Condon, Bix Beiderbecke, Pee Wee Russell, Benny Goodman, Wild Bill Davidson, Louis Armstrong, King Oliver, and Earl "Father" Hines. They played a mixture of dixieland and swing.

Calloway lived in Blanche's apartment. He enrolled at Crane College and played on the College basketball team. He was good enough to try out for the Harlem Globetrotters and to receive an offer to join them. Calloway sang part time while taking courses at Crane. Eventually, he sang more and more and studied less and less, until finally he dropped out of college.

Calloway became the house singer and later master of ceremonies at the Sunset Cafe, where Louis Armstrong played. Eventually, Calloway replaced the bandleader and, for the first time, had a band of his own—the Alabamians. Although he conducted, he continued to sing blues, dixieland, and ballads. He looked for ways of stimulating the audience, of entertaining them.

Calloway stayed with the band when it left the Sunset Cafe to go on the road with the ultimate destination of New York City. New York was the place to be. Louis Armstrong played at Connie's Inn, Fletcher Henderson at Roseland, Duke Ellington at the Cotton Club, and King Oliver and Chick Webb at the Savoy Ballroom.

` Calloway rented a room in Fletcher Henderson's house in Harlem. Henderson was known for a style of music that became known as "swing." His band had many well-known musicians, including Coleman Hawkins on clarinet and tenor sax and Benny Carter on alto sax, soprano sax, and clarinet. Later, Henderson teamed up with Benny Goodman and wrote and arranged many songs for him.

Calloway urged his band to move away from the old-style, un-hip tunes that they had played traveling around the Midwest. New York was used to jumping jazz and swing numbers, and the band had to change to be accepted in the City. Unfortunately, the Alabamians were a corporate band, in which the members made the decisions, and Calloway was unable to convince them to replace songs like "Come Up and See Me Sometime" and "Bye, Bye Blues."

In November 1929, the Alabamians opened at the Savoy Ballroom, where the audience was used to Baltimore native Chick Webb's "Savoy Tempo," a quick, two-four rhythm that was easy to dance to. The band lasted only one night of a two-week contract. Calloway was out of work; Louis Armstrong got him hired as a singer for a revue entitled *Connie's Hot Chocolates*. Fats Waller was the pianist and songwriter. Calloway sang songs such as "Ain't Misbehavin" and "Rhythm Man." Subsequently, the show went on the road.

While *Hot Chocolates* was playing in Boston, an agent came up from New York City to ask Calloway to lead the Missourians, a band that had played at the Savoy Ballroom. Although the Alabamians had not impressed people at the Savoy, the bandleader had. The Missourians had originated in Kansas City where Count Basie played second piano for them. Although the Missourians were also a corporate band, they increasingly were managed by Calloway. He signed a ten-year agent's contract that was much more favorable to the agent than to Calloway.

The band's first job in the City was at the Crazy Cat on the West Side in midtown. Every night at 11:00 p.m., their show was broadcast live to the New York City area; they became well-known. One night after the show, two men representing the mob asked Calloway to play at the Cotton Club, which was the most prestigious place to perform in the City. Calloway mentioned that he knew that Duke Ellington was playing there and was told that Ellington was going on tour and then making a movie. Calloway told the men about his long-term contract with his agent. They advised him not to worry about it but to be at the Cotton Club at 2:00 p.m. the next day for rehearsal. The mob doubled his salary.

The Cotton Club, where the bandstand was a replica of a Southern plantation, produced two revues a year. Sunday night was the big night. Expensive cars lined up outside the club bearing the elite of New York Society. Lady Mountbatten dubbed the Cotton Club "the aristocrat of Harlem." Many Cotton Club shows were created by Harold Arlen. Ted Koehler wrote the lyrics and worked on the sets. The revues were a combination of vaudeville and burlesque accompanied by sophisticated music and dancing.

Calloway became the band manager, and the name of the band was changed to Cab Calloway's Cotton Club Orchestra. Later, in the 1930s, Dizzy Gillespie, Illinois Jacquet, and Jonah Jones played for the band, which was on the radio frequently and made records. When they were not playing at the Cotton Club, they traveled the New York-New Jersey theater circuit.

In 1931, Calloway and his new agent, Irving Mills, wrote "Minnie the Moocher" and had their first hit. It became the band's theme song, replacing "St. James Infirmary." Subsequently, Calloway wrote over 100 tunes. One of the hits of the Cotton Club revues that year was Arlen's and Koehler's "I've Got the World on a String." The band did many benefits around New York City and made an extended tour of the South.

Next, Calloway and the band went to Hollywood to make the movie, *The Singing Kid,* with Al Jolson. The music was by Harold Arlen. This was the first of ten movies in which the band performed. They also made many short subjects.

In 1935, the Cotton Club Orchestra made a successful tour of Europe. Duke Ellington's band had traveled around Europe two years previously. Calloway's band opened at the London Palladium. The Prince of Wales, who had enjoyed the their records, and the King of Greece attended the concert. European crowds were enthusiastic. The band's last stop was Paris, where they met many expatriate black musicians, including Sidney Bechet.

Upon their return to the U.S., the band toured the Midwest as well as Texas and Oklahoma. By 1941, the Cotton Club Orchestra had fifteen members, including Dizzy Gillespie and Jonah Jones on trumpet, Milton Hinton on bass, and Cozy Cole on drums.

In 1943, Calloway was in the movie *Stormy Weather* with Lena Horne, Bill "Bojangles" Robinson, and Fats Waller. Ted Koehler of the Cotton Club revues wrote the script. It was Calloway's favorite movie. By 1947, Calloway could no longer get bookings for the band, so he had to break it up. It was one of the most difficult things that he ever had to do. He tried to find other jobs for the band members.

Times were lean for Calloway until 1950, when he was asked to play the role of Sportin' Life in a Broadway revival of *Porgy and Bess.* George Gershwin had seen many of the revues at the Cotton Club in the 1930s and modeled his Sportin' Life character on Calloway. Leontyne Price was Bess and William Warfield was Porgy for the initial European tour. *Porgy and Bess* ran for three and a half years, including a final year in London. After *Porgy and Bess*, Calloway formed a small combo and toured the United States, the Caribbean, South America, and Europe.

In 1957, Calloway had a role in the movie *St. Louis Blues* with Nat King Cole, Eartha Kitt, Pearl Bailey, Ella Fitzgerald, and Mahalia Jackson. Calloway was also in *The Cincinnati Kid,* written by Ring Lardner, Jr., and Terry Southern; it starred Steve McQueen, Edward G. Robinson, Ann Margret, Karl Malden, Tuesday Weld, and Joan Blondell.

In 1967, Calloway played Horace Vandergelder opposite Pearl Bailey in the Broadway production of *Hello, Dolly!* The musical ran for over three years. When *Hello, Dolly!* played in Washington, D.C., Calloway and Bailey were invited to the White House by President Lyndon Johnson. In 1980, Calloway was in the film *The Blues Brothers* with John Belushi and Dan Ackroyd. Calloway sang "Minnie the Moocher," giving younger audiences the opportunity to see him perform.

On April 25, 1992, Calloway visited Rochester to do a benefit on behalf of Action for a Better Community. That October, he opened the Rochester Pops Orchestra concert series by singing some of his old standards. In 1993, Calloway received an honorary doctorate from the University of Rochester. While he was in town, the Cab Calloway Orchestra performed at the Nazareth College Arts Center. Also in 1992, a plaque and monument commemorating his career was dedicated in Otto Henderberg Square, a small park on Sycamore Street in the Swillberg neighborhood.

Cab Calloway died on November 18, 1994, after suffering a stroke the previous June. He was survived by his wife, Nuffie, whom he had married in 1953, and five daughters.

## William Warfield (1920-2002)

"Warfield's life has been full. His career has lasted over four decades and has included success in all areas to which a protean singer could aspire. His mastery of the concert stage was established with his first Town Hall recital and confirmed by countless appearances in all parts of the world. He is a consummate oratorio singer. He has appeared with great orchestras and great conductors, all of whom have applauded his musicianship. He has achieved a mythic identification with the baritone roles in *Porgy and Bess* and *Showboat.* Television and film have recorded his triumphs as singer and actor. Critical opinion regards him as one of the great singer-actors of the [twentieth] century."     Richard A. Long, Foreword,
*William Warfield: My Music & My Life*

William Caesar Warfield, the oldest of five sons, was born in West Helena, Arkansas, on January 22, 1920, to Bertha McCamey Warfield and Robert Warfield, a Baptist minister. Robert Warfield moved the family to Rochester in 1925.

Warfield considered himself lucky to be raised in Rochester and "wouldn't have traded my Rochester childhood for any other." In *William Warfield: My Music & My Life,* Warfield observes:

> Rochester in the Twenties and Thirties was a place where the "colored" and the Polish and the Irish and the Italians grew up in the same mixed neighborhood, where the ethnic differences that separated us were usually no more significant than the varied aromas that wafted out of our mother's kitchens ... while we played together in our adjoining back yards....
>
> From our safe vantage in Rochester, ... we were safe in our melting pot, surrounded by a vigorous tradition of tolerance. People went out of their way to trumpet the principles of brotherhood and mutual accommodation; they believed in those principles, and were proud of them, and proclaimed

163

> them inseparable from the idea of America itself....

> If my first gift was the gift of life given me by my family, my second was given me by my extended family in Rochester. They gave me the chance to form my character in a climate of tolerance and remarkable goodwill.

Warfield's interest in music began when he sang in the choir at the Mt. Olivet Baptist Church satellite Aenon Missionary Baptist Church, where his father was assistant pastor. Bertha Warfield had a fine soprano voice that was always remembered by her oldest son. Rev. Warfield, a self-taught pianist, also had a fine voice. At the age of nine, young Warfield began his piano lessons, which continued during his years at Washington High School, where he also sang in the choir.

In 1937, Warfield entered the annual competition sponsored by the National Educators League for a full music scholarship to a nationally recognized school. He won first prize at the national competition in St. Louis. He could have attended Juilliard or Curtis, but he chose to enroll at the Eastman School of Music.

At the Eastman School, in addition to music courses, Warfield took courses in French, German, and Italian. Professor Elsa Miller believed that lieder and arias were composed to be recreated. She insisted upon fluency, not merely pronouncing the words properly. Also, Warfield took dramatics classes, studied acting manuals, and joined the local community players.

During early World War II, Warfield was drafted into the U.S. Army and was assigned to Jefferson Barracks, Missouri, for basic training. There he experienced segregation and racial prejudice for the first time. His drill sergeant resented him because he had a college education. During training, the University of Rochester notified him that he had enough credits to graduate with his class that spring.

After basic training, Warfield was assigned to ordnance; specifically, he was assigned as a "human mule" to haul ammunition for artillery training exercises. He petitioned the colonel of his regiment to be reassigned so that he could use his language skills.

Warfield was transferred to Camp Ritchie, Maryland, a "G-2," or military intelligence post. His mission was to train military intelligence teams for assignments throughout Europe. His major responsibility was manager of a theater used during the day for training films and for entertainment in the evenings.

Warfield met many show business people at Camp Richie, including a playwright, a press agent, and actor Larney Goodkind, who was to play an important role in Warfield's career as his manager. Goodkind, who had been a talent scout for Universal Pictures prior to the war, was from a musical family and had many contacts in show business

Warfield sang in chapel programs and recitals at Camp Richie. He became known as, in his words, the "big black sergeant who sings opera." However, he began to branch out from classical music to popular music and boogie-woogie.

In December 1943, Billy Rose, who was preparing a production of *Carmen Jones*, heard about Warfield from a University of Rochester contact and asked Warfield to audition for the part of Husky Miller. He was offered the part, but Rose's request for "detached service" from the Army for him was denied.

While stationed at Camp Richie, Warfield had many opportunities to visit New York City and Washington, D.C., on three-day passes. He met New York City socialite Mary Schlesinger, who had a summer home near Camp Richie. She provided important contacts for him in New York.

At Schlesinger's parties in her New York apartment during the War, Warfield observed in his autobiography that he was perceived as the "exotic black man who spoke French and Italian and German, played Schubert and sang Verdi, and who was currently working for G-2." In his own view, "I was young Bill Warfield, this wide-eyed kid who's living in the barracks, first time away from home in Rochester, New York."

In January 1946, Warfield was discharged from the Army and returned home to Rochester. All five Warfield sons came back from the war safely. Rev. Warfield had a new assignment as pastor of Mt. Vernon Baptist Church. Warfield's brother Thaddeus was minister of music there for many years as well.

Warfield enrolled in the graduate program at the Eastman School to earn a M. A. to prepare himself for teaching, which he looked forward to doing. The spring semester had barely started when Dr. Howard Hanson, Director of the Eastman School, called Warfield into his office to tell him that Herman Levin, producer of the Broadway musical hit, *Call Me Mister,* wanted him to audition for the lead in the show on the road.

Warfield was offered the part and returned to Rochester to discuss the offer with Dr. Hanson, who suggested that he seize the opportunity; he could always return to the Eastman School. He took Dr. Hanson's advice.

*Call Me Mister,* a social satire with music and lyrics by Harold Rome and a piece by Noel Coward, was one of the big hits of the Broadway season. Warfield made many friends on the road tour across the country, including dancer Bob Fosse and comedians Carl Reiner and Buddy Hackett, who kept the cast entertained.

When the road show closed, Warfield returned to New York, where he registered with Actors' Equity and General Artists Corporation to schedule auditions. He took voice lessons with professor Otto Herz of the American Theatre Wing, who was also assistant conductor of the New York Opera Company. In addition, Warfield studied with Yves Tinayre, who had been a celebrated lyric tenor, to expand his classical repertoire. These studies, which Warfield could not afford on his own, were subsidized by the G.I. Bill as part of the Veterans Training Program.

Warfield's career took off when he rediscovered Larney Goodkind, who had left Universal Pictures and wanted to return to music. Goodkind obtained parts for him in an off-Broadway play, *Set My People Free,* and a musical, *Regina.* When the run of *Regina* ended, Warfield went on the road in a series of nightclub engagements.

In 1947 and 1949, Warfield entered the Naumburg Foundation's vocal competition. First prize was an all-expenses-paid recital at New York's Town Hall. On both occasions, he made it to the finals but was disappointed to miss out on the best opportunity to advance his career.

Just before Christmas of 1949, when Warfield planned to return to Rochester to sing Handel's *Messiah* with the Oratorio Society, he performed at the Club Norman in Toronto. He was invited to join financier Walter Carr at his table. Carr could tell that Warfield had classical music training and asked why he was performing in night-clubs and not on the stage. Warfield replied that he was studying and rehearsing for the concert stage, but that he also had to pay the rent.

Carr asked him what it would take to advance his career. Warfield replied that a Town Hall debut in New York with decent reviews would spur agencies to promote him. Carr then asked what a Town Hall debut would cost and was told about $1,000. Carr gave him an advance of $600 and asked him to have Goodkind work out the details.

Carr told Warfield that when he was a young man, his career had been stalled, and he needed help to take advantage of an opportunity. A mentor sponsored him, and he made a resolution to help someone else later. Carr wanted to help Warfield get out of the clubs and onto the concert stage.

Warfield's debut at Town Hall was on March 19, 1950. Ross Parmenter's review in the New York *Times* included the following observations:

> William Warfield, the baritone who was heard earlier this season in Marc Blitzstein's musical drama, *Regina,* showed yesterday afternoon in his first New York recital at Town Hall that he is also a highly gifted concert singer. It was an auspicious debut.... He is endowed with a noble voice, warmth of temperament, a feeling for the stage, and great sincerity.... Perhaps the most striking thing about him yesterday, aside from his splendid voice, was his range of style....

> The baritone called his first group "Songs of the Believer," and he mingled the spirituals of his own people with the religious music of Schuetz, Perotin, Handel, and Monteverdi. This revealed another facet of his talent, for he also has the gifts of the oratorio singer.

> Mr. Warfield held his listeners with everything he did, and they reveled in his voice for its pure sound, from its warm, rich depths to its particular-

ly beautiful soft high tones. And he won them still further in his encores, when he supplanted Otto Herz at the piano and played his own accompaniments for two Jubilee Shouts.

Other reviews included raves entitled: "Unusual Baritone" in the *Saturday Review,* "Great New Voice" in *Newsweek,* and "William Warfield Scores in Recital" in the New York *Times.* The response to Warfield's debut at Town Hall was immediate and glowing. It generated an offer from the Australian Broadcasting Commission to tour Australia. He performed thirty-five concerts in Australia without repeating any pieces.

When Warfield returned from Australia, he was invited by MGM to play the role of "Joe" in a remake of the musical *Showboat,* the role popularized by Paul Robeson in the 1936 movie. The role included singing "Old Man River." After he completed the movie, Warfield returned to New York for a second Town Hall recital, which allowed him to expand his repertoire, and then he toured for Columbia Artists.

In 1950, Warfield was asked to play the role of Porgy in a American National Theatre and Academy production of *Porgy and Bess.* He went with the director and the financial backer to hear a Juilliard production of *Falstaff* starring Leontyne Price, a somewhat shy young woman who was obviously bound for stardom. They were impressed, and Price was asked to play the role of Bess; Cab Calloway played Sportin' Life. During rehearsals and the road show, Price and Warfield, despite the difference in their ages, fell in love. He proposed to her in Chicago. They were married in August 1952 at the Abyssinian Baptist Church in Harlem and left immediately for a successful tour of Europe with *Porgy and Bess.*

Because of commitments with Columbia Artists, Warfield was unable to play the role of *Porgy* on tour in the United States. Not only was it difficult for Warfield to give up the opportunity to play Porgy opposite his wife's Bess, but it was tough on the marriage as well when he went on the road with Columbia Artists.

In January 1954, Warfield and Price gave the first of only three concerts they ever did together at the Academy of Music in Philadelphia. Also that year, Warfield was awarded the Alumni Citation by the Eastman School of Music. Two years later, Warfield and Price performed Handel's *Messiah* with the Philadelphia Orchestra. After these successful concerts, Price moved toward operatic roles. She was asked to sing *Aida* with the Metropolitan Opera Company but decided to obtain additional seasoning in Europe instead. After her successes in Europe, Price returned home for her debut with the San Francisco Opera. The couple's careers took different paths. By 1957, their marriage was strained, and they separated the following year. They remained friends and confidants and were supportive of each other's career. They did not divorce until 1972.

In 1956, 1958, and 1959, Warfield toured for the State Department as a "musical ambassador." The first tour, with Eugene Ormandy and the Philadelphia Orchestra, was a successful five-week tour to seventeen cities in Europe; the high point was reached at La Scala in Milan. Next, a tour of Africa was followed by an around the world tour. Also in 1957 and 1959, Warfield starred as "De Lawd" in Marc Connely's *Green Pastures* on NBC television.

In 1961, Warfield was cast as Porgy in *Porgy and Bess,* staged by the Light Opera Company at City Center. Leesa Foster was Bess; her understudy was Barbara Conrad, mezzo-soprano of the Metropolitan Opera Company. Critic Howard Taubman of the New York *Times* wrote, " Mr. Warfield is a superb Porgy. His playing has dignity and humility and his singing has the kind of nuance, control, and potency that one rarely encounters in the Broadway theatre."

Judith Crist of the New York *Herald Tribune* added: "Mr. Warfield is more than a fine baritone. He is a fine actor and his portrait of the crippled beggar of Catfish Row is brilliant in its blending of tenderness and strength, in its pathos and compassion. His performance is beyond compare ... an unforgettable Porgy." In 1964, the production was revived, and it was performed at the World's Fair that year. Also in 1964, Warfield and Price teamed up in a recording of *Porgy and Bess* for which they won a Grammy Award.

In 1974, Warfield was awarded New York City's Handel Medallion. The following year, he performed at Carnegie Hall to commemorate the twenty-fifth anniversary of his Town Hall debut. Many noted performers attended, including Marian Anderson and Leontyne Price. The following year, Warfield gave a performance, in a speaking role for which he became known, of Aaron Copland's *Lincoln Portrait.* He performed it in German in Vienna and in French in Paris on a bicentennial tour with Leonard Bernstein. In 1984, Warfield won a Grammy Award for *Lincoln Portrait* performed with the Eastman Philharmonia in Rochester.

Warfield always had an interest in teaching. In 1974, he became a professor of music in the School of Music at the University of Illinois at Champaign-Urbana. Subsequently, he became chair of the voice faculty.

Warfield visited relatives in Rochester three or four times a year. He performed in Rochester occasionally, for example, in 1975 concerts with the Rochester Oratorio Society and the Rochester Philharmonic Orchestra and at the Memorial AME Zion Church. He also sang with the Finger Lakes Community Orchestra in 1976 and with the Rochester Pops Orchestra in 1985.

In 1977, the William Warfield Scholarship Fund for talented vocalists was established at the Eastman School of Music. In 1990, Warfield attended a performance in Kilbourn Hall in the Eastman Theatre to benefit the scholarship fund.

Warfield received honorary doctor's degrees from the University of Arkansas, Lafayette College, Boston University, Augustiana College, and James Milliken University. In 1984, he served as president of the National Association of Negro Musicians.

Warfield retired from the University of Illinois in 1990. He continued as a visiting professor at Eastern Illinois University and as an adjunct professor at Northwestern University.

In 2000, Warfield narrated Joseph Schwantner's *New Morning for the World,* based on the words of Martin Luther King, Jr., at the Eastman Theatre. After the performance, which commemorated his eightieth birthday, Warfield received the Alumni Achievement Award from the Eastman School of Music. It named its music education program for Rochester city schools the William Warfield Partnership. Mayor William A. Johnson, Jr., presented Warfield with a plaque proclaiming the week of his birthday William Warfield week.

William Warfield died on August 25, 2002, in Chicago, Illinois, of complications from injuries suffered in a fall.

Powers Block, Corner of Main and State Streets

## *George Ellwanger (1816-1906) / Patrick Barry (1816-1890)*

"Patrick Barry from Ireland and George Ellwanger from Germany became leaders in the forties [1840s] in the development of the ... nursery business. Their discovery of the fact that the vast expanse of Lake Ontario's seldom-frozen waters, a few miles to the north, provided a temperature stabilizer that safeguarded young seedlings from the deep freezes that threatened growers in less-favored localities encouraged them to develop nurseries that soon became the principal suppliers of the demands of western settlers for fruit trees and bulbs.

While Ellwanger journeyed back and forth to Europe and imported fresh plantings, his partner, Barry, became the leader in organizing the Genesee Valley horticultural fair and other agricultural fairs that drew thousands of valley farmers into the City on repeated occasions and promoted development of fruit culture in lakeshore towns east and west of the Genesee. These developments foreshadowed the transformation of Rochester from a milling town to a horticultural center in the years ahead."      Blake McKelvey,
*Rochester on the Genesee: The Growth of a City*

George Ellwanger was born in Würtemberg, Germany, on December 2, 1816. His father was a vineyardist in the beautiful Rems valley. As a young boy, Ellwanger helped his father in the vineyards. It was hard work, but he enjoyed it. He saw that uncertainties in the weather could undo much of their hard work. As he grew older, he realized that the economy of southern Germany at that time was not strong.

Ellwanger decided to immigrate to America, but first he had to learn a marketable trade. He chose the nursery and florist business. In 1830, he paid 100 gulden (forty dollars) to become an apprentice to the foremost horticulturist in Stuttgart. For four years, he worked hard from dawn to dusk without pay to learn his trade.

In early 1835, Ellwanger took passage on a sailing vessel to New York, where he arrived on June 24 after a sixty-two-day voyage. He traveled on the Erie Canal to Buffalo. Along the way, the canalboat made a stop in Rochester to drop off freight. He was impressed with Rochester: its proximity to Lake Ontario, its healthy vegetation, its access to Canada via steamship, and its door to the West—the Erie Canal.

Ellwanger settled in Rochester in September 1836 and went to work for Reynolds and Bateham's, the only horticultural firm in western New York. By the following spring, he was the manager. Two years later, when the owners dissolved their partnership, he took over the firm. In 1839, he purchased eight acres to start Mt. Hope Nurseries and planted an extensive test orchard of fruit trees. He learned from these specimens and used them to propagate selected varieties that thrived in the northern climate.

In October 1840, Ellwanger became a citizen of the United States. In December that year, Ellwanger and other German immigrants erected the first Christmas tree in Rochester in front of the German Lutheran Church on Grove Street. Hundreds of Rochesterians watched as candles on the tree were lit. This ceremony became an annual social event at Christmastime.

Ellwanger's partner, Patrick Barry, was born on a farm outside of Belfast, Ireland, on May 24, 1816. He taught school for two years before immigrating to America. In May 1836, he arrived in New York and obtained a position with the Linnaean Nursery of William Prince & Son in Flushing. He worked for four years at the oldest and most comprehensive nursery in the United States.

Barry moved to Rochester in the summer of 1840 and in October that year formed, in partnership with Ellwanger, Mt. Hope Garden and Nurseries. They moved equipment from Ellwanger's old nursery off Sophia Street and made extensive plantings around the almost completed greenhouses on the new site.

Ellwanger and Barry added greenhouse plants to their business, added eight more acres in 1843, and doubled their acreage the following year. In 1845, Ellwanger traveled to Germany and France to collect stock for the nursery, leaving Barry to run the business. Upon Ellwanger's return, they introduced dwarf and low-branched fruit trees to America. Expansion of the West provided a large market for the nursery; they provided fruit trees to the original orchards in California. Their Rochester location gave them not only the temperature moderation provided by Lake Ontario but also an eight-day advantage in shipments to the West.

Mt. Hope Garden and Nurseries's attention to the identity of each variety in its shipments and its ability to pack and ship product well made its reputation. Prior to the construction of the Panama Canal, the nursery was the first to pack fruit trees to withstand the long sea voyage and the journey across the Isthmus of Panama to California. After Admiral Perry opened the markets of Japan to the West, that country sent large orders to Ellwanger and Barry for fruit trees, ornamental trees, flowers, and seeds.

An early Barry article was "Horticulture in Western New York" in 1842. Two years later he became editor of the Horticultural Department of the *Genesee Farmer,* a position that he held until 1852. In 1848, Barry visited all of the leading nurserymen in Europe, paying particular attention to pruning methods. Upon his return, he began his book, *The Fruit Garden,* which he published in 1851.

Also in 1848, Ellwanger and Barry were among the organizers of the American Congress of Fruit Growers in New York City and the North American Pomological Convention in Buffalo. They were instrumental in later combining the organizations. Barry was the president of the Western New York Horticultural Society for over thirty years. He was also served as a member of the board of control of the New York Agricultural Experiment Station and president of the New York Agricultural Society.

In 1853 and 1854, Barry served as editor of *The Horticulturist.* Perhaps his most important written work was his "Catalogue of the American Pomological Society," the principal reference for American fruitgrowers and a guide used worldwide.

By 1851, Mt. Hope Garden and Nurseries had grown to 100 acres; one section had over 200,000 dwarf fruit trees. Over the next ten years, their acreage quadrupled. The February 19, 1876, issue of *American Rural Home* reported:

> We think that we are speaking within grounds when we say that the Mt. Hope Nurseries in this city, founded and perfected by Messrs. Ellwanger and Barry, are the most complete nurseries on the American continent....

> They then had 650 acres in nursery, divided as follows: Fruit trees, 450 acres; ornamental trees,

shrubs, plants, etc., 120 acres; vineyard for testing grapes, and bearing small fruit plantation, thirty acres; specimen trees, fruit and ornamental, twenty-five acres; lawn and grounds around office, and [sixteen] plant-houses, twenty-five acres.

The specimen fruit tree ground contains nearly 2,000 varieties, exclusive of grapes and small fruits. The specimen ornamental ground is proportionately extensive, and contains the most complete collection in this country. Every new tree or plant that promises to be of value for this country is promptly added.

Many other nurseries thrived at this time in Rochester, including those of James Vick, Hiram Sibley, and Joseph Harris, all of whom subsequently specialized in the seed mail-order business. They produced comprehensive sales brochures and, in effect, eliminated the middleman—the retail store. James Vick was particularly active. When he outgrew his thirty-five acres on East Avenue, he purchased sixty-five acres north of the city overlooking Lake Ontario. Vick's East Avenue seed garden was subsequently divided into the residential area of Vick Park A and Vick Park B.

Ellwanger and Barry were active in the community. Ellwanger served as a board member of several banks and business enterprises, including the Eastman Kodak Company. Barry served as president of the Flour City National Bank and the Mechanics Savings Bank as well as the Rochester Gas Company and the Flour City [Powers] Hotel Company.

In the 1870s, Ellwanger and Barry became active in real estate. They participated in the construction of 118 houses between South and Mt. Hope Avenues, including Cypress and Linden Streets. In 1890, Ellwanger and Barry donated a pavilion and twenty acres of land to the City for Highland Park and dedicated it to the children of Rochester.

After the death of Patrick Barry in 1890, William Barry carried on his father's interests and, like his father, was president of the Western New York Horticultural Society for many years. George Ellwanger, who had become a patriarch of Rochester, died in

November 1906. His son, Henry Ellwanger, who of his three sons had been the most involved with floriculture and horticulture, predeceased him in 1896.

Mt. Hope Garden and Nurseries closed in July 1918, two years after the death of William Barry. The dominance of Rochester nurseries lasted until late in the second decade of the twentieth century and then passed to other regions of the country, particularly the Northwest.

## *Maj. Gen. Elwell Otis (1838-1909)*

"No other Monroe County individual ever has been so feted as was Elwell S. Otis on June 15, 1900 [on his return from the Philippine Islands]. A triumphal arch, a miniature Arc de Triomphe, was erected at East Avenue and Main Street East, and an estimated 150,000 persons jammed the route of a testimonial parade. President McKinley ordered what was called the "cream" of the U.S. Army in the eastern United States to take part in the parade. Nothing like all this had been seen in Rochester before or since." Andrew Wolfe,
"Soldier Hero, Old Style," *Saints, Sinners, and Salesmen*

Elwell Stephen Otis was born to William and Mary Ann Late Otis in Frederick, Maryland, on March 25, 1838. In 1841 at the age of three, he moved with his family to a 1,000-acre farm that extended between Emerson Street and Lyell Avenue and from Myrtle Street to Mt. Read Blvd. The farm was mainly in the Town of Gates; the homestead was on Lyell Avenue.

Otis graduated Phi Beta Kappa from the University of Rochester in 1858 and earned a law degree from Harvard Law School three years later. He practiced law in New York until September 1862, when he entered the Union Army as captain of company D, 140th New York Infantry, in the regiment of Rochesterian Colonel Patrick O'Rorke.

Otis served in General Warren's V Corps during the Civil War and was promoted to lieutenant colonel in December 1863. He commanded his regiment after his colonel was killed during the Battle of Spotsylvania. In October 1864, during the Battle of Petersburg, Otis suffered a head wound, and he was given a medical discharge from the army in January 1865. For bravery in action, he was promoted to brevet colonel and brevet brigadier general of volunteers.

When the regular army was reorganized after the war, Otis was appointed lieutenant colonel in the 22nd Infantry and joined his regiment in Dakota Territory. In further recognition for his bravery during the Battle of Spotsylvania, he was promoted to brevet colonel in the regular army. In 1874 and 1875, he was assigned as Assistant Inspector General of the Department of Dakota. He served in many Indian campaigns, including the campaign of Little Big Horn in 1876 and 1877. In 1878, his book, *The Indian Question,* published in New York, related his thoughts on Indian service.

In February 1880, Otis was promoted to colonel of the 21st Infantry and later that year moved with the headquarters and two companies of his regiment to Ft. Leavenworth, Kansas. General William Sherman, Commanding General of the U.S. Army, selected Otis to establish a training school for young officers. Three infantry regiment companies, four cavalry troops, and a light battery of artillery were placed under his command.

Otis established the School of Infantry and Cavalry, which evolved into the Army Staff and Command School and has been in continuous existence since its founding. He remained its commandant until June 1885. In the fall of 1893, he was appointed chief of the recruiting service, and he was promoted to brigadier general in November 1893. He commanded the Department of Colombia until the spring of 1897, when he was reassigned to the Department of Colorado.

In May 1898, Otis was promoted to major general of volunteers and ordered to report to San Francisco with the expedition fitting out for duty in the Philippine Islands. Upon his arrival in the Philippines in August, he was given command of the VIII Army Corps and relieved General Wesley Merritt as commander of the Department of the Pacific and as military governor of the Philippines. Otis served on the first Philippine Commission that was presided over by Jacob Schurman, president of Cornell University. Schurman's secretary was Frank Gannett, founder of Gannett Newspapers.

Otis faced a complex and tense situation in relieving Spanish civil and military officials in all of the Islands and in establishing an American government. Aguinaldo, leader of the insurgents, maneuvered for position in the outskirts of Manila. The new government was established and peace with the insurgents was maintained until early February 1899 when a U.S. Army sentry shot a Filipino soldier who ignored challenges to be recognized. The situation in Manila was tense for several days until the insurgents were beaten off and scattered.

Otis cleared the Philippines of brigands, strengthened the

American government, and enforced civil law. He was a forceful man who did not shrink from responsibility. He made many decisions with little direction from Washington. His adaptation of Spanish law to the requirements of the new government formed the basis of civil government in the Philippines that exists to this day.

Otis served in the Philippines until May 1900, when he was relieved by General Arthur MacArthur, father of Douglas MacArthur. Otis was promoted to brevet major general for his service in the Philippines and to major general in the regular army in June 1900.

Upon return to the United States, Otis was feted with the largest parade in Rochester until that time. He arrived in Rochester in the private coach of the president of the Buffalo, Rochester & Pittsburgh Railway the evening before the testimonial parade. A crowd cheered his arrival at the New York Central railroad station as the 54th Regimental Band played "America." After a 13-gun salute, he was welcomed by James Cutler, chairman of the reception committee, and Henry Hathaway, president of the Chamber of Commerce. His staff went to the Genesee Valley Club for a "smoker."

Regular Army units from all over the eastern U.S. arrived in Rochester and set up encampments in Maplewood Park and along the banks of the Genesee River. Over 12,000 federal troops, several National Guard companies, veterans of the Civil War and the Spanish-American War, the Rochester Fire Department, members of various societies, and school children marched in the parade on June 15, 1900.

Main Street and East Avenue were decorated for Otis Day, and bunting and flags were displayed on all public buildings and stores. It reminded the crowd of 150,000 along the parade route of a Fourth of July celebration, but on a larger scale. A smaller version of the Arc de Triomphe designed by architect Claude Bragdon had been erected at East Main Street and East Avenue. The legend on the white arch proclaimed: "Welcome to Maj. Gen. Elwell S. Otis, Greeting and Honor."

Band concerts kicked off the festivities. The sixty-nine-member U.S. Marine Band played many pieces, including "The Admiral Dewey March," "The Man Behind the Gun," and "Stars and Stripes Forever." A baseball double-header was played between Montreal and Rochester at Culver Field. That evening, speeches were made by the guest of honor and many others, including General Joseph Wheeler; Dr. David Jayne Hill, Assistant Secretary of State and former president of the University of Rochester; and James Sherman of Utica, who subsequently became Vice President of the United States.

Evening concerts were provided at two locations: The 54th Regimental Band played many pieces, including "Good Bye, Dolly Gray" and "There'll Be a Hot Time in the Old Town Tonight" at Clarissa Street, and the Marine Band entertained at the Court Street bridge. Events of Otis Day were concluded with an impressive display of fireworks over the Court Street bridge.

Otis commanded the Department of the Lakes in Chicago until March 1902 when he retired and returned to Rochester to live at the family homestead. He died on October 21, 1909, and was buried in Mt. Hope Cemetery. In 1929, his body was reinterred to Arlington National Cemetery. Elwell S. Otis School on Otis Street was named for one of Rochester's heroes.

# CHAPTER 7

# THINKERS / POLITICIANS

### Marion Folsom (1893-1976)

"He [Marion Folsom] has done all sorts of important and difficult things, such as quietly piloting through Congress the first complete revision of the tax laws since 1876. He has been a pioneer in working out the terms of the new brand of American conservatism that has come to power in the Eisenhower administration. And, above all, he has been a leading contributor to a gigantic change in the basic shape of our society."                    Newspaper journalist Joseph Alsop

While an officer of the Eastman Kodak Company, Marion Folsom became an early promoter of unemployment insurance and was a principal author of the Social Security Act of 1935. He served the administrations of Presidents Roosevelt, Truman, and Eisenhower in various capacities and helped to shape the organization and role of the U.S. Government in social services.

Marion Bayard Folsom was born to William and Margaret Folsom on November 23, 1893, in McRae, Georgia. He began working in the family general store at the age of twelve and soon recommended changes, including improvements to his father's bookkeeping system. He enrolled at the University of Georgia and graduated in 1912 at the age of eighteen. Two years later he earned a Master of Business Administration degree with highest honors from Harvard University.

George Eastman personally interviewed Folsom for a position with the Eastman Kodak Company. After accepting the job offer, Folsom spent the summer touring Europe while visiting managers of the branches of Eastman Kodak abroad. He began his career with the Company on October 1914 in Rochester. For the first three years, he reported to Frank J. Lovejoy, general manager of the Company.

When the U.S. entered World War in 1917, Folsom volunteered for service in the U.S. Army and was assigned to Officers Training Camp. He was commissioned second lieutenant and received orders to France. The ship transporting him across the English Channel was torpedoed by a German submarine. He survived to see action in France with the Twenty-sixth Division and was promoted to captain.

When Folsom rejoined Eastman Kodak after the war, he organized the company's first comprehensive statistical department. In 1920, as statistical secretary to the president, he was responsible for cost-benefit studies. The following year, he became assistant to president Eastman and performed a wide variety of high-level tasks. In 1930, he was promoted to assistant treasurer and joined the ranks of upper management of the Company. He was civic-minded and became active in the Chamber of Commerce, the Rochester Council for Social Agencies, and the Y. M. C. A., as well as in Rochester's hospital planning.

Folsom developed humanitarian views and realized that the obligations of a corporation were not just production, sales, and profits. Spurred by Folsom, Eastman Kodak began to broaden its outlook on labor management relations, particularly by sponsoring employee bonuses, paid vacations, and wage dividends. In 1921, Folsom proposed that Eastman Kodak establish company unemployment insurance to aid employees who had been laid off. His suggestions would not be taken seriously for another ten years.

Eastman's early thoughts on company retirement plans were negative. Nevertheless, he asked Folsom to check on what other companies were doing about employee benefits. Folsom prepared a plan for employee life insurance, retirement annuities, and total disability benefits that was implemented on January 1, 1929.

The Great Depression hit Rochester hard but not as hard as many other U.S. cities. By 1933, twenty-five percent of American workers were unemployed. Half of Rochester's thirty-nine clothing companies closed permanently. The shoe industry also suffered substantially. City work-relief projects, the Rochester Unemployed Co-operative League labor exchange, and the Bureau for Homeless Men helped but provided little relief to the unemployment problem.

Folsom was the main architect of the Rochester Plan, an unemployment insurance plan sponsored by eight large and six small Rochester companies that covered 26,000 workers or one-third of the City's work force. No money was deducted from employees' paychecks; the companies paid for the plan. Each company was responsible for its own employees' program. The Rochester Plan was announced on February 18, 1931, by James Gleason, president of Gleason Works and chairman of the Industrial Management Council of the Rochester Chamber of Commerce.

Folsom served on the Rochester Unemployment Committee and was a founder of the Rochester Public Employment Center (RPEC). Frances Perkins, New York State Industrial Commissioner in the administration of Governor Franklin D. Roosevelt, sponsored a bill permitting the State to accept private funds to support unemployment exchanges such as the RPEC.

Folsom viewed unemployment insurance as an element of employment stabilization that motivated companies to retain employees. When employees were laid off, companies had to make unemployment insurance payments. Furthermore, when the economy improved, companies had to hire and train new employees that were not as productive as the ones that they had laid off. Thus unemployment insurance helped to lower labor costs, stabilize the workforce, and to some extent minimize swings in the business cycle.

The Rochester Plan was successful, but its application was too narrow; it did not cover enough of Rochester's workers. Until 1934, Folsom had endorsed private plans such as the Rochester Plan. However, he realized that public participation was required if a sufficient number of workers were to be covered. In other words, a partnership with government was needed. He realized that the future was with federal-state unemployment insurance.

During 1934-35, Folsom served on Secretary of Labor Frances Perkins's Advisory Council on Economic Security, which contributed heavily to the creation of the Social Security Act of 1935. The Act authorized every state to formulate its own unemployment insurance law. Folsom also served on Congressional commissions responsible for revising the Social Security Act in 1937-38 and 1948.

In 1935, Folsom was elected treasurer of the Eastman Kodak Company. From 1947 until he retired in 1969, he served on the board of directors of the corporation.

After serving on the Council on Economic Security, Folsom served as a founder of the Committee for Economic Development in 1942, as a member of the Federal Advisory Council on Social Security, and as a division executive of the National Defense Advisory Commission. From 1944 to 1946, he was staff director for the House Committee on Postwar Economic Policy and Planning and served as vice chairman of the Advisory Committee on the Merchant Marine in President Truman's administration.

In 1953, Folsom resigned from Eastman Kodak to become Under Secretary of Treasury in President Eisenhower's administration. In carrying out the responsibilities of this position, Folsom oversaw the first complete revision and codification of the U.S. tax laws since 1876. He also directed a study of old-age and survivors insurance that resulted in an amendment to the Social Security Act in 1954.

In 1955, Folsom replaced Oveta Culp Hobby as the Secretary of Health, Education, and Welfare and became responsible for overseeing the social security environment that he had helped to establish. Columnist Joseph Alsop commented on Folsom's work on the first national old-age insurance bill in 1934: "This bill became the foundation stone of the vast structures of social security and welfare over which Folsom now presides. He can claim to be the only man who has contributed to every phase of the Social Security system's growth."

Folsom returned to Eastman Kodak in 1958 until his retirement in 1969. In 1969-70, he served on the Federal Advisory Council on Employment Security and on the National Health Advisory Council from 1970 onward. He was awarded the Albert Einstein medal for citizenship and the Bronfman prize for public health achievement. Brown University, University of Rochester, Swarthmore College, Syracuse University, and Tufts University conferred honorary degrees on him.

On September 28, 1976, Folsom died following a stroke. He was buried in Arlington National Cemetery. His accomplishments included changing business attitudes from the limited view that a salary was all a company owed an employee toward the realization that corporate goals encompass more than productivity and growth. He believed in using the power of government to achieve social progress.

## George Aldridge (1856-1922)

"This is the story of a man who virtually ruled the City of Rochester for two score years.... His friends gave him nothing but words of praise. His enemies—and there were not many—admitted his exceptional ability to lead a political party.... That the man had the kind of personality that endears one to the hearts of many, is obvious. He loved the role of leader. He ruled wisely and well and when he made mistakes, he recognized them and made amends."     Clement Lanni, *George W. Aldridge, Big Boss, Small City*

Aldridge's father, George Aldridge, Sr., served as alderman of the first ward beginning in 1872 and was president of the Common Council. In 1873, he was acting mayor after Mayor Carter Wilder resigned. While growing up, young Aldridge had a role model to emulate. In 1880, he ran for public office for the first time as a member of the Executive Board that controlled the fire, police, and public works departments. He accepted the Republican nomination reluctantly and did not campaign. He lost and was chided by his friends for three years. In 1883, Aldridge ran again for the Executive Board. This time he worked hard to get votes, and he won.

Aldridge was a big, forceful man who understood human nature. He knew how to horsetrade, and he knew how to use patronage. He was the dominant member on the three-member Executive Board, which included a lifelong Aldridge follower and a Democrat. He considered where his patronage would do the most good. He knew how to evaluate the weaknesses of others. Aldridge became known as a man who kept his word and as a charitable man. He visited the sick, and he helped the unfortunate.

Aldridge always dressed well. He paid attention to his personal appearance and was respected by his associates. He spoke openly with his close political and social friends. He had an excellent working relationship with Rochester's newspapers. He gave reporters, all of whom respected him, good material for their columns. However, they protected their source. He rarely gave formal statements to the press, and it was uncommon for him to be quoted in the newspapers. He believed: "Never write when you can say it; never say it when you can nod your head." One of his mottoes was (within reason) "Deny nothing, claim everything."

Aldridge surrounded himself with members of both parties. If people were loyal to him, it did not matter to him whether they were Republicans or Democrats. He placed Democrats as well as Republicans in the fire and police departments, regardless of whether they were Catholics, Protestants, Masons, non-Masons, of Irish descent, of German descent, or Native Americans. To him, they were all votes.

At that time, comprehensive election laws did not exist. It was not necessary to register to vote or to enroll in a party caucus. Republican and Democratic caucuses were held on different days. A person could change parties from one election to the next. In fact, if he were bold enough, he could vote in both party caucuses. However, his neighbors knew to which party he belonged.

In a sense, Aldridge was a combination of leader and boss. Theodore Roosevelt explained the difference between the two: "The leader leads, and the boss drives." Aldridge led the party well and adapted to changing conditions. He selected capable men for public office, men with sizable followings in their wards who could strengthen the boss's position.

The only Democratic mayors during Aldridge's control of the Republican party were mayors William Carroll in 1890-1892 and George Warner in 1896-1900. Aldridge lost some of his city patronage during those years, but he managed to keep many of his followers in office. Also, he was able to maintain control of county, state, and federal patronage.

When Aldridge granted a favor; he expected a favor in return and kept track of preferments granted. He was sometimes criticized by members of his own party for bestowing favors on Democrats. He responded, "Well, he has done some things for me you know, and we must not forget our friends." Miller Kelly was the Democratic leader of the fifteenth ward. He was ward alderman from 1880 to 1905, and no more loyal Aldridge Democrat existed in Monroe County. Everyone knew it, and Kelly never denied it.

In 1894, Aldridge ran successfully for mayor. Thirty-eight-year-old Aldridge won the election by a plurality of 2,752 votes, and his followers celebrated at the Powers Grill. In Aldridge's inaugural address, he called for greater efficiency in the fire and police departments, as well as in the public works and waterworks departments.

James Cutler, leader of the twelfth ward and later two-term Rochester mayor, said of Aldridge: "As a leader he is bold and steadfast for the right. His integrity in official and private life is unquestioned. An army of stalwart friends, not restrained by party lines, will make this victory sweeping and complete."

In the election, Aldridge had done everything that he could to give a plurality in Monroe County to Levi Morton, the Republican candidate for governor. Democrats claimed that Aldridge was seeking appointment as State Superintendent of Public Works. On January 1, 1895, the State Legislature convened, and Aldridge was confirmed by the State Senate for that position. Aldridge was widely known in the State. Republican party boss Thomas Platt had invited Aldridge to planning meetings at the Fifth Avenue Hotel in New York City, headquarters of the Republican State Committee.

While serving as State Superintendent of Public Works, Aldridge did not give up his hold on Monroe County politics. In his new position, he attempted to ignore Governor Morton's guidelines and was prevented from doing so. Aldridge placed many of his cronies in positions along the Erie Canal. He was accused of spending too much money on work on the Canal.

In particular, Aldridge was blamed for improper classification of material excavated. For example, excavated rock was paid for at the rate of $1.25 per cubic yard, and earth was paid for at $.24 per yard. Some of the Superintendent's men were being paid $1.25 per yard for earth, claiming that it was rock. Although no evidence was found that required prosecution, Aldridge's reputation was tarnished.

Back in Rochester, Merton Lewis had been appointed to fill the unexpired term of Mayor Aldridge. Lewis was opposed by Joseph Alling, an educated man of considerable wealth and high principles, who wanted to loosen the City's control over the Rochester school district. Idealist Alling promoted improvements to the school system and reorganization of the school district.

The dynamic Alling backed Democrat George Warner for mayor in the next two elections. Warner won, and Aldridge had to capitulate to Alling in keeping the mayor's office out of education and in providing a new charter, called the "White Charter," which allowed the mayor to make appointments that previously had been made by the Executive Board controlled by Aldridge.

Although he had beaten Aldridge on these issues, Alling held him

187

in high regard. According to biographer Lanni, he told Aldridge: "If I were able to give you $50,000 (big money in those days) to run the politics of this city, I would do it. You are worth it." Alling also observed: "The surprising thing about Aldridge was his ability to pick men. While I would be pondering over a name, Aldridge would suggest one who would fit admirably." Alling added: "Organizations are always tempted to give people as poor a government as they will put up with, but Aldridge gave as good a government as the exigencies of his political organization provided."

From 1902 to 1906, James Cutler served two terms as mayor. Aldridge found him to be a man who thought for himself; Cutler did not consider himself controlled by Aldridge. When Hiram Edgerton succeeded Cutler in the mayor's office, he and Aldridge formed a compatible working relationship. The Rochester *Herald* referred to them as "I and Hi."

Aldridge submitted his name for lieutenant governor to test the waters. He was not nominated, but his name gained state-wide recognition. In 1896, Aldridge ran for governor. Initially, Republican boss Platt supported him. When Platt saw Aldridge's candidacy gain momentum, he became concerned about losing his State party boss role to Aldridge if he became governor. Then, Platt backed Frank Black of Rensselaer County, who was elected. Aldridge continued to support Platt, and a few months later the State party boss became U.S. Senator Platt.

On March 9, 1910, Thomas Platt died, and, one day later, Congressman James Perkins died. Aldridge was confronted with the alternative of being State party boss or running for Congress. He had always wanted to hold elective office; however, as soon as he decided to run for Congress, opposition became vocal. The State Superintendent of Insurance discovered questionable payments made to State officials by fire insurance companies. In 1901, $5,000 had been paid to the Republican State Committee and a check for $1,000 had been given to Aldridge, which he said was a legitimate gift to the Monroe County Republican Party.

Aldridge lost the election, and the Rochester *Herald* predicted the end of party machine domination in Rochester. Aldridge continued as State committeeman and ruled the party locally until he died, twelve years later.

In 1920, George Eastman proposed the city manager form of

government for Rochester. Two anecdotes have been told about Eastman and Aldridge, who became friends after Aldridge helped the Eastman Kodak Company obtain an easement across several of his friends' properties for a water line between Lake Ontario and Kodak Park. One story is that Aldridge once asked Eastman to be mayor, and later agreed to a city manager form of government if Eastman would be the first city manager. In the other story, Aldridge turned down one of Eastman's requests with the comment: "George, you run Eastman Kodak Company, and I'll run the city."

Aldridge became ill in December 1920 while attending the Republican National Convention in Chicago. He instructed his partner-delegate to vote for Warren Harding from the first to the last ballot. To reward Aldridge, President Harding offered Aldridge the position of Commissioner of Internal Revenue, Treasurer of the United States, or Collector of the Port of New York. He accepted the collectorship. In that position, when he was offered bribes, he replied, "I can use the money but I never got any that way, and I never will."

George Aldridge was serving in the Collector's office when he died on June 13, 1922, while playing golf at the Westchester Biltmore Country Club. Hundreds gathered at the New York Central railroad station when his body was returned to Rochester. His body lay in state in the rotunda of the Monroe County Courthouse. Hiram Edgerton got up from his deathbed and was carried to pay his last respects to his old political friend. Edgerton died two days later.

President Harding sent a letter of condolence. Governor Nathan Miller and former Governor Charles Whitman led the funeral procession, followed by U.S. Senators James Wadsworth, Jr., and William Calder. Thousands paid their respects. Editor Louis Antisdale of the Rochester *Herald* wrote:

> When one considers the combination of lovable attributes that were assembled in this rare personality, it is easier to understand how this man became the actual, the admitted though unofficial ruler of a great city for a stretch of time longer than the reigns of most European monarchs of our day. The elements of manliness, of generous sympathy with the unfortunate, of loyalty to friends ... have an intensely human appeal.

Besides the talents and instincts of the political managers and directors, there were deep-planted in the nature of George Aldridge's love of Rochester, pride in its greatness and growth, joy in its manifestations of comfort, of happiness, of prosperity.... There is still no denying that this master of Rochester for more than a generation planned and schemed to the end that Rochester might be great and renowned and envied among the cities of America.

## *James Cutler (1848-1927)*

"Educated as an architect, Mr. Cutler combined ... the qualities of both artist and engineer. These qualities were developed and disciplined for him by years of successful practice of his profession. When his inventive mind turned him into the channels of manufacture and business activities, his interests and experience widened to include industrial relations and finance. All of these qualities he early devoted to a careful and intelligent study of civic problems and public affairs, long before he was called to any public office.... His study of civic problems of his home city led him to be one of the advocates of a more adequate charter for the city ... which, on January 1, 1908, placed Rochester among the first-class cities of the State with its own fundamental civil law."                                    Rush Rhees,
"The Gift and the Donor," *The Rochester Historical Society*

James Cutler was the architect for the Kimball Tobacco Company factory and the seven-story Elwood Building at the corner of State and Main Streets. As plans for the building were being made, Frank W. Elwood asked Cutler to devise an efficient means of sending mail from the upper floors of the building down to the first floor for collection by the Post Office. Cutler had to consider many design criteria, including controlling the speed of mail traveling down the chute to minimize breakage and temperature differences between upper and lower floors that might cause condensation, dampening packages being mailed.

Because many high-rise buildings were being constructed at the time, demand for mail chutes was heavy. Cutler patented his design and founded the Cutler Manufacturing Company in 1884 to meet the demand for his product. At the time, mail chutes were being manufactured from many other designs that were inferior to Cutler's. In a town in Indiana, a local contractor installed a mail chute made to his own design. When mail sent from the building seemed to be disappearing, the mail carrier responsible for picking up mail from the building was accused of interfering with the U.S. Mail and sent to prison.

A year later, the mail chute was repaired and the lost mail was found in a space in the wall between floors. A soldered seam had opened up, diverting the mail. The innocent mail carrier was released from prison. Cutler gained business from this incident. From then on, the U.S. Post Office would not permit mail carriers to collect mail from mail chutes other than those manufactured by Cutler.

Cutler was an early advocate of a safe municipal water supply for Rochester that met the demands of a growing city. He made engineering studies and compared Rochester's needs with that of other municipalities, learning from their experiences. Later, as mayor, he authorized construction of and oversaw early work on Cobb's Hill reservoir and the second water conduit from Hemlock Lake to Rochester's south side.

As a student of civic problems, Cutler was also an advocate of improving the City's charter. He was a sponsor of the White Charter, which when implemented on January 1, 1908, placed Rochester in the forefront of cities in New York State in civil law. He also was a significant contributor to many amendments to that charter. Cutler's first assignment in City government under the White Charter was Commissioner of Public Safety.

In November 1902, Cutler was elected mayor of Rochester and assumed that office on January 1, 1903. He was an active mayor who introduced new accounting procedures and increased the authority of the city purchasing agent. Also, he pressured the Erie Railroad to elevate its track south of the Court Street dam to eliminate a flood hazard.

Mayor Cutler improved Rochester schools by expanding East High School and by approving the construction of West High School in 1905. He pushed for building two new grade schools and the expansion of several others. He approved salary increases for teachers and implemented an enriched program of courses. He advocated changes that elevated Rochester schools to a much higher level.

As mayor, Cutler avoided political infighting, and he usually had the support of the City Council. He pushed for increased recreational use of parks. He was in office when George Eastman and Dr. H. S. Durand provided their gift to the City for Durand-Eastman Park, a boost toward the establishment of a notable park system.

Cutler served two terms as mayor of Rochester and continued to be active in the affairs of the City even after stepping down as mayor. He was a leader in the preparation of a city plan for Rochester's civic development. City planners studied local problems, recommended solutions, and guided construction of Rochester's streets and public buildings.

Cutler was active in the Municipal Art Commission that grew out of the City Planning Board's preparation of the city plan. He gave considerable time and effort to the City Planning Board and the Municipal Art Commission until several years before his death in 1927. According to historian Blake McKelvey, James Cutler was often described as "the best mayor Rochester ever had."

Rochester Free Academy, Fitzhugh Street

## Hiram Edgerton (1847-1922)

"He had a vision of the City Beautiful, a city of parks and play-grounds, a city of happy homes and enduring, uplifting institutions ... a city where men, women and little children would have room to grow in the vitality of physical health and the graces of mental and spiritual enlargement.... This dream of the City Beautiful came to Hiram H. Edgerton, and he gave his life to making the dream come true. He forgot the interests and ambitions which other men seek; he gave himself to Rochester so that today there is scarcely one of the great and beautiful things which we possess in this city of schools and buildings and parks and other institutions of public welfare which does not somewhere have his personality stamped upon it."

Rev. C. Waldo Cherry, D.D, "Eulogy," 1922

Hiram Edgerton participated in the public affairs of Rochester for over fifty years. He was a building contractor who constructed many of the city's buildings, and he was mayor of Rochester for fourteen years.

Hiram Haskell Edgerton was born on April 19, 1847, in Belfast, New York, to Ralph and Octavia Penhollow Edgerton. Edgerton attended the Genesee Seminary in Belfast prior to moving with his family to Rochester in 1858, where he attended the Rochester Free Academy and the Rochester Business Institute. He began working at his father's lumber yard at the age of sixteen and took over the business and a retail coal yard upon his father's death in 1868.

In 1881, Edgerton became a building contractor and evolved as a leader in that field. He built the Wilder Building, the downtown Rochester Post Office, forty churches, and many manufacturing plants. He rebuilt the Sibley, Lindsay, and Curr building after a dis-astrous fire and built the Granite building. He was the prime contrac-tor for the Buffalo, Rochester & Pittsburgh Railway Company. His reputation for quality and reliability earned him contracts in other cities in New York State and surrounding states.

Edgerton was a member of the Rochester Board of Education from 1872 to 1876 and president of the board for two terms. He served as president of Rochester's Common Council from 1900 until 1908. In 1903, he served briefly as interim mayor of Rochester prior to being elected to that office for seven consecutive terms from 1908 until 1922. After serving as mayor, he was appointed superintendent of municipal construction, permitting him to complete the projects that he had approved as mayor.

One of Edgerton's accomplishments was the creation of Exposition Park on the site of the old Industrial School. In its initial configuration, Exposition Park housed the public library, the municipal museum, the Rochester Historical Society, Jefferson Junior High School, an extensive playground, and a bathhouse. Exposition Park had facilities for athletic events and other buildings that were used by the Rochester Exposition Association for conventions, exhibits, and shows, e.g. large national horse shows. After Edgerton's death, Exposition Park was renamed Edgerton Park.

Accomplishments of Edgerton's tenure as mayor included the completion of Cobb's Hill reservoir, construction of a third water conduit from Hemlock Lake, erection of flood control walls along the Genesee River, deepening of the River, and completion of plans for a new bridge across the Genesee.

During Edgerton's administration, over eighty acres were added to what is now the Monroe County Park System. Ontario Beach Park was obtained for the City in 1920, and construction was begun for a new street and railroad in the bed of the old Erie Canal, which had been rerouted south of the City. Rochester's aviation field was established during Edgerton's tenure as mayor, and the Village of Charlotte and sections of Brighton and Lincoln Park became part of the City of Rochester.

Twenty-five new school buildings were built during Edgerton's terms as mayor and seventeen schools were remodeled. Seventeen new firehouses were built, and the fire department was expanded from 200 to 500 firemen. He created the Bureau of Playgrounds and Recreation, which served a model for other cities. By 1921, twenty-five playgrounds were in operation. He was instrumental in founding the Rochester Public Library and in establishing library branches throughout the city.

Edgerton was Rochester's mayor during World War I. He supported the loan campaigns and the food and fuel administration and was instrumental in establishing the Home Defense League that served as an auxiliary police force. He is remembered for going to the railroad station when men went to war and for greeting them when they returned. He honored them with veterans' banquets and commissioned the printing of a World War Service Record documenting the role of Rochester's servicemen in World War I.

Edgerton was a popular mayor, especially with the working classes. He was not considered a typical politician. He strived continually for the betterment of his city and was very approachable and open to ideas for improving Rochester.

When he stepped down as mayor, he said, "My confidence in the future of Rochester is unbounded, and my faith in the people is limitless. I am sure they will permit no backward steps. I leave office with the consciousness of having tried to do my full duty according to my ability. Let me assure the people of my deep affection for them and of my abiding faith in our city."

Edgerton died on June 18, 1922. His last thoughts were of Rochester, and his last words were: "I want to go to Highland Park tomorrow." Hiram Haskell Edgerton, who served his city well, was buried in Mt. Hope Cemetery.

## *Kenneth Keating (1900-1975)*

"Kenneth Keating certainly stands with the outstanding public servants of our state in this [twentieth] century. He was a warm, delightful person, whose great asset was personal—his rapport with people, and their admiration and confidence in him as a man and as an official whom they liked and in whom they placed their trust."

Governor Hugh Carey

Kenneth Keating was a brilliant Rochester lawyer, a successful town attorney, a U.S. Army colonel in World War II, a highly regarded Congressman for six terms, a ranking U.S. Senator, and a State Court of Appeals Justice. He finished his government career as Ambassador to India and Ambassador to Israel

Kenneth B. Keating was born on May 18, 1900, in Lima, New York, to Louise Barnard Keating and Thomas Keating, proprietor of a general store in the village of Lima. Louise Keating, a graduate of the Genesee Wesleyan Seminary in Lima who had taught in several western New York communities, home-schooled her son until he was seven. She began young Keating's education at the age of three; he could read by the age of four. One year later, he was doing third-grade-level work.

When he was seven, Keating entered the Lima school system in the sixth grade, where he performed at the top of his class. In high school, debating was his strength. He won many speaking competitions in Livingston County and surrounding counties and was known as "the boy orator of Lima." He defeated competitors who were five to ten years older than he was. A classmate asked what the key was to his academic success. He responded, "I spend the summer studying the subjects of the coming year."

Keating entered the Genesee Wesleyan Seminary when he was thirteen and graduated two years later with top honors; he gave the class valedictory address. He won a scholarship to the University of Rochester and began studies there at the age of fifteen. The difference in age with his classmates did not bother him. A strong ability to get along with others and a sense of humor helped him to adjust to his new environment. In his freshman year, he was elected chairman of the class nominating committee and worked on the student newspaper. He also captained the debating team of his class and ran on the track team.

During World War I, Keating was sent to Officer Training Camp of the Student Army Training Corps at the age of eighteen. However, the war as over before he finished training. He returned to the University of Rochester where he graduated with honors and was elected to Phi Beta Kappa. He was class valedictorian and was chosen Ivy Orator.

Keating taught for a year at East High School in Rochester before enrolling at the Harvard Law School in the fall of 1920. In 1923, he graduated in the top ten percent of his class and subsequently joined the Rochester law firm of Harris, Beach, Folger, Remington, and Bacon. Working long hours coupled with possessing a sharp legal mind made him a successful young attorney.

At thirty, Keating was elected to the board of directors of one of Rochester's largest banks and became attorney for the Town of Brighton. By the late 1930s, he was considered one of the City's top attorneys. In 1940, he attended the Republican National Convention. His law practice was prospering, and he had a loving wife and daughter; at the age of forty-one, it was not likely that he would be drafted. However, motivated by a life-long interest in public service, he volunteered for the U.S. Army. In the spring of 1942, he received a commission as major and was assigned to lend-lease activities.

In mid-1943, Keating was promoted to lieutenant colonel and assigned as chief lend-lease negotiator at the headquarters of Lord Louis Mountbatten, Supreme Allied Commander of the China-Burma-India Theater and cousin of the King of England. Keating's people skills served him well in a difficult environment. Inevitably, strain existed between Westerners and Easterners, as well as between British and Americans on occasion. The negotiating task provided opportunities to prevent graft and bribery.

In 1944, Keating was promoted to colonel in the General Staff Corps. The following year, he was awarded the Legion of Merit with a citation for outstanding service. Lt. Gen. Raymond Wheeler, the U.S. Army commander, commended him highly for his service in the China-Burma-India Theater and for his contribution to the success of the Allies in the theater. He returned home in 1946.

Keating ran for Congress in 1946 and won an upset victory over the incumbent. He was part of the "Class of 46" in the House of

Representatives, when many Republicans were swept into office. He served as a Congressman from 1947 until 1959 and established a reputation as a "progressive Republican." He was active in helping persons displaced as a result of World War II, and he became an expert on the countries of Eastern Europe. Keating concentrated on the issues of civil rights, immigration, international affairs, and anti-Communism.

In 1958, Keating was asked to run for the Senate. Many of his colleagues thought that he could not win because it appeared that the Democrats were going to dominate the election. He ran against New York City's popular District Attorney Frank Hogan and won. Although he now served in the upper chamber, he continued to work hard on the details and to help the little man.

Civil rights were one of Keating's major interests. He had been a sponsor of the Civil Rights Act of 1957, and he made major contributions to the Acts of 1960 and 1961. One of his significant contributions was his major role in the enactment of the Civil Rights Act of 1964. In addition to his ongoing interest in immigration, he also was active in the areas of farm policy and social security.

Keating became involved early in the 1962 Cuban Missile Crisis. A visitor to his office told him about Russian missile activity in Cuba. Keating asked the State Department to take action. When they failed to act, he spoke on the Senate floor of the threat ninety miles from our shores. The government assumed that he was acting on political motives until they realized that he was right. U-2 spy-plane flights over Cuba showed that the missiles were not "defensive," as the State Department had been insisting. Keating had stood his ground despite verbal abuse directed at him.

Keating was one of first to recognize the potential of Israel in the Middle East. Also, he sponsored the Twenty-third Amendment to the Constitution, which granted residents of the District of Columbia the right to vote, and legislation in 1964 to establish the first national park in New York State, Fire Island National Seashore.

In the election of 1964, Keating found himself at odds with his own party. He was a personal friend of Barry Goldwater, but he did not agree with the viewpoints of the Republican Presidential candidate. Keating had fundamental differences of opinion; he said that he could not compromise on principle.

In 1964, Keating ran against "carpetbagger" Senate candidate

Robert Kennedy from Massachusetts. He knew that this campaign would be difficult—running against a national figure who was well-financed and who had strong Democratic party support. Keating lost because he had two significant factors against him: Goldwater lost the election dramatically, and the sympathy vote for Robert Kennedy resulting from his brother's assassination was strong. Keating returned to the practice of law at the New York City firm of Royal, Koegel, and Rogers (future Secretary of State William P. Rogers). In 1965, Keating was elected to the New York State Court of Appeals.

In 1969, President Richard Nixon appointed Keating Ambassador to India. He served during the India-Pakistan conflict after which Bangladesh was created. Keating counseled the State Department against favoring Pakistan in the conflict. However, the Nixon-Kissinger policy supported Pakistan. India's victory in the war was swift. Keating was popular in India, but he served as ambassador during a period of anti-American sentiment. He was recalled during the summer of 1972.

Keating campaigned for Nixon in the election that fall and was appointed Ambassador to Israel. He established a good working relationship with the Israeli government and again was popular in the country in which he served. Senator Jacob Javits observed that Keating's service in Israel was "a source of security and reassurance to Israel's people and to millions of Americans who have been so devoted to its mission." Even after he stepped down as ambassador, Keating was invited to Washington, D.C., to participate in policy-making sessions on the Middle East.

Keating died in May 1975, two weeks before his seventy-fifth birthday. President Gerald Ford observed that Keating was known "for his statesmanship, gentle grace, and commitment to peace. Seldom has one man led a more versatile and more useful public life."

Warner's Castle, Mt. Hope Avenue

# CHAPTER 8

# ECCENTRICS / ARCHITECTS

### William Morgan (1774-1826)

"Journalistic rivalries acquired a new intensity with the outbreak of anti-Masonry in 1827. It was perhaps not surprising that the Genesee boomtown became the focal center of this movement, for the building of the aqueduct and other stone structures had attracted a number of working masons to Rochester, and together with other enterprising men drawn to the village, many aspired to membership in the popular Masonic lodges. Some, but not all, were admitted, and William Morgan, who became a member shortly before completing his job assignment in Rochester, but who found himself excluded when he moved to Batavia, determined to cash in on the secrets he had learned by publishing a full account of the mysterious rituals."

Blake McKelvey, *Rochester on the Genesee: Growth of a City*


William Morgan was born in Culpepper County, Virginia, on August 7, 1774. He served in the army in the War of 1812, married Lucinda Pendleton in Richmond, Virginia, in the fall of 1819, and moved to Toronto, Canada, where he worked in a brewery. In 1823, he worked as a mason/bricklayer on Aqueduct bridge that carried the Erie Canal over the Genesee River in downtown Rochester. Later, he worked on other mason/bricklayer jobs in Batavia, Le Roy, and Rochester.

Morgan was admitted to the Wells Lodge of the Masons in Rochester as a visitor and was awarded membership in the Royal Arch Masons in Le Roy. He broke with the Masonic Order when he was not hired to work on the Masonic lodge being built in Le Roy. He moved to Batavia with his wife and two young children in 1826, where he applied for membership in a Royal Arch Masons chapter being formed. Officials there knew Morgan as one who had more than an occasional drink and who was a loose talker. They denied him membership. He was determined to get even with the Masons.

Morgan decided to publish the secrets of the order with the help of David C. Miller, publisher of the Batavia *Republican-Advocate.*

Miller had received the first degree of the Masonic Order; Morgan had received the first three degrees. The Masons became aroused by this threat to reveal the first three degrees of the Order, and they attempted to talk him out of it. They published an item in the Canandaigua *Messenger*: "If a man calling himself William Morgan should introduce himself to the community, they should be on their guard, particularly the Masonic fraternity. Morgan was in the village on May 1, and his conduct here and elsewhere call forth this note.... Morgan is considered a swindler and a dangerous man."

Miller and Morgan were prosecuted for debts, but both raised bail and stayed out of jail. Attempts were made to burn down the building that housed Miller's press. On September 11, 1826, Morgan was served a warrant for the theft of a shirt and a cravat from a Canandaigua tavernkeeper. He was taken to Canandaigua where the charge was dismissed. He was then jailed in Canandaigua for a small debt owed to another Canandaigua innkeeper. Loton Lawson, accompanied by three other Masons, paid the debt and secured Morgan's release.

The men seized Morgan as he left jail and led him to a carriage. Morgan lost his hat in a minor scuffle and was heard crying out, "Murder." The carriage traveled through Victor and Pittsford, and was in Rochester before dawn. A fresh team of horses was acquired at Hanford's Landing on the Genesee River. The carriage traveled westward along Ridge Road. The men stopped briefly at a house along the ridge as they traveled through Clarkson, Gaines, and Ridgeway.

Morgan was taken to Fort Niagara, where he was kept in the powder magazine until arrangements could be made to send him to Canada. His "guard" rowed him across the Niagara River, but the Canadians backed down—they did not want him either. When Morgan did not return to New York, people asked, "Where is William Morgan?" An anti-Masonic movement began to build. Morgan's book was entitled: *Illustrations of Masonry by One of the Fraternity Who Has Devoted Thirty Years to the Subject.* Sales were sluggish; people were more interested in what happened to Morgan than they were in his exposé of passwords and secret grips.

Morgan's body was never found. With no *corpus delecti*, no proof of death, no one could be charged with his murder. However, Thurlow Weed, a Rochester editor, pried information out of John

Whitney, one of Morgan's abductors. Whitney told Weed that Morgan had been promised a farm in Canada, so he willingly went out again in a rowboat on the Niagara River. When they were out on the River, his captors tied a rope around him with a weight on the other end. Morgan struggled and bit off the thumb of one of his captors, but they maneuvered him into the water. Whitney never signed a confession regarding the incident; nothing could be proved in court.

However, Loton Lawson, along with Nicholas Chesebro, Edward Sawyer, and John Selden, were all convicted of kidnapping Morgan from the Canandaigua jail. They served brief jail terms. Twelve indictments were handed down at trials in Genesee, Monroe, Niagara, and Ontario Counties, and Sheriff Bruce of Niagara County spent two years and two months in jail. Whitney was jailed for one year and three months, and others served short jail terms. Sixty-nine Masons were involved in the abduction. Their action had an unanticipated, adverse impact on their fraternal order.

A new political party, the Anti-Masonic Party, was formed, and 112 delegates, including eleven ex-Masons from eleven states, attended its initial meeting. In 1831, the Anti-Masonic Party met in Baltimore to nominate a candidate for President of the United States. It was the first third party in the United States, the first party to hold a nominating convention, and the first to publish a platform of party principles.

The number of Masonic lodges in New York State declined from 360 in 1826 to 75 in 1836; membership declined from 22,000 to 4,000 over that ten-year period. The impact of William Morgan on the events of his era was significant, but it was out of proportion to his deed.

## *Margaret Fox (1834-1893) / Kate Fox (1835-1892)*

"When Margaret and Kate Fox of Rochester became famous in the late 1840s for their mysterious rappings, they helped to establish Spiritualism as a serious cult in the United States, and their curious manifestations baffled some of the shrewdest men of their day. John Fox, their father, was a hard-headed Methodist who found it difficult to accept the strange occurrences under his own roof as his daughters became the elite of the spirit world. It all began when he took a small farmhouse that was said to be haunted. Years earlier, a peddler was supposed to have been murdered on the premises, and now neighbors believed that his ghost walked the night." Ishbel Ross,
*Charmers and Cranks*

John Fox, his wife, Margaret, and his two youngest daughters, Margaret and Kate, moved to Rochester from Bath, Canada, in 1844. In December 1847, the blacksmith and his family moved into a house on the corner of Parker and Hydesville Roads in the hamlet of Hydesville, near Newark.

Michael Weekman, who had lived in the house in 1846 and early 1847, moved out because his family had heard mysterious noises, and he had failed to find the source of the rapping sounds. Shortly after blowing out the candle in her bedroom one night, Weekman's eight-year-old daughter had felt cold, clammy hands on her face. The neighbors thought that the house was haunted. John Fox and his wife were devout Methodists; they did not believe the rumors.

In early 1848, the Fox family heard mysterious rappings in the walls of their house for the first time. Margaret and Kate both felt cold hands pass over their faces. On March 31, 1848, the teenage girls, one fourteen and one thirteen, decided that they would attempt to communicate with the source of the rappings.

Kate called out, "Here Mr. Splitfoot, do as I do," and snapped her finger three times. Three raps were heard in response. Margaret clapped her hands four times and said, "Do just as I do." Four raps were heard on the wall near her. Then Kate held up four fingers and asked, "How many fingers am I holding out?" They heard four raps. Kate pointed out to her mother that the source of the knocking could see as well as hear.

They received no response to the question, "Are you a man?" However, they received a multiple-rap response to the question, "Are you a spirit?" William Duesler, a neighbor who devised a code by assigning a number to a letter of the alphabet, learned that the spirit's name was Charles B. Rosma. He also learned that Rosma was a peddler who had been murdered in the house and buried in the cellar. When Duesler and several other neighbors dug in the cellar the next morning, they found a human skull, human hair, and quicklime.

Some people thought that modern Spiritualism was born that evening of March 31, 1848. They believed the "conversation" that night with the spirit of Charles Rosma was the first communication between this world and the next. Sir Arthur Conan Doyle referred to the event as "one of the great points of psychic evolution." That spring, the rappings became more frequent, and people began to visit the house. One day there were 500 visitors.

In *The Spirit Rappers*, Herbert G. Jackson, Jr., observes:

> In July of 1848, two events of note took place less than twenty-five miles apart in western New York. Elizabeth Cady Stanton and Lucretia Mott convened the first Women's Rights Convention at Seneca Falls, and the cellar floor of the empty Hydesville "spook house" was ripped up in a two-day quest for the corporeal remains of a murdered peddler.
>
> The period was one of religious and social ferment, a period that had witnessed the rise—and in some cases the fall—of Mormonism, Mesmerism, Shakerism, Fourierism, phrenology, Swedenborgianism. Thousands of Millerites had believed that 1843 or 1844 would see the end of the world.
>
> It was also a time of serious economic depression and recovery, abolitionism, feminism, and temperance crusades....

The girls' older sister, Leah Fox Fish, decided to capitalize on the attention that her family was receiving in the press. Leah, a widow who lived in Rochester, scheduled "sittings" to display her sisters' talents. People called these sittings "séances." Leah moved her young sisters into her home on Troup Street in Rochester. In November 1849, she rented Corinthian Hall, the largest hall in the City, for public demonstrations of her sisters' ability to communicate with the next world.

Advertising circulars for the meeting promised a "full explanation of the nature and history of the mysterious noises supposed to be supernatural, which have caused so much excitement in this city.... The 'mysterious agencies' have promised to give the public an actual demonstration of the sounds, so that they may know that the sounds are neither made nor controlled by human beings."

Two of Leah's friends were among the earliest to spread the word of Spiritualism. Isaac Post and his wife, Amy, who were Quakers, were the first ones that Leah invited to hear the rappings. E. W. Capron, a young businessman from Auburn, was another of the early believers.

Many people had difficulty believing the Fox sisters' revelations. Skeptics attempted to disprove them, including three doctors from Buffalo. The Buffalo *Commercial Advertiser* published a letter prepared by three physicians from the University of Buffalo. They concluded:

> Now, it was sufficiently clear that the rappings were not vocal sounds; these could not have been produced without movements of the respiratory muscles, which would at once lead to detection. Hence, excluding vocal sounds, the only possible source of the noises in question, produced, as we have seen they must be, by voluntary muscular contractions, is in one of the more movable articulations of the skeleton.

> From the anatomical construction of the voluntary muscles, this explanation remains the only alternative. By an analysis, prosecuted in this manner, we arrive at the conviction that the rappings, assuming they are not spiritual, are produced by the action of the will, through voluntary movements of the joints.

> Various facts may be cited to show that the motion of
> the joints, under certain circumstances, is adequate to
> produce the phenomena of the rappings; but we need
> not now refer to these. By a curious coincidence,
> after arriving at the above conclusion respecting the
> source of the sounds, an instance has fallen under our
> observation, which demonstrates the fact that noises
> precisely identical with the spiritual rappings may be
> produced by the knee joints.

The doctors cited the example of a woman from Buffalo who could make rapping sounds with her knees. Leah Fox responded by suggesting that the doctors examine Margaret during a séance. They learned that there were no raps if Margaret's feet, while she was seated, were placed on chairs in front of her, and her knees were held firmly. Leah explained that the spirits did not respond, because they thought that Margaret was being mistreated. Margaret became nervous and tired from the negative comments in the press and of the publicity that the doctors had received.

Leah took her sisters on a tour of Albany, Troy, and New York City. In Albany, a minister accused the Fox sisters of blasphemy against the Holy Scriptures. He filed a complaint against them with the police who took no action. However, an unruly mob disrupted their séance. Margaret's and Kate's demonstrations in New York were attended by James Fenimore Cooper, William Cullen Bryant, and *Tribune* editor Horace Greeley.

The interest of Greeley and his wife, Mary, in the Fox sisters was triggered by grief over the death of their son and their hope of communicating with him. The Greeleys invited the Fox sisters to hold séances in their home. Their guests included singer Jenny Lind, the "Swedish nightingale." Mary Greeley sincerely believed that she had been able to communicate with her son. Horace Greeley did not actually believe that contact had been made, but his name associated with the cause of Spiritualism helped to promote the Fox sisters. Greeley documented his thoughts about the Fox sisters:

> Their conduct and bearing is as unlike that of
> deceivers as possible, and we think that no one
> acquainted with them could believe them at all capa-

ble of engaging in so daring, impious, and shameful a juggle as this would be if they had caused the sounds. And it is not possible that such a juggle should have been so long perpetrated in public, and yet escape detection. A juggler performs one feat quickly and hurries to another. He does not devote week after week to doing the same thing over and over deliberately, in view of hundreds who sit beside him or confronting him in broad daylight, not to enjoy but to detect his trick.

A deceiver naturally avoids conversation on the subject of his knavery, but these ladies converse freely and fully with regard to the origin of these "rappings" in their dwelling years ago, the various sensations they caused, the neighborhood excitement created, the progress of the developments—what they have seen, heard, and experienced first to last. If all were false, they could not fail to have involved themselves in a labyrinth of blasting contradictions, as each separately gives accounts of the most astounding occurrences at this or that time. Persons foolish enough to commit themselves without reserve or caution could not have deferred a thought of thorough self-exposure for a single week....

Greeley offered to finance Kate's education. She went to school but tired of it and returned to her Spiritualist activities.

In the fall of 1852, Margaret Fox and her mother traveled to Philadelphia, where she met Arctic explorer Elisha Kent Kane. Kane, member of a leading Philadelphia family, had sailed as ship's doctor on an 1850 expedition to find the lost English explorer, Sir John Franklin. They failed to find Franklin, but the expedition placed Kane's name before the American public. He was in line to command the next search expedition to the Arctic.

Kane visited Margaret and her mother and was immediately captivated by the young Spiritualist. For him, it was love at first sight. He pursued her and encouraged her to go to school and to give up her interest in Spiritualism. During the early spring of 1853, Margaret realized that she was in love with Kane. Kane promised to marry her upon his return from his next voyage to the Arctic. In May 1853, he sailed for the North.

In Kane's absence, Margaret went to school in Philadelphia and later in Albany. Kane's expedition was unsuccessful in finding Franklin; however, they discovered Kennedy Channel, which Robert E. Peary used on a later expedition. Kane's trip was concluded with a 1,300 mile, eighty-three-day trek to a Danish town in Greenland.

Since Kane's family discouraged his courting Margaret, he made no attempt to contact her upon his return to New York. His parents looked upon her as their son's friend, not his fiancée. Margaret was shocked by this treatment. Kane prevailed, however, and he and Margaret were married in a Quaker ceremony. Shortly after their marriage, Kane sailed for England to report to Lady Franklin about the search for her husband and to confer with several scientific societies. He became ill and stayed in England only a short time. Upon his return, he went to Havana to recuperate in the sun.

On February 16, 1857, Kane died. Upon her husband's death at the age of thirty-six, Margaret gave up her Spiritualist demonstrations. In accordance with her husband's wishes, she became a Catholic. Kane had suggested this because he thought that it would end her connection with Spiritualism, and, briefly, it did. Subsequently, she went on a tour to England with Kate, and while there demonstrated her psychic powers to Thomas Carlyle.

Upon their return home from England, Margaret and Kate renounced the methods by which they had inspired the Spiritualist movement. On October 21, 1888, at the Academy of Music in New York, Margaret gave a demonstration of how she and her sister had made the rapping sounds. She removed the shoe and stocking from her right leg and showed the audience how she made the noises with her big toe. She said that her sister, Leah, had urged her two younger sisters not to reveal the secret. The New York *Herald* commented on the event:

> By throwing life and enthusiasm into her big toe, Mrs. Margaret Fox Kane produced loud spirit rappings ... and dealt a blow to Spiritualism, that huge and worldwide fraud which she and her sister Kate founded in 1848. Both sisters were present, and both

denounced Spiritualism as a monstrous imposition and cheat. The great building was crowded, and the wildest excitement prevailed at times. Hundreds of Spiritualists had come to see the originators of their faith destroy it at one stroke. They were greatly agitated at times and hissed freely....

Mrs. Kane's confession: "That I have been instrumental in perpetrating the fraud of Spiritualism upon a too confiding public, many of you already know. It is the greatest sorrow of my life. It is a late day now, but I am prepared to tell the truth, and nothing but the truth, so help me God....

Many here will scorn me; but if they knew the sorrow of my past life they would pity, not condemn. When I began this deception, I was too young to know right from wrong. I hope God Almighty will forgive me and those silly enough to believe in Spiritualism."

On November 20, 1889, Margaret recanted and said that she really did have psychic powers, but that she had been talked into saying that she and her sister made the rapping sounds with their big toes. Margaret said that she had lied when she spoke out against Spiritualism, as documented by biographer I. G. Edmunds in *The Girls Who Talked to Ghosts: The Story of Katie and Margaret Fox*:

Would to God that I could undo the injustice that I did the cause of Spiritualism. I was under the strong mental influence of persons who hated it. They made me say things that were untrue.... At the time I spoke against Spiritualism, I was in great need of money. Persons I prefer not to name took advantage of this. The excitement also helped upset my mind.... It was all false. My belief in Spiritualism has not changed. When I said those dreadful things, I was not responsible for my words.

Margaret and Kate were welcomed back into the Spiritualism movement and remained active in it until their death.

Many factors contributed to the growth of Spiritualism in the United States, particularly in the Northeast and Midwest. During the 1840s and 1850s, many economic, political, and social changes happened in America. Financial panics occurred in 1837 and 1857. A new generation of political leaders was taking office, replacing the one that had led the country in its early years. Population and urbanization were increasing rapidly, particularly with the growth in immigration in the 1840s.

In *Spiritualism in Antebellum America,* Bret E. Carroll summarizes the impact of these changes:

> These unsettling developments combined to produce spiritual malaise, discomfort, discontent, and above all a search for order among many Americans. Most of those attracted to Spiritualism found their deities distant, their cultural and social surroundings disturbing, and their ministers and churches ineffectual in addressing the resulting uneasiness.
>
> Fearing that spiritual values and religious institutions were losing their influence on American society, they experimented with new religious ideas and practices and joined their contemporaries in a variety of cultural, social, moral, and scientific (or quasi-scientific) reform movements. They hoped to find more satisfying forms of religious belief and expression and, like many religious Americans before and after them, to realize a society and a cosmos that they feared was spiritually empty.
>
> This restless searching ... was a major theme of nineteenth-century culture. Those who embraced the Spiritualist religion often had backgrounds suggesting restless disapproval of the status quo and an openness to new and progressive philosophies. They usually came from such liberal religions as Swedenborgianism, Universalism, Quakerism, and,

to a lesser extent, Unitarianism, Transcendentalism, and Rationalism, each of which contributed not only members to the Spiritualist movement but also ideas to its religious ideology.

They often moved through one or more of these beliefs before drifting to Spiritualism. They also tended to be committed to one or more of such causes as temperance, women's rights, abolitionism, communitarianism, phrenology, and Mesmerism, as well as dietary, dress, marriage, and medical reform. Their desire for order and spiritual fulfillment eventually led them to seek communion with spirits and to create their own religion.

Beginning in the 1830s, commercialization and industrialization changed the nation dramatically. The growth of technology displayed by the building of manufacturing plants, railroads, and telegraph systems required the public at large to adapt. The expansion of a capitalistic market economy led to an increase in materialism and economic uncertainty. Moral values seemed to be declining.

In *Spiritualism and Society*, Geoffrey K. Nelson comments on the phenomenon of Spiritualism:

During the period of most rapid expansion [1848-1870] there was no central organization of Spiritualists, and there were very few local organizations of any permanence. The movement in this period was virile and fluid in the extreme, consisting of local groups of enthusiasts who seldom formalized their organization into anything like a church. Beyond a vague belief in the existence of God, the immortality of the human spirit, and the ability of spirits to communicate with the living, there was little agreement on doctrine.

The spirits themselves had various opinions regarding the nature of God and varied answers to other theological and natural problems. This was not strange to Spiritualists though since they believed that the human soul does not become all wise on entering the spirit world, but takes with it all its earthly preconceptions and beliefs. Only gradually do spirits acquire further knowledge. It is therefore not strange to find that in their beliefs about God, the Spiritualists varied from the agnostic position through Unitarianism to conventional Christian beliefs.

According to the estimates of N. P. Willis, editor of the *Home Journal*, in 1853, 40,000 Spiritualists were active in New York in approximately 300 circles. They were very active in Brooklyn, particularly in Williamsburg.

The decline of Spiritualism had many facets. Examples of mediums who used fraud and deception became public knowledge, turning off many followers, particularly intellectual supporters. Many churches had attacked the Spiritualist movement from the beginning, implying that it was the work of the devil and, in any case, was not really Christian.

The press, with its tendency for sensationalism, was particularly unkind to the movement. Newspapers tended to neglect the Spiritualist interpretation of an event and to concentrate instead on their own viewpoint on the phenomenon of the movement. It was illegal to demonstrate Spiritualism in public in the State of Alabama. Generally, Spiritualism was not perceived to have lived up to its early promise.

In *The Heyday of Spiritualism*, Slater Brown provides an overview of the decline of Spiritualism:

> Though America had produced the first and some of the most remarkable mediums, the lack of any competent and disinterested body of investigators left the Spiritualists without any critical ballast to keep their ship on an even keel. As their numbers increased (by 1855, Spiritualists claimed over two million adherents to the faith), so did their critical standards decline.

Mediums gifted with genuine clairvoyant powers became lax, now that there was no real pressure to use them. Like ... clairvoyants, they drew on their own imaginations during a séance rather than on their psychic faculties. Daydreams ... were frequently offered as as inspired visions of life.... Physical manifestations, inexplicable as many of them were, came to be ignored as of secondary importance to the communications from exalted spirits of the past.

Spiritualist journals [by 1856, there were scores] published any report of psychic experience that drifted into the office, with no effort on the part of the editors to check the information or credibility of the correspondent. Occasionally, hoaxes, perpetrated by some prankster, would occupy a journal's pages.... With so many diverse and corrupting elements at work—commercialism, overcredulity, secondhand evidence, hoaxes, and downright fraud—it was difficult to separate the chaff from the wheat, the false from the genuine.

In their later years, the Fox sisters had no regular source of income. Margaret and Kate attempted to earn money as mediums, but their income from this activity was small. Both drank heavily. Kate died on July 2, 1892, in a seedy rooming house in New York. Margaret, who was ill and living in poverty, died on March 8, 1893, at the home of a friend in Brooklyn. Both were buried in Greenwood Cemetery. The women, who had been celebrities in their youth, died in obscurity.

On November 21, 1904, a group of children playing in the cellar of the Fox home in Hydesville found an over fifty-year-old skeleton when a foundation wall crumbled. Many area residents believed that this was the skeleton of the peddler who had been murdered in the house. People wanted to believe the stories that had circulated for over half a century.

In 1915, the Hydesville house was moved to the Spiritualist camp at Lily Dale in the Chautauqua region where it was destroyed by a fire in 1955. A marker on the site at Lily Dale notes: "The Birthplace of Modern Spiritualism—Upon This Site Stood the Hydesville Cottage, the Home of the Fox Sisters." It includes the words: "There is no death; there are no dead."

## *"Red Emma" Goldman (1869-1940)*

"The legacy of Emma Goldman's thirty years of activism in America has always been controversial. In several areas, however, her achievement is indisputable. More than anyone else, she sought to integrate a commitment to social revolution with a concern for the inner psychological liberation of the individual. She was almost alone among immigrant radicals in resisting a narrowly economic interpretation of social injustice and in stressing cultural, psychological, and sexual issues. At a time when most of the Left, anarchist and socialist, argued that the emancipation of women would occur with the defeat of capitalism, Goldman insisted—as feminists had long argued—that women's issues must be addressed now, not postponed to a hypothetical future."                                          Alice Wexler,

*Emma Goldman: An Intimate Life*

Emma Goldman was born in 1869 in Kovno, Russia. In 1882, the Goldman family moved to St. Petersburg, where Goldman worked as a seamstress in a glove factory. She had an unhappy home life. Her mother was cold to her; the family's favorite was Emma's older half sister, Helena. Her autocratic father was bitter because of his business failures. Another older sister, Lena, had immigrated to the United States, married, and settled in Rochester. In 1885, Emma and Helena joined their sister, Lena.

Goldman worked as a seamstress making overcoats ten and a half hours a day for $2.50 a week. She asked her boss for a raise so that she could buy books and theater tickets as she had in St. Petersburg. He refused and told her that her thoughts were too fancy for a worker in a clothing factory. She quit that job and got a job in a smaller factory for $4.00 for a six-day week. Goldman was disillusioned with life in America.

In 1886, Goldman's parents and two brothers moved to Rochester, where the family lived in an apartment on Joseph Avenue. A boarder, Jacob Kirshner, lived with the family. Goldman and Kirshner were married when she was seventeen, but they divorced within a year.

In her 1931 autobiography, *Living My Life*, Goldman wrote about finding "an escape from the gray dullness of Rochester existence" at the weekly Socialist meetings in Germania Hall. At a meeting of the Socialists, she heard of the Chicago Haymarket bombing. Six extremists were sentenced to death without proof of their guilt. Goldman was deeply moved by the injustice of the incident. It drove her to read anarchist literature and to become a staunch anarchist. She began to participate in the activities of the far Left wing in the class war.

Goldman realized that she could be more active in Left wing activities if she lived in New York City, which also offered many more cultural activities than did Rochester. In August 1889, with $5.00 in her handbag, a sewing machine, and some clothing, she arrived in the big city. She brought along her hatred of capitalist society's institutions. She was welcomed heartily into anarchist groups, where she met Alexander Berkman, a fiery liberal, and Johann Most, a radical editor. Both were influences on her life as an extremist.

Most helped her to improve her speaking style. Goldman became an intense speaker who effectively projected her beliefs. She went on a lecture tour to speak on behalf of the Haymarket prisoners and spoke at the German Union in Rochester, where she was vocal about the City's clothing "sweat shops."

Goldman believed in "free love." At one time, she shared rooms with two lovers, Berkman and a young artist, at the same time. In 1892, Berkman traveled to Pittsburgh to kill Henry Frick, who had led the attack against strikers at the Homestead Works of the Carnegie Steel Company. Berkman stabbed Frick once and shot him three times, but he did not succeed in killing him. Berkman, who was captured in Frick's office with a stick of dynamite in his mouth, received a twenty-two-year prison sentence, of which he served sixteen years.

After completing training, Goldman worked as a nurse and continued her radical activities. She was editor of the publication, *Mother Earth*, until the government shut it down during World War I. She lectured widely. She was billed as lecturing on drama, a subject that she knew well, but she managed to convey her political viewpoints interwoven with the discussion of drama. In 1893, she was convicted of inciting a riot in Union Square and served a year in jail on Blackwell's Island. She ran the jail's infirmary while serving her sentence.

Goldman was in St. Louis when she heard of the shooting of President McKinley in Buffalo in 1901. She saw a newspaper containing a picture of his assassin, Leon Czolgosz, and the headline,

"Emma Goldman Sought." She recognized Czolgosz as a young extremist, who had called himself Fred Nieman, with whom she had talked in Cleveland. However, they had not talked about McKinley, and Goldman had nothing to do with the assassination.

Czolgosz had told police that he knew Goldman, thus triggering a search for her. Police searched the homes of her relatives in Rochester. She traveled from St. Louis to Chicago, where she was taken into custody. She was interrogated in jail for several days. She claimed that she was beaten before she was released. Although she was cleared from any participation in the shooting of President McKinley, she was associated with it in the public's mind. She later claimed that she was suspected in participating of every act of violence in the United States after 1901.

Goldman was definitely a free spirit. She advocated atheism and the overthrow of the government. She spent fifteen days in the workhouse for promoting birth control. She smoked two packs of cigarettes a day at a time when few women smoked. She and Berkman advocated resisting the draft during World War I and were both jailed for two years. Upon their release from prison in September 1919, they were deported to Russia along with 250 other Socialists and Communists.

Goldman looked forward to living in Communist Russia, but she became more disillusioned there than she had been in America. The distrust, oppression, and terror under the new Communist government were no better than conditions under the Czars. After two years, she left Russia for Sweden and then Germany. She lectured in England and France about the shortcomings of the Russian experiment. She married a Welsh miner, James Colton, to obtain British citizenship that would ease her entrance into Canada.

While she lived in Canada, President Roosevelt approved a ninety-day visa for her to visit the United States. She spoke to the City Club forum in Rochester, a conservative forum, and told them, "I am no more respectable than I ever was. It is you who are a little more liberal. Your city and the action of the State of Illinois in the Haymarket cases made an anarchist out of me." She died in Toronto in 1940 at the age of seventy. Emma Goldman sought nontraditional solutions to problems of social injustice until she died.

## Claude Bragdon (1866-1946)

"Architecture, you know, is related to space in the same way that music is related to time, that is to say, one of its functions is to divide and subdivide space rhythmically and harmoniously. The site happens to be a triangle ... and if the whole building is to conform to an equilateral triangle, every part of it must do the same.... So, like the equal and regular beats into which music is divided, I first marked off my paper into a number of equilateral triangles.... On this pattern of triangles I traced the plan of my building.... The interior proportions of the dome I established by means of a single equilateral triangle. The same principle applied to the elevation yielded equally satisfactory results."    Claude Bragdon, *The Frozen Fountain*

Claude Bragdon was a noted Rochester architect who designed many of the city's landmarks, including the New York Central Railroad Station (razed and replaced), the Chamber of Commerce Building, the Bevier Memorial Building, the First Universalist Church, the Maplewood Branch of the YMCA, the Country Club of Rochester (also razed and replaced), and many residences.

Bragdon also undertook design projects outside of Rochester, including the Livingston County Court House in Geneseo, the Library and Historical Building in Canandaigua, and the Hunter Street Bridge in Peterborough, Canada. He was the recipient of the Silver Medal of the Architectural League of New York and three-time winner of the League's President's Medal.

In 1938, in *More Lives Than One,* Claude Bragdon observes that Greek Revival architecture in the United States was followed after the Civil War by the Cast-Iron Age, whose architects were of "mediocre ability." Victorian Gothic and French Second Empire styles were popular at this time. Those architects were followed by the Romantic Henry Hobson Richardson whose massive designs included semicircular arches and clustered columns. Richardson attempted to translate Spanish Romanesque architecture into American building design. The individualistic style of Richardson, who designed Trinity Church in Boston, did not last much beyond his lifetime.

Architecture in the United States, influenced by material and util-

Chamber of Commerce, South St. Paul Street

itarian concerns, became eclectic. Architect Louis H. Sullivan of Chicago attempted to provide discipline for his fellow American architects. He designed the Transportation Building for the 1893 World's Columbian Exposition in Chicago. The work of most architects was displayed in the Court of Honor enclosure. Its beauty was perceived to be "alien and ancient" and had no relation to the Machine Age that the Exposition was supposedly ushering in.

Sullivan's Transportation Building, which imitated no earlier designs, was relegated to a site behind the enclosure. In the opinion of Frank Lloyd Wright, a pupil of Sullivan, the designs displayed in the Court of Honor delayed architectural evolution in the United Stated by fifty years. Architects from Europe were influenced by Sullivan's design. Modern European architecture, in turn, influenced American Modernism.

Until this time, high-rise building designs varied from one section to another; different designs were usually used for lower floors, middle floors, and upper floors. Sullivan advocated a "form follows function" approach in which the first floor had display windows and second and higher floors were uniform to indicate the "tallness" of the building.

Bragdon began as an architectural draftsman. His first project as an architect was the Hunter Street Bridge over the Otonabee River in Peterborough, Ontario. Frank Barber of Toronto was the engineer. In *More Lives Than One,* Bragdon described the working relationship between the two men:

> The engineer's function in such a collaboration was to discover and develop that particular form of bridge which should best meet the given requirements from the triple standpoint of efficiency, economy, and endurance; but the function of the architect, aside from his general recognition as a purveyor of beauty, was not so easy to define. In the effort to do so we got nowhere until a single word, struck out in the heat of discussion, settled the difficulty and illuminated the subject with new light. That word was "dramatize," and the architect became thenceforth the dramatic artist, his [or her] function being to express, as eloquently as possible, everything that

223

First Universalist Church, South Clinton Avenue

needed to be or could be expressed—to make clear
that "beautiful necessity" whereby the bridge was as
it was and not otherwise.

Barber chose a single arch design for the span of 235 feet.
Bragdon designed the arcade supporting the roadway with semi-ellip-
tical arches that diminished toward the center of the arcade. They
were pleasing to eye as well as functional.

Bragdon was influenced by a trip to England, France, and Italy in
1895. He was particularly impressed by the architecture of Venice. In
his opinion: "Venice is a shattered rainbow, built into a city.... In
Venice everything seems to labor under the beautiful necessity of
being beautiful." In Italy, he was influenced by the use of color and
the care paid to city planning and the setting in which a particular
design flourishes. He was also impressed by the asymmetric plan and
the classical architectural detail of the Palazzo dei Diavoli near Siena.
He returned home convinced of the "impotency" of American architecture.

In 1898, Bragdon designed the Livingston County Courthouse in
Geneseo. He chose the Colonial style for this work because it
reflected "the period in which our taste was truest and finest."
However, he continued to look for original styles; he realized that, in
a sense, the Colonial style was another form of eclecticism.

In 1905, Bragdon designed the Country Club of Rochester. Two
guidelines for the building were holding cost down and providing a
clubhouse that would be easily adaptable to multiple uses. The design
was virtually symmetrical with long, low lines. The clubhouse
reflected a sense of proportion and harmonized with its setting and its
function.

Bragdon received an architectural commission and worked
between 1908 and 1910 on the First Universalist Church in
Rochester, one of the projects with which he expressed his satisfaction. His design provided a grouping of symmetrical components
around a central core. The Romanesque style possibly reflected the
influence of Richardson.

Bragdon considered the New York Central railroad station, which
opened in 1913, his most important commission in Rochester. His
goal was to design a monument to the New York Central and to the
City that was practical, economical, and functional. He avoided the

example of Charles F. McKim's Pennsylvania Station in New York City, which did not look like a railroad station. Bragdon viewed it as a "Temple of Fatigue."

After several false starts, Bragdon reminded himself: "This is a railway station!" He went down to the tracks and watched—and felt—the locomotives. His design for the railroad station was based on five tangential circles like the wheels of a locomotive engine. In Bragdon's words: "Of these the two end ones defined the height and width of the office divisions at right and left of the waiting room, and the three remaining circles circumscribed the great round-arched windows which gave it light."

Bragdon was a man of varied interests. In addition to architecture, he had serious interests in the theater, in mathematics, and in music. The latter two interests were displayed in his railroad station project. In choosing a proportion for the waiting room, he drew upon a system that he describes in his book, *The Beautiful Necessity:*

> What might be called the "musical parallel" by reason of the employment of those numerical ratios subsisting between the consonant intervals within the octaves—namely: 1:2, the octave; 2:3, the fifth; 3:4, the fourth; 4:5, the major third; and 4:7—the subminor seventh. The waiting room is twice as wide as it is high and twice as long as it it wide—the interval of the octave; or, if one prefers to name it so, the proportions of a root-four rectangle of Dynamic Symmetry. There also occur the ratios of 2:3 and 4:7—the fifth and diminished seventh. The beauty of the proportions of this room impress everyone as particularly fine.

Bragdon viewed architecture as "frozen music."

Bragdon's musical interest was displayed just before the station was officially opened when the waiting room was bare. He invited Marie Russak, a noted oculist who previously had been an opera singer, to tour the building. Bragdon described the visit:

> As we were standing in the gallery overlooking the waiting room, she ran up the notes of the diatonic

scale in her full, powerful voice. At the utterance of a certain note the entire room seemed to become a resonance chamber, reinforcing the tone with a volume so great as to be almost overpowering: the walls, the ceiling, the entire building seemed to cry aloud. "There!" said the singer as the sound died away in overtones, "Now your railway station has found its keynote—now it is alive."

Despite all of this architectural, mathematical, and musical effort, the station was razed in two phases and replaced by a small, utilitarian station of no particular architectural note. Unfortunately, it was another example of urban renewal taking precedence over historic preservation. Utica, New York, found a way to preserve its historic railroad station; Rochester did not.

In 1911, Bragdon left architecture to follow his interests in the theater. He moved to New York City and became a set designer for Walter Hampden's theatrical productions. From this time onward, his interest in architecture was restricted to writing books and numerous articles expounding his theories and criticisms of modern architecture. He never really found the replacement for popular eclecticism in architecture that he was seeking when he gave up his practice.

Rochester Savings Bank Building, Liberty Pole Way

## A. J. Warner (1833-1910) / J. Foster Warner (1859-1937)

"He [Andrew Jackson Warner] was an untiring worker, at his office day and night, wholly devoted to his business, suffering nothing to interfere with the prompt fulfillment of his engagements.... His artistic soul delighted in harmony in all things, thus music was a great pleasure. He was of a social, friendly nature and found enjoyment in the company of his Masonic brethren at such hours as he allowed himself off duty. He was a Unitarian in religious belief but took no interest in politics and no part in public life."

*Memorial Encyclopedia of New York,* 1916

Andrew Jackson Warner was a noted Rochester architect who left his mark on the City. He designed the Powers Block (which included the Powers Hotel, the Powers Art Gallery, the Powers Law Library, and offices for 1,000 clients), the Ellwanger and Barry building, and the Monroe County Savings Bank.

Warner's designs also included City Hall (now Irving Place), St. Mary's Hospital, the Wilder Building, Brick (Second) Presbyterian Church, First Presbyterian Church (now Central Church of Christ), Asbury Methodist Church (now Bethel Christian Fellowship), St. Bernard's Seminary, the Mt. Hope Cemetery Gatehouse, Rochester Free Academy, and Warner's Castle. His work includes many other sites in Rochester and around New York State, such as the Erie County Municipal Building, the Buffalo State Hospital, Corning City Hall (now the Rockwell Museum of Western Art), and the Richardson-Bates House in Oswego.

Warner was born on March 17, 1833, in New Haven, Connecticut, to Amos and Ada Austin Warner. Ada Austin was from Canandaigua, and two of her brothers—Henry and Merwin Austin—were architects. In 1847, Warner moved to Rochester and joined his uncle Merwin's architectural practice as an apprentice and draftsman.

In 1853, Warner entered into an architectural partnership with his uncle Merwin Austin. He left the partnership in 1857 when Austin refused to give him an increase in salary. His uncle gave him dire warnings about trying to make it on his own; nevertheless, Warner became one of Rochester's best-known architects. His work obviously was affected by the time in which he lived: a time of economic

City Hall, Broad and Fitzhugh Streets, now Irving Place

prosperity, rapid expansion of the city, and equivocal taste.

On March 22, 1855, Warner married Kate Foster, whose mother was from a pioneer Pittsford family. They had four children; two of whom died in infancy. The surviving sons, William Amos Warner and J. Foster Warner, became architects.

Warner was known as a hard worker and a stern taskmaster. He was particularly demanding of his sons when they joined his architectural firm. When Foster was leaving for his honeymoon in Niagara Falls in April 1883, his father's parting words were: "Just remember to be back at work on time on Monday morning." He meant it.

In 1867, Warner formed a partnership with Charles Coots that lasted until 1872, when Coots left to design the Genesee Brewery building before moving from Rochester. That year, Warner's nephew, Frederick Brockett, began training with him. Frederick's brother, William Brockett, followed in 1873.

Warner worked independently until 1875, when he formed a partnership with James G. Cutler who had designed the Kimball Tobacco factory and the Elwood building. Cutler left the partnership in 1877. In 1882, the firm of Warner and Brockett was established. It lasted until 1893, one year prior to Warner's retirement. Frederick Brockett continued the practice after his uncle's retirement.

J. Foster Warner's first major project with his father's firm was the 1882 design for the Power's Hotel. He also designed the George Eastman House, the Monroe County Courthouse (now City Hall), the Third Monroe County Courthouse (now the Monroe County Office Building), Rochester Savings Bank, the Eastman Laboratory for Physics and Biology of the University of Rochester, the Granite Building, the Sibley, Lindsay, and Curr department store, Soule House on East Avenue, and the Ontario County Courthouse.

J. Foster Warner was known for "classical symmetry, forms, and details." In 1889, he established his own architectural practice. He was known as an extroverted, stubborn, polished individual who was popular with the ladies and drove fast cars. He was a director of the Rochester Telephone Company, the first president of the Rochester Chapter of the American Association of Architects, and chairman of the City Planning Commission. From 1890 until 1910, he was one of the most distinguished Rochester architects.

A. J. Warner and J. Foster Warner were leading architects for over fifty years. Their influence on Rochester's cityscape was significant.

Third Monroe County Courthouse, West Main Street,
now the Monroe County Office Building

Monroe County Courthouse, Church Street, now City Hall

First Presbyterian Church, South Plymouth Avenue,
now Central Church of Christ

# CHAPTER 9

# RELIGIOUS LEADERS / ECCLESIASTICS

## Charles Grandison Finney (1792-1875)

"Charles G. Finney ... was the most widely known of many great revival preachers in the pre-Civil War United States. His campaigns from 1824 to 1834 in the so-called 'Burned-over District' of upstate New York and in Philadelphia, New York City, and Boston made his name synonymous with the final stage of the Second Great Awakening as it has been traditionally understood. In 1835, at age forty-three, Finney moved to Oberlin, Ohio, where he became professor of theology and later president of Oberlin College. Oberlin was known for its abolitionist stance, for its acceptance of black students, and as a pioneer in coeducation for women." Charles E. Hambrick-Stowe, *Charles G. Finney and the Spirit of American Evangelism*

Revivalism was viewed as a return to religion, i.e. being born again, and as an awakening of new church members. Religious fervor and mass evangelism were elements of revivalism. Charles Grandison Finney was the most prominent evangelist of the Second Great Awakening in the United States (1800 to 1835). He spoke out against urbanization and industrial revolution and advocated a return to a more simple, pious life.

In 1831, Finney came to Rochester for a revivalist meeting that was one of the largest until that time. His sermons included "The Carnal Mind Is Enmity Against God" and "The Wages of Sin Is Death." Finney's impact on the region's ferment was significant. As described by David Maldwyn Ellis in *New York: State and City:*

> Charles G. Finney and his colleagues not only converted hundreds of thousands but stimulated many reform movements. Upstate became the nursery for many humanitarian movements. Among the reformers were Theodore Weld and Gerrit Smith, who sought to abolish slavery; Elizabeth Cady Stanton

and Susan B. Anthony, persistent fighters for women's rights; and John B. Gough, a reformed drunkard who enthralled thousands with his lurid tales of degradation. Finney attracted support from such wealthy men as the Tappan brothers, silk merchants in New York City....

Finney, a tall man with a serious demeanor, was a captivating speaker who advocated the dual responsibility of an individual's commitment to God, including saving souls and working toward a better society. He declared: "Genuine faith always results in good works and is itself a good work." He believed that all men could be saved. He advocated charity, humility, tolerance, temperance, and humanitarianism and provided an alternative to the stern requirements of Calvinism.

In the summer of 1831, Finney was invited to Rochester to preach at the Third Presbyterian Church and to bring members of the three Presbyterian churches closer together. According to Basil Miller in *Charles Finney,* "On investigation, he discovered the outlook to be dark indeed, for there was dissension among the Presbyterian churches of the City as well as little spiritual life in evidence. Wickedness abounded, dance halls flourished, and a low moral tone marked the City. After much prayer, Finney said, 'My mind became entirely decided ... that Rochester was the place to which the Lord would have me go.'"

Within a month of Finney's arrival in Rochester, "Christians of different denominations are seen mingling together on the Sabbath and bowing at the same altar in the weekly prayer meetings." He preached three sermons each Sunday and conducted at least four services during the week at the three Presbyterian churches and occasionally at Baptist and Methodist churches as well. He spent over six months in Rochester.

According to Rev. Kenneth S. Fox, pastor of the Open Door Mission: "Charles Grandison Finney's coming to town was the pivotal experience that changed Rochester. The influence of Finney's powerful message is still felt in Rochester because it was passed down in so many different ways. Parents who heard the evangelist told their children. Ministers and Sunday-school teachers carried the word to their flocks. And generation after generation of

Rochesterians stayed in the city and preserved the Finney legacy."
In his memoirs, Finney observed:

> I never preached anywhere with more pleasure than
> in Rochester. They are a highly intelligent people,
> and have ever manifested a candor, an earnestness
> and an appreciation of the truth excelling anything I
> have ever seen, on so large a scale in any other place.
> I have labored in other cities where the people were
> even more highly educated than in Rochester. But in
> these cities the views and habit of the people were
> more stereotyped; the people were more fastidious,
> more afraid of measures than in Rochester.

Finney brought over 400 new families—635 new members—into
the church in Rochester. Many leaders of the community were among
the converts that included Samuel D. Porter, who became an active
reformer in the 1840s; Alvah Strong, a leader of the local Baptist
church and later of the University of Rochester; and abolitionist
spokesman Henry B. Stanton who later married Elizabeth Cady,
leader of the Women's Rights Movement.

Finney's second revival in Rochester was held in 1842 at Brick
Presbyterian Church. His third revival in Rochester was in 1855, during an economic downturn. Finney conducted a series of noontime
prayer services that were well attended. This revival stimulated the
efforts of the temperance movement and the Bible societies and
spurred many businessmen to lead the Sabbath schools. Finney
observed: "What was quite remarkable in the three revivals that I wit-
nessed in Rochester, they all commenced and made their first
progress among the higher classes of society."

Nevertheless, the working class also participated in the revival.
According to Basil Miller in *Charles Finney,* "Merchants arranged to
have their clerks attend the day services. 'This became so general
throughout the City that in all places of public resort, in stores and
public houses, in banks, in the street and in public conveyances and
everywhere, the work of salvation that was going on was the absorb-
ing topic.' The soul-saving continued until 'It seemed as if the whole
City would be converted.'"

Rev. F. D. Ward, a Rochester missionary to India, noted:

"Rochester has become what it is religiously very largely through the agency of revivals." In his "Reminiscences of Early Rochester," Dr. Augustus H. Strong agreed: "Rochester owes more to revivals of religion than it owes to its providential location or to the energy of its people; for without these revivals, it is questionable whether there would have been anything like the education or the enterprise that characterized the city."

Later, Finney taught at Oberlin College in Ohio, which had been founded in 1833 by ministers from New England and New York. By 1846, the College had developed its own ideology, a combination of liberal religion, practical training, and the politics of reform. The spiritual leader of the Oberlin community was Professor of Theology Finney, who had impressed the parents of Antoinette Brown, the first woman minister, at a series of revival meetings in Rochester during the winter of 1831.

Charles Grandison Finney died on August 15, 1875. President Fairfield of Oberlin College spoke to the first graduating class after Finney's death: "Your destiny will be in a measure shaped by what he was and what he did. And here is our relief and satisfaction in closing up such a career of usefulness and power. There is to be no real loss. From that burning and shining light, in which for so long a season we were permitted to rejoice, a thousand other lights have been kindled, and thus the darkness of the world shall be more and more enlightened."

## *Brigham Young (1801-1877)*

"When a furious mob murdered [Joseph] Smith, Young assumed the leadership of the Mormon survivors and redirected their vision toward new goals. Far beyond the Mississippi, in heretofore unsettled territory, lay the Great Basin to which he led the remnants of the Church and its followers. There Young supervised the building of a new Society that soon attracted thousands of newcomers from other parts of the Union and from Europe as well. The account of his life is thus an American success story, a rise from poor beginnings to power and wealth.... It is also a story that illuminates important features of the social history of the United States—religious enthusiasm, the pioneering spirit, and the encounter with the American West."

Oscar Handlin, Preface, Brigham Young<br>and the Expanding American Frontier

Brigham Young, sixth child and third son of John and Abigail Howe Young, was born on June 1, 1801, in Whitingham, Vermont. John Young was a farmer who moved frequently because of increasingly worn-out soil. Abigail Young was a relative of Elias Howe, one of the inventors of the sewing machine, and Samuel Gridley Howe, an eminent nineteenth-century reformer.

In 1802, John Young moved his family to Smyrna, Chenango County, New York. He cleared land for farming and built a log dwelling in an area known as Dark Hollow. The family's next move was to Genoa in Cayuga County, east of Cayuga Lake. Brigham was introduced to hard work at an early age, including logging and driving teams of horses. The family was poor and hired Brigham out to neighbors to earn additional income. He attended the Drake School House and was tutored by his mother.

The Youngs were Methodists who initially had been New England Congregationalists. In Brigham's opinion, his parents were "the most strict religionists that lived upon the earth." The children were not allowed to use words such as "devil" and "I vow." Brigham held back from joining the Methodist church or any other church. He said a prayer to himself: "Lord, preserve me until I am old enough to have sound judgment, and a discreet mind ripened on a good, solid foundation of common sense."

Abigail Young died in 1815, just after Brigham's fourteenth birthday. He had been close to his mother; in his words: "Of my mother—she that bore me—I can say no better woman lived in the world." His older sister Fanny, who had helped care for him as a child, returned home and became the stabilizing influence in the family. Brigham developed into an independent individual with a deliberate manner.

In 1815, the family moved again—to the Sugar Hill district of Schuyler County near Tyrone. Their farm had many maple trees, and they supplemented their income by making maple sugar that could be bartered for flour and other necessities. In 1817, John Young married Hannah Dennis Brown, a widow with several children of her own. He broke up his household and moved in with his new wife. John Young told sixteen-year-old Brigham: "You now have your time; go and provide for yourself."

Young moved to Auburn, where he became an apprentice to learn the trades of carpentry, glazing, and painting. One of his early projects was the finish carpentry and painting of the new home of Judge Elijah Miller, the father-in-law of William H. Seward, a future Governor, U.S. Senator, and Secretary of State. The Seward Mansion, which Seward inherited from Judge Miller, has an ornate fireplace mantel crafted by Young who also worked on the construction of the Auburn Theological Seminary.

In 1823, Young moved to Port Byron, a fast-growing town on the new Erie Canal. He worked in a furniture repair shop, a wool carding mill, a pail factory, and a boatyard. One of his employers noted: "He would do more work in a given time and secure more and better work from his help without trouble than any man they have ever employed." In 1824, Young joined the Methodist church. He insisted on being baptized by immersion, although that was not the usual Methodist practice at the time.

On October 5, 1824, Young married Miriam Works, a beautiful blonde whom he had met while working at the pail factory. Their daughter, Elizabeth, was born in Port Byron. In 1828, the family moved to Oswego, where he worked on the construction of a large tannery. When the tannery was finished the following year, he moved his family to Mendon, south of Rochester, where his father and several of his sisters had settled. Young built a house at the corner of Cheese Factory and Mendon-Ionia Roads. He also constructed a large undershot water wheel on Trout Creek that flowed through his property, which provided power for grindstones, lathes, and saws.

While living in Port Byron, Young had heard "rumors of a new revelation, to the effect of a new Bible written upon golden plates ... at Palmyra. I was somewhat acquainted with the coming forth of the Book of Mormon ... through ... the newspapers [and] many stories and reports." Young saw a copy of the *Book of Mormon* when Samuel Smith, brother of Joseph Smith who had found the golden plates on Hill Cumorah, visited Mendon to preach about Mormonism and to sell copies of the "golden Bible."

In January 1830, Young, his brother Phineas, and his good friend and neighbor Heber Kimball traveled to Columbia, Pennsylvania, the location of the nearest Mormon church, to observe Mormons interpreting their religion, prophesying, and speaking in tongues. Young returned to Mendon and then visited his brother, Joseph, a Methodist minister in Canada, to ask his opinion of the new religion.

That April, John, Sr., Joseph, and Phineas were baptized into the Mormon religion, followed by Young who was baptized by Elder Eleazer Miller in the stream behind his home in Mendon. He said that before his clothes "were dry on my back [Elder Miller] laid his hands on me and ordained me an Elder, at which I marveled. According to the words of the Savior, I felt a humble, child-like spirit, witnessing unto me that my sins were forgiven." Ordination as an Elder gave Young the authority to preach the Gospel. The rest of the family followed him into the new religion.

Young liked many aspects of Mormonism: its similarities to Puritanism, with its emphasis on common sense; its espousal of "Christian Primitism," an attempt to restore Christianity as it existed in the time of Jesus Christ; its authoritarianism, which required unquestioning loyalty to the Mormon prophet Joseph Smith; and its lay priesthood, which provided a path to status and influence.

In June 1830, the Young's second daughter, Vilate, was born. The childbirth temporarily incapacitated Miriam. Young took part-time jobs so he could do more of the household chores while Miriam was bedridden. The family remained poor and contracted small debts.

On September 8, 1832, Miriam Young died of tuberculosis. Young and his two daughters moved in with his friend, Heber Kimball. That fall, Young and Kimball traveled to the main Mormon settlement in Kirtland, Ohio, east of Cleveland, to meet Joseph

Smith—founder of the Church of Jesus Christ of Latter Day Saints. Upon meeting the charismatic Mormon prophet, Young spoke in tongues and asked the Latter Day Saints leader's opinion of his gift. Smith "told them that it was of the pure Adamic language.... It is of God, and the time will come when Brother Brigham Young will preside over this church."

Young returned to Mendon to preach Mormonism. He traveled around upstate New York and Canada baptizing converts. In September 1833, he moved to Kirtland to be near Joseph Smith and the center of Mormon activity. He courted Mary Ann Angell, a former Baptist from Seneca, New York. In February 1834, Young and Angell were married by Sidney Rigdon, an influential Mormon leader. Early the following year, Smith appointed Young one of the the Council of Twelve Apostles, which was modeled on the apostles of the New Testament. They were responsible for overseeing the Mormon churches and missionary activity.

From 1835 through 1837, Young traveled around upstate New York, New England, and Canada spreading the word of Mormonism. On a return visit to Kirtland during this time, he supervised the completion of the Kirtland Temple. Smith encountered difficulties in Kirtland when he attempted to establish a Mormon-controlled bank. Because of his indebtedness and his plan to print his own money, Smith was denied a State banking charter. He established the bank anyway; unfortunately, it failed in the Panic of 1837.

In 1838, Young was drawn into the conflict between Mormons and non-Mormons in Missouri who were concerned about the Mormon's economic and political control of the region. A series of armed clashes began in Gallatin, Missouri, when non-Mormons attempted to prevent Mormons from voting. Three Mormons were killed at Crooked River, Caldwell County, and seventeen were killed and fifteen wounded seriously at Haun's Mill, Caldwell County, by an unruly mob of over 200 men.

The Governor of Missouri, Lilburn Boggs, called out the Missouri militia and issued the order that the Mormons "must be exterminated or driven from Missouri, if necessary, for the public good." Joseph Smith turned himself in to the authorities and his brother, Hyrum, and Sidney Rigdon were arrested. Young was the senior member of the Council of the Twelve Apostles who was not in captivity. He appealed to the Missouri Legislature for compensation for Mormon property that had been seized. A token payment was made, and, due to threats to their lives, the Mormons left Missouri for Illinois.

In 1839, Young made his last visit to upstate New York while en route to England on a successful mission that more than doubled Mormon membership there. He promoted the increase in the number of English Elders and the immigration of English Mormons to America. Over the next six years, over 4,000 immigrated to the United States. He also established a Mormon periodical, the *Millennial Star*, in England. Young clearly established a reputation as an efficient administrator and organizer.

Smith escaped from his six-month captivity and established the center of the Mormon faith in Nauvoo, Illinois. In July 1841, when Young returned to Nauvoo, he found that it had become a rapidly growing city of 3,000 that would expand to 10,000 by the end of 1841. The Nauvoo Charter gave Mormons comprehensive powers of self-government, although they could not pass any laws contrary to the Illinois and U.S. Constitutions. The mayor and City Council formed their own municipal court, and the City controlled its own militia, the Nauvoo Legion.

Young was elected to the Nauvoo City Council and appointed editor of the Nauvoo newspaper, *The Times and Seasons*. His commitment to Mormonism was severely tested in 1841, when Joseph Smith endorsed the practice of polygamy for the Latter Day Saints. Smith may have been influenced by the practices of the Oneida Community in New York State when he supported the concept of plural marriage. Initially, Young was appalled by the practice. He said, "It was the first time in my life that I had desired the grave." When he expressed his views to Smith, he was told, "Brother Brigham, the Lord will reveal it to you."

Young was faced with the dilemma of either practicing polygamy or defying the prophet Joseph Smith. Eventually, he accepted the concept of plural marriage. He married four times between 1842 and 1844. His wives all lived in their own houses.

The practice of polygamy was the greatest source of difficulties for the Mormons, both within and outside of the Church. Nauvoo was envied as the most prosperous city in Illinois; however, its self-government was not easily accepted by non-Mormons. Smith realized that he must look to the Far West as "a place of refuge" where "the devil cannot dig us out." In February 1844, Smith asked the Council of Twelve to send a delegation west toward California and Oregon to build a temple and to establish a government of their own.

The delegation to the West was delayed by Smith's decision to run for the Presidency of the United States in 1844 as an independent candidate. Young and other Mormon leaders did much of the campaigning for the candidate. Smith had problems of his own back in Nauvoo. A group of dissidents led by William Law split off from the Latter Day Saints because of disagreements with Smith's policies, particularly polygamy. Law and his associates established a competing newspaper, the Nauvoo *Expositor.* Smith asked the City Council to destroy the press and all copies of the newspaper, a blatant violation of freedom of the press.

Anti-Mormon feeling intensified around Nauvoo, and Smith, his brother, Hyrum, and two other Mormon leaders gave themselves up to county authorities in Carthage. On June 27, 1844, a large, organized mob entered the jail at Carthage, killed Smith and his brother, and wounded another Mormon leader. Young, who was campaigning for Smith in Massachusetts at the time, returned to Nauvoo by a round-about route to avoid assassination.

Young's only serious rival for the Mormon presidency was Sidney Rigdon. Young's forceful speech, his alignment with the Council of Twelve, and his confidence that the Church would make the right decisions made him the clear choice. Although Smith's brother, William, supported Young's election to the presidency, he later attempted to replace him. Anti-Mormon sentiment continued to run high, and Illinois Governor Thomas Ford repealed the Nauvoo charter and disfranchised both the City police and the Nauvoo Legion. Earlier, Ford had ordered the return of their State-supplied weapons.

Illinois justice was unable to convict the killers' of Joseph Smith and his brother. Anti-Mormon mobs burned barns and crops on farms around Nauvoo. Young realized that they would have to abandon Nauvoo soon and settle in a frontier sanctuary. Texas was considered as a possible site, as were California, Oregon, and the Island of Vancouver. Young ruled out Oregon and Vancouver because they were involved in ongoing border disputes between the United States and Great Britain. He favored the Great Basin because it was remote and virtually uninhabited by whites.

In February 1846, the main body of settlers left Nauvoo. Young organized twenty-four companies of 100 each and personally selected the leader of each company. Mormons were unable to sell most of their property, and that which was sold went for a fraction of its value. Both Utopian Robert Owen and the Catholic Church looked at the property, particularly the Temple, but decided not to purchase it. Before leaving Nauvoo, Young was continually threatened with arrest. The Mormons' trek was the largest and best-organized of all migrations to the West.

They spent the first winter on Potawatomi Indian lands just north of Omaha, Nebraska. Young supervised the building of 538 log houses and 83 sod houses for 3,483 people. In early 1847, he assumed personal responsibility for the pilot company of 159 pioneers, seventy-two wagons, sixty-six oxen, and ninety-two horses. The company, whose goal was to chart the path to the Great Salt Lake Valley for others to follow, used artificial horizons, a circle of reflection, and sextants but did not employ professional guides.

Initially, the company traveled the Oregon Trail along the Platt River, averaging ten miles a day. They used dry buffalo dung as fuel for their fires. They encountered hostile Pawnees and friendly Sioux Indians. On July 7, 1847, they reached Fort Bridger on the Green River. John C. Fremont's description of the Great Salt Lake Region was favorable; however, Jim Bridger, the famous scout, told them that the Indians in the area were unfriendly, and that the area's cold nights would prevent the growth of crops. When they reached within fifty miles of the Great Salt Lake (near Ogden, Utah), another scout gave them a favorable report of their destination, including its agricultural potential.

On July 24, 1847, Young got his first view of the Great Salt Lake Valley from the the mouth of Emigration Canyon and said, "This is the Place." Compared with Nauvoo, the Salt Lake Valley was dry and remote. Bounded by majestic snow-capped mountains, it was forty miles long from north to south and twenty-five miles wide. Young laid out the city with streets eight rods wide in a perfect grid.

During the winter of 1847-48, Young reorganized the First Presidency of the Church and appointed Heber Kimball First Counselor and his own cousin, Willard Richards, Second Counselor. Also, Young assumed the designation of prophet, seer, and revelator that had been held by Joseph Smith. By spring of 1848, the settlement had grown from 300 to over 5,000 people.

The first crop was severely reduced by an invasion of crickets that they could not get rid of until seagulls came from the Great Salt Lake to consume them. The Mormons benefitted economically during 1849, when wagonloads of gold prospectors passed through on their way to California. They repaired the travelers' harnesses and wagons and sold them supplies.

During 1849 and 1850, Young sent two representatives to Washington, D.C., to lobby for statehood for Utah. He preferred to skip territorial status because it would involve federal observers who could limit his control. President Taylor denied the request for statehood; however, upon Taylor's death, President Fillmore granted territorial status to Utah, which was named for the Ute Indians in the region. Mormons had called it Deseret. Young was chosen as Utah's first territorial governor, and Mormons were appointed as Associate Justice of the Territory's Supreme Court, U.S. Marshal, and U.S. Attorney.

Young counseled staying on friendly terms with the Ute Indians in the area. He asked the Mormons to "feed them and clothe them ... never turn them away hungry" and "teach them the art of husbandry." In his opinion, "It was cheaper to feed the Indians than to fight them." From 1850 to 1855, the number of Mormons in the Salt Lake Basin grew to 60,000, mainly from the East but including 15,000 from Great Britain.

In May 1857, President Buchanan sent 2,500 federal troops to Utah to remove Young as territorial governor. As had occurred earlier, anti-Mormon sentiment was rampant, principally due to their belief in polygamy. Young accepted President Buchanan's appointed governor, Alfred Cumming, but refused to let troops enter Salt Lake City. Young threatened to burn every structure built by the Mormons if the army entered the City. Mormons vacated the City until July 1858, when peace was made with the federal government.

The settlement continued to expand. Young was a good businessman and by the late 1850s Salt Lake City prospered from lumbering, lumber mills, and tanneries. On August 23, 1877, Young became ill and was diagnosed with cholera. His condition worsened, and he died on August 27, exclaiming the name of the founder: "Joseph! Joseph! Joseph!" John Taylor, senior member of the Council of Twelve, became president of the Church in 1880.

Brigham Young provided leadership for the Mormon Church at a critical period in its history that enabled it to become the largest religion established in the United States. He contributed heavily to the growth of the American frontier and is considered one of the great colonizers of the United States.

## *Reverend Algernon Crapsey (1847-1927)*

"In successive stages of my career I have been influenced by the master minds of Newman, Darwin, and Karl Marx.... In this process of growth I could no longer think within the confines of the literal interpretation of the creeds of the [Episcopal] Church of which I was a member and minister. In my effort to interpret the creeds in light of my increasing knowledge I came in conflict with the authorities of my Church, was accused, tried, and condemned as a heretic. I then renounced my ministry and changed the pulpit for the platform."

Algernon Sidney Crapsey, *The Last of the Heretics*

Reverend Algernon Crapsey, Rector of St. Andrew's Church, was an Episcopalian minister whose belief in Darwin's theory of evolution brought him into conflict with the authorities of his church. He was accused, tried, and condemned as a heretic. He admitted to being a heretic, which he defined as "one who thinks and gives voice to his own thought; chooses his own way; does not submit easily to authority."

In 1905, Dr. Crapsey began a series of lectures/sermons on the subject of religion and politics that attracted large audiences and provided material for one or two newspaper columns a week. He began his lectures by tracing the relationship of church and state down through the ages. By his tenth lecture, he had reached the time of the Rochester of his day. He condemned the degree of commercialization in not only the City but also the church. Most listeners thought that he was being too critical.

Dr. Crapsey's difficulties began with the next lecture in which he attacked churchmen of the day for not letting scientific knowledge influence their interpretation of the Scriptures. Initially, he approached the topic by making a general statement, but then he proceeded by questioning the credibility of the virgin birth. This drew an immediate response from the audience, other local ministers, and, of course, from the local press. The Episcopal bishop, Bishop Walker, visited Rochester to investigate the incident. Dr. Crapsey's last sermon in the series on the social Gospel was virtually unnoticed.

In 1924, Dr. Crapsey summarized his earlier thoughts in *The Last of the Heretics:* "I asserted that Jesus was born and that He lived as we live; that He died as we die; that the story of the immaculate birth was unknown to Him, to His Mother, or to the early Christian church. For that I was tried and convicted and deprived of my pastorate. What was heresy in 1906 is now orthodoxy."

The trial of Dr. Crapsey, which was conducted by church officials in Batavia, raised questions that dominated sermons in Rochester for some time. Dr. Crapsey had his defenders, mainly liberal churchmen who supported his appeal of the conviction. He published his lecture in a book, *Religion and Politics,* which sold well. Unfortunately, most of its readers concentrated on his position on the credibility of the virgin birth and ignored his broader social message.

In December 1906, Bishop Walker terminated Dr. Crapsey as rector of St. Andrew's Episcopal Church. Fifty prominent Rochesterians requested that he prepare a series of lectures to be delivered locally. The manager of the Lyceum Theater volunteered the use of his building for a series of Sunday evening lectures in January. Large crowds attended his lectures, and he received invitations to speak at Temple B'rith Kodesh and the Unitarian Church. This interest motivated Dr. Crapsey and his supporters to form a new Brotherhood of nonsectarian members. Beginning on October 6, 1907, the Brotherhood continued the series of Sunday evening services at the Lyceum Theater and did settlement work in the slums.

Before resuming the services, Dr. Crapsey traveled to Europe to attend the Hague Peace Congress. Upon his return to Rochester, he gave his first lecture in the series for the Brotherhood to an overflow audience. The lecture was entitled: "The New Theology in England and Its Relation to the Social and Political Life of the Country." That winter, Dr. Crapsey gave thirty lectures about intellectual and social issues facing the church in Rochester and in the nation.

Dr. Crapsey's lectures in the Lyceum Theater continued for seven years, with subjects ranging from his philosophical views to his thoughts on social problems. By 1912, his lectures were all about the "gospel of Socialism." Although he was not comfortable with its materialistic aspects, he served as an organizer of the Socialist party in Rochester in a critical election year. As Dr. Crapsey became more liberal, he moved away from the views of his principal backers in the Brotherhood. In 1913, the Brotherhood dissolved, and its featured speaker became a parole officer for the State Industrial School at Industry, the area's reform school.

The Crapsey home became a community center. Mrs. Crapsey prepared meals for needy families and for people who were ill. Their daughter, Adelaide, started a sewing club that made clothing with donated material for poor children. A Bible study group met at the Crapsey home weekly. Dr. Crapsey organized gardening activities using vacant lots in the city, which were allocated to needy families. This gardening activity was modeled on a successful program that had begun in Philadelphia in 1908. In 1910, Dr. Crapsey's son, Paul, succeeded his father in running the Rochester program, which continued for three more summers.

In 1924, Dr. Crapsey wrote his autobiography, *The Last of the Heretics,* which City Historian Blake McKelvey called "the most stimulating book written in Rochester during these years." Dr. Crapsey cited the influence that Newman, Darwin, and Karl Marx had on him: "Under the inspiration of Newman, I became a Neo-Catholic and High Church clergyman of the Protestant Episcopal Church. Under the guidance of Darwin, I became an Evolutionist, a rationalist and a disciple of the Higher Criticism.... From first to last, I have been a Humanist...."

## Bishop Bernard McQuaid (1825-1909)

"Bernard McQuaid never allowed sentiment, much less sentimentality, to interfere with duty. The Episcopal motto he had taken was *'Salus animarum lex suprema':* 'The supreme law is the saving of souls.' The motto testified to his awareness of his new responsibility. He entered upon this responsibility as a man of both experience and courage. A teenager from Lima was in the audience when Bishop McQuaid was installed in office. Years later this Lima lad, now Archbishop Edward Quigley of Chicago, used to recall McQuaid's words in his inaugural sermon: 'I come here without fear, knowing what is to be done.' Ability and fearlessness were to be the hallmarks of his whole regime."                          Father Robert F. McNamara,
*The Diocese of Rochester 1868-1968*

Bishop McQuaid was known for his contributions to education, principally Catholic parochial education. He said, "The schools are my greatest glory." He was held in high esteem by his peers and his superiors, and he participated in the 1869-70 Council of the Vatican in Rome. He sponsored the establishment and support of orphanages in the Rochester Diocese and was the author of a number of articles, including "Our American Seminaries" and "Christian Free Schools." Highly regarded by Protestant and Jewish clergy in Rochester, he was a civic-minded individual who served on the Rochester Parks Commission.

Bernard J. McQuaid was born in New York City on December 15, 1825, to Bernard and Mary Maguire McQuaid, immigrants from Ireland. When he was an infant, his family moved to Jersey City, where his father worked in a glass factory. Young McQuaid's mother died in 1827, and his father, who remarried, died five years later. His stepmother was not interested in raising him, so she placed him in the Roman Catholic Orphan Asylum on Prince Street in Manhattan where he was guided by Sister Elizabeth Boyle. She instilled in him the strong personal qualities of perseverance and self-reliance.

McQuaid attended Chambly College, a preparatory seminary near Montreal, Quebec. In 1843, he began his studies at St. Joseph's, the New York diocesan seminary on the campus of Fordham University. In 1846, the Jesuits replaced the Vincentian fathers at the seminary. McQuaid was ordained on January 16, 1848, and was subsequently assigned to St. Vincent Church in Madison, New Jersey, and later to St. Patrick's Church in Newark.

While in the Diocese of Newark, Father McQuaid was instrumental in founding Seton Hall College and Seminary. He developed his talents in finance, oratory, and education. In 1866, Father McQuaid was named vicar general, second-in-command, of the Diocese of Newark. Early in 1868, he was consecrated as Bishop of Rochester. The Bishop of Newark had tried to retain him, even though it was said that Father McQuaid's "zeal sometimes runs over and floods his neighbor's field."

Father McQuaid arrived in Rochester in 1868 to become the first bishop of the newly created Diocese of Rochester. The Diocese was comprised of eight counties, 4,431 square miles, and a population of 377,000, of whom 54,500 were Catholics.

One of the first issues that Bishop McQuaid addressed was the ongoing debate about Christian free schools. He lectured in Corinthian Hall, asserting that public education in a democracy should be available to all children. He believed that public funds should be provided to all religious denominations for Christian free schools with teachers that had the confidence of Christian parents.

Protestant churches leaders agreed with this proposal; they thought that religion was being underemphasized in public schools. Reading the Bible in public schools was one of the issues. Subsequently, it was banned along with other religious instruction in public schools. Finally, after six years of lobbying, the Rochester Free Academy was built in March 1874 and occupied by 300 students and nine teachers.

The Free Academy was popular among Protestant as well as Catholic students. By 1888, student enrollment approached 700, causing overcrowded conditions. The school day was divided into halves, underclassmen in the morning and upperclassmen in the afternoon. Bishop McQuaid offered free parochial education to all Catholic children. By 1890, the percentage of Rochester's Catholic children in grade schools was higher than all cities except Newark and Philadelphia. Just under 7,000, taught principally by nuns of the Sisters of St. Joseph, were enrolled at fourteen parochial schools.

Bishop McQuaid's greatest contributions were in primary education and in establishing St. Andrew's Preparatory Seminary and St.

Bernard's Theological Seminary. He had less success in secondary education and never fulfilled his goal to found a college, even though he considered buying the buildings in Lima when the Methodist Seminary moved to Syracuse.

Fortunately, Bishop McQuaid was successful in establishing three high schools for girls: Academy of the Sacred Heart, St. Mary's Academy, and, in 1871, a high school operated by the Sisters of St. Joseph that subsequently became Nazareth Academy. In 1878-79, he was unsuccessful in his first attempt to convince the Jesuits in Buffalo to establish a boy's high School in Rochester.

By July 1893, the Catholic church had sixteen parishes in Rochester serving 41,836 churchgoers. The church building program had boomed during the 1880s. The next major building project for the diocese was St. Bernard's Seminary on Lake Avenue. The Seminary was officially dedicated by Bishop McQuaid in August 1893, the evening before his silver jubilee at the Cathedral. He had ensured a capable staff of professors by sending selected scholars to Rome during the 1880s. The emphasis was on broad cultural education rather than study in theology only.

In October 1898, the seventy-fifth anniversary of the parish, St. Patrick's Cathedral was consecrated. It was also the thirtieth anniversary of Bishop McQuaid's installation as Bishop of Rochester and the fiftieth anniversary of his ordination. In 1905, Father Thomas F. Hickey was appointed Titular Bishop of Rochester to assist the aging Bishop McQuaid.

In 1906, Bishop McQuaid finally got his Catholic high school for boys—Cathedral High, which later became Aquinas Institute. In 1908, Bishop McQuaid dedicated the new Hall of Theology at St. Bernard's Seminary. Bishop Bernard J. McQuaid died in 1909 and was interred in Holy Sepulcher Cemetery on Lake Avenue. A half century after his death, McQuaid Jesuit High School was named for him.

## *Bishop Fulton J. Sheen (1895-1979)*

"On October 26, 1966, Pope Paul VI officially named Fulton Sheen Bishop of Rochester, New York. It was shocking, front-page news. Sheen was seventy-one and lacked parish and administrative experience. He was now to leave the Society of the Propagation of the Faith, where he had been a striking success. The New York *Times* reported that he had raised more than $100 million during his sixteen years as director. A later examination showed the total sum to have approached $200 million. In 1950, donations amounted to $3.5 million; in 1965, the figure had skyrocketed to nearly $16 million."

Thomas C. Reeves, *America's Bishop: The Life and Times of Fulton J. Sheen*

In addition to his success with the Society of the Propagation of the Faith, Msgr. Sheen was a highly regarded television personality. He was also known for converting Heywood Broun, Henry Ford II, Fritz Kreisler, and Clare Boothe Luce, among others, to the Catholic faith.

Bishop Sheen had a strong academic background. Following his ordination after attending St. Paul's Seminary in Minnesota, he did graduate work at the Catholic University of America in Washington, D.C., and at the University of Louvain, Belgium, where, in 1923, he earned a Doctorate in Philosophy. He was invited to work on an Agrégé en Philosophie degree, which was considered a super Ph.D. While working on this degree, he studied in England and Rome and wrote a book, *God and Intelligence,* which many considered his finest written work.

Upon completion of his graduate work, Father Sheen was invited to become a Professor of Thomistic Philosophy at Columbia University and to assist Msgr. Ronald Knox in establishing a Catholic college at Oxford University. He received many other teaching offers, including one that he wanted to accept, to organize and become the first department head of the philosophy department at the seminary in Detroit.

However, Father Sheen's superior, Bishop Dunne of Peoria, Illinois, appointed him assistant pastor at St. Patrick's parish in Peoria. He spent the next year in routine parish work. Finally, the bishop called him into his office and told him that he was being assigned as Professor of Philosophy at the Catholic University in Washington, D.C. When Father Sheen asked the bishop why he had not sent him there upon his return from Europe, the bishop replied, "Because after the success you had in Europe, it was rumored that you would obey nobody. I wanted to find out if you were obedient and would do what you were told."

Many church members thought that in appointing Msgr. Sheen Bishop of Rochester, Cardinal Spellman was removing his adversary from the Archdiocese of New York to reduce the possibility that Msgr. Sheen would succeed him as archbishop. Differences between the two men had been ongoing for ten years, partly because Msgr. Sheen had demanded and maintained total control of the funds that he had received as head of the Society of the Propagation of the Faith.

In 1966, Cardinal Spellman was seventy-seven years old, two years beyond the age at which the Pope had asked bishops to resign voluntarily. The cardinal wanted to continue as archbishop so that he could chose his successor. Pope Paul VI granted Cardinal Spellman his wish. According to Thomas C. Reeves in *America's Bishop:*

> The cardinal knew that removing his antagonist from the archdiocese would not be easy. Fulton was highly popular with Vatican Propagation officials due to his fund-raising abilities, and he was known to be on excellent terms with the Holy Father. He was the most widely known and popular Catholic priest in America. Spellman must have known how to get his way with Paul VI, however. A perceptive student of the cardinal has called him "perhaps the closest equivalent of a twentieth century American Richelieu that our secular republic has produced."

Msgr. Sheen was asked to come to Rome for an audience with the Pope and was told of the decision to transfer him from the Archdiocese of New York. He was offered a choice of two archdioceses and five dioceses; he chose Rochester. Msgr. Sheen would replace Bishop Edward Kearney, a popular eighty-two-year-old bishop who had productively led the diocese since 1937.

Two weeks after Cardinal Spellman announced his continuance in office, he called a press conference to announce that Pope Paul VI had appointed Msgr. Sheen Bishop of Rochester. The cardinal and the new bishop stood together for a half hour allowing photographers to take pictures. One writer observed: "Both were beaming."

Cardinal Spellman commented: "Just as every priest looks forward to the day when he can be a pastor, so I am sure, every bishop dreams of having a diocese of his own—not because of worldly ambition, but simply because a bishop by calling is a shepherd, and a shepherd seeks a flock." Bishop Sheen said, "I am a soldier in the army of the church. The general has told me to go to Rochester and I love it. I am a lover of souls, and in Rochester I will be even closer to priests and people."

The Roman Catholic Diocese of Rochester contains twelve counties and is spread over 7,455 square miles from Lake Ontario in the north to the Pennsylvania state line in the south, and from Livingston County, bordering on the Diocese of Buffalo, to the west and to Chemung County, bordering on the Diocese of Syracuse, to the east. In 1966, the diocese had 450,000 Catholics, about 36 percent of the population of the twelve counties making up the diocese, which had 10,350 students in parochial schools and over 2,000 trained lay teachers.

Bishop Sheen arrived in Rochester at a time when the decrees of Vatican Council II were being implemented. The vernacular Mass, instead of the Mass said in Latin, had been introduced in 1964, pastors were redesigning altars so that priests faced the congregation while saying Mass instead of having their back to them, and many more hymns were being sung.

Other changes were taking place during the sixties. In his autobiography, *Treasure in Clay,* Bishop Sheen notes:

> The sixties had a peculiar philosophy, which affected every person regardless of his faith or lack of faith. It may be described in two ways: first, what was generally good in the sixties was the shift from the individual to the social. In the sixties, a social consciousness arose in which the love of neighbor was too often purchased at the cost of neglect of God; at times, individual justice was ignored so long as one was fighting for social justice.

The second characteristic of the sixties, which seems to be in contradiction but is not, was the emphasis on the "me." The "I" of each person is accepted as the valid criterion. In the beginning is not the Word, but in the beginning is the I and it was good. Anything that stands opposite the self is a negation of self. This became as Sartre put it, "My neighbor is hell"; and by "neighbor" Sartre included even God, for God opposes the self as the absolute. As a consequence of these two assumptions, a sense of personal guilt and sin began to vanish, The only sins were social sins. This made it difficult for religion and morality in the sixties....

On December 14, 1966, Bishop Sheen was greeted by 3,000 people at the Greater Rochester International Airport. Upon his arrival, he commented that he had been "helping 800 dioceses in the world" and that "I have an ardent desire to spend myself and to be spent, to get my arms around Rochester." Referring to his role as a television personality, he said, "Now you've seen me live, and I'm sure you're disappointed."

The following day, Bishop Sheen's 90-minute installation ceremony was held in Sacred Heart Cathedral, attended by Cardinal Spellman, seven of his auxiliary bishops, thirty-three other bishops, the lieutenant governor of New York, the mayor of Rochester, clergy of all denominations, Clare Booth Luce, and lay people, who made up half of the congregation.

In an apostolic letter, Pope Paul VI declared: "Everything that you have so tirelessly accomplished in the past, by deed and by the spoken and written word to feed the sheep of Christ's flock has won you universal acclaim. We now nourish the fond hope that in the future you will undertake even greater things."

One ongoing difference of opinion between Bishop Sheen and Cardinal Spellman, Archbishop of New York, concerned the war in Vietnam. Bishop Sheen was anti-war and supported the Pope's stance on the conflict. Cardinal Spellman was pro-war. Bishop Sheen called for withdrawal of U.S. troops from Vietnam. Cardinal Spellman, in his role as head of the Military Ordinariate, told American forces in Vietnam: "They were holy crusaders engaged in Christ's war against the Vietcong and the people of North Vietnam."

In his travels around the diocese, Bishop Sheen met Father Michael Hogan at St. Francis DeSales Church in Geneva. The Bishop, who needed a personal secretary for office work and typing, chose Father Hogan as his secretary to handle appointments and administrative tasks. He called Father Hogan "a joy and an inspiration."

Among his unspecified duties, Father Hogan served as the Bishop's chauffeur. A local Dodge-Plymouth dealer lent the Bishop a new car every year. One day, Bishop Sheen commented to his chauffeur, "When the good Lord was on earth, He had to go around Jerusalem on an ass; but it is my privilege, thanks to you, to be driving a Plymouth around the diocese." Father Hogan responded, "Yes, but you still have an ass to drive you."

Bishop Sheen's accomplishments included the installation of certified audits of diocesan finances, consultation with priests of the diocese on appointments, and the provision of homes for low-income families. Education was another of his priorities; soon after his arrival in Rochester, he directed that the salaries of all teachers in parochial schools be increased. He also improved the seminary in Rochester by bringing in professors with national reputations.

In addition, Bishop Sheen's tenure as Bishop of Rochester was notable for his ecumenical efforts. On January 30, 1967, he spoke to 2,300 people in a synagogue. Rabbi Herbert Bronstein introduced him by saying that one would have to look back to the fifth century to observe a parallel to that evening's gathering. A month later, Bishop Sheen and Rabbi Marc Tannenbaum, Director of Interreligious Affairs of the American Jewish Committee, spoke to an audience of 900 Christian and Jewish leaders. After concluding his talk, Bishop Sheen embraced Rabbi Tannenbaum, who called it "an embrace that seemed to close an alienation gap of 1,900 years."

Unfortunately, one incident in Bishop Sheen's tenure as Bishop of Rochester cast a shadow over his many accomplishments. One of his long-term concerns was the shortage of low-cost housing for the poor. He decided to give some church property to the U.S. Department of Housing and Urban Renewal (HUD). He wrote to Robert Weaver, Secretary of HUD, offering a gift of one of the parishes in the inner city of Rochester, whose property was to be used for construction of housing for the poor. President Lyndon Johnson's

Great Society was looking at many ways of helping the disadvantaged at this time.

Bishop Sheen had obtained permission to do this from the Board of Consultors, the Apostolic Delegate, and from the Vatican. Unfortunately, local urban renewal officials had not been consulted. Officials from HUD visited Rochester and chose the Church of St. Bridgit, which occupied a square block in the inner city. The parish had a dynamic pastor, Father Francis Vogt, but the congregation had shrunk to under 100 parishioners. The property of St. Bridget's included one and a half acres of property, a church, a rectory, and a school—all valued at $680,000. The parish was in a neighborhood scheduled for urban renewal; in fact, demolition of some buildings had already begun.

Father Vogt was against giving his parish away and suggested that the congregation be consulted. He said, "There is enough property around without giving away the church and the school." The bishop wanted to move along with his plan and said there was not enough time to do that because he wanted to announce the plan on Ash Wednesday. Auxiliary Bishop Hickey recommended delay; however, Bishop Sheen issued a press release on February 29, 1968, announcing the arrangements that he had made with HUD.

The morning after the announcement, six Monroe Community College students, who were volunteers at the parish, picketed outside the Bishop's offices. They carried signs with the messages "God's House Belongs to His People" and "Save St. Bridget's." The parish received many telephone calls; all of the callers were opposed to the deal with the federal government. The Bishop's office received many letters from bitter parishioners. Bishop Sheen visited a parochial school, and his car was surrounded by several hundred protesters, many of whom threw pebbles at it.

The Priests' Association of Rochester drafted a letter with twenty-two signers requesting that St. Bridget's be spared. Subsequently, over 100 additional priests signed the letter. The Rochester *Democrat and Chronicle* sided with the protesters and strongly disagreed with the Bishop's action. Bishop Sheen was overwhelmed by the negative response. His experience up to this time had been one of obedience to the authority of the church.

On March 3, Bishop Sheen cancelled his offer to HUD and was not available for discussion of the topic. The *Democrat and*

*Chronicle* headline was "ST. BRIDGET'S SPARED; JOY REIGNS." One of the main points of contention was that the bishop had not sought the opinion of the people of the parish. Later, Father Vogt said that if the bishop had asked them, they probably would have agreed to giving away the church and the school.

This incident sparked Bishop Sheen's decision to move on from being the bishop of a diocese. While watching the pickets, he told Father Patrick Collins, "That night, that very night, I resigned as Bishop of Rochester. It took Pope Paul VI some time to accept it. But, that night, as far as I was concerned, I left Rochester." After this event, his outlook was not as upbeat as it had been, and he was not as willing to take on new projects.

However, Bishop Sheen's interest in low-cost housing was not lessened. On April 16, 1968, the Bishop Sheen Housing Foundation was established. Seventy members donated ten dollars a week to start a housing fund. When the Bishop retired as Bishop of Rochester, eighteen low-income families had been provided with homes. In 1980, the Bishop of Rochester, Bishop Matthew Clark, combined the Housing Foundation with the housing commission run by the Episcopal Diocese of Rochester, forming the Bishop Sheen Ecumenical Housing Foundation.

On September 20, 1969, Bishop Sheen celebrated his fiftieth year as a priest. He wrote a twenty-page booklet that he sent to friends; he asked that there be no gathering to celebrate the occasion. His retirement was announced in mid-October. At the age of seventy-four, the announcement noted that he was retiring due to age.

Msgr. Joseph Hogan was named as his successor. Bishop Sheen was permitted to name his successor, and he chose the highly educated, popular brother of his secretary. Bishop Sheen noted: "I am resigning the Diocese. I am not resigning work. I am not retiring, I am regenerating." He said that he planned to move back to New York City, where he maintained a small apartment, "to teach any place I can, do TV, and enter into dialog with unbelievers."

Bishop Sheen was given the honorary title of Archbishop of Newport on the Isle of Wight. He noted that he was honored to be archbishop of an ancient church seat but quipped: "It is very much like being made a Knight of the Garter. It is an honor to have the Garter, but it does not hold up anything." Later, he was appointed Assistant at the Pontifical Throne. He considered this an honor "because my heart was always at the throne of Peter."

In a CBS interview with Mike Wallace, Bishop Sheen noted that he might have gone farther in the church "but I refused to pay the price." Wallace asked him what the price was. Without being specific, he responded, "Well, I felt it would be disloyalty to my own principles, and I think to Christian practice."

Statue of Mercury atop the Kimball Tobacco Factory
Courtesy West, a Thompson Company

# CHAPTER 10

# ROCHESTER STORIES

### The Statue of Mercury on the Rochester Skyline

Originally, the statue of Mercury was erected on top of the chimney of the Kimball Tobacco Factory. Now it is located atop one of the buildings off Broad Street of West, a Thompson company, which was previously known as Lawyers' Cooperative Publishing Company.

Initially, William Kimball specialized in producing chewing tobacco using a patent bailer invented in 1869. He had backed Oscar W. Allison of Rochester, who had obtained the patents to a cigarette cutting machine. With it, Kimball became one of the first in the United States to produce cigarettes on a large scale. His business began to boom in 1880 when he manufactured 91.5 million cigarettes.

Kimball outgrew his factory at 34 Court Street on the east side of the Genesee River in 1881; he built a new factory on a island on the west side of the River. As the market for cigarettes grew, he phased out the manufacture of chewing tobacco and cut tobacco and concentrated on producing cigarettes. By 1883, the Kimball Tobacco Company had 800 employees, more than any other Rochester company. The revenue from cigarettes was $1.2 million that year. His best-selling brands were "Old Gold," "Peerless," "Three Kings," and "Vanity Fair." Eventually, Kimball produced a million cigarettes a day.

Kimball realized that many Victorian Rochesterians had reservations about his product; therefore, he made a special effort to ensure that his new factory was tastefully designed. The factory had a twelve-foot square, 150-foot-tall smokestack to carry carry fumes away from city streets. In 1885, the massive smokestack became a pedestal for a twenty-one-foot-tall statue of Mercury designed by Kimball's brother-in-law, J. Guernsey Mitchell. The statue of Mercury, the Roman god of commerce and messenger for the other gods, became the symbol of Rochester's skyline.

In 1890, the Kimball Tobacco Company was purchased by the American Tobacco Company. William S. Kimball died on March 25, 1895. The American Tobacco Company closed its Rochester operations in 1905. When the tobacco factory and its smokestack were razed in the mid-twentieth century, the statue of Mercury was placed in storage. The public wanted Mercury restored to the skyline, however. In 1974, Thomas Gosnell, CEO of Lawyers' Cooperative Publishing, contracted for a tower to be built on top of one of the firm's buildings to serve as the new pedestal for a restored Mercury.

The location of Mercury on the Kimball Tobacco Company smokestack, in the path of escaping smoke and acid fumes, had caused pitting of the statue. The pinholes in the statue had to filled and the statue refurbished before it was mounted on the new tower, where it reigns as Rochester's popular skyline symbol. The statue is owned by the City of Rochester.

## *Buffalo Bill's Rochester Connection*

William Frederick "Buffalo Bill" Cody was an army scout, a buffalo hunter, an Indian fighter, and Wild West Show performer. The Cody family moved to Rochester in 1874 and resided at 434 Exchange Street. They lived briefly at the Waverly Hotel on State Street and then moved to 10 New York Street, off Jefferson Avenue.

Cody was tall and broad-shouldered, with long, black, curly hair and a well-trimmed goatee and mustache. He smoked cigars and wore a wide-brimmed hat and a black coat with tails. A gold watch chain with large links hung across his vest. He was an extroverted, minimally educated product of the frontier.

Cody was born on February 26, 1846, in LeClair, Iowa. At the age of twelve, he killed his first Indian—to foil an attack on a wagon train. During the Civil War, he fought as a "Jayhawk" with a guerrilla band in Kansas. He joined the Union Army as a scout and was promoted to captain. In 1865, he married Louise Fredereci of St. Louis.

After the war, Cody became a U.S. Cavalry scout in campaigns against the Native Americans, who called him "Pahaska," the long-haired one. He left the army and worked as a hunter, a pony express rider, a stage coach driver, a trapper, a wagon master, and a wagon-train courier. He became known as "Buffalo Bill" after he killed 4,280 buffaloes in a year and a half to furnish meat for men building the Kansas Pacific Railroad. Also, he operated as a guide on buffalo hunts for celebrities such as General Philip Sheridan, Grand Duke Alexis of Russia, and James Gordon Bennett, the New York publisher.

Elmo Judson, using the pseudonym Ned Buntline, placed Buffalo Bill before the American public and made him famous. Judson wrote hundreds of stories in which Buffalo Bill was the hero. Cody's popularity, particularly in the East, encouraged him to go on the stage. His first thespian effort was *The Scout of the Plains* in Chicago. The play was poorly written, and the acting matched the quality of the play; nevertheless, it had considerable action and shooting, and the audience loved it. Later, the cast included Kit Carson, Jr., Bill's friend, Texas Jack, and Wild Bill Hickok.

By 1874, Cody had decided that a traveling company was not a good environment for his wife and three young children; he moved his family to Rochester. In 1875, Buffalo Bill starred at the Grand Opera House, later the Embassy, in his new home city. By that time,

Native Americans had joined the cast. When they were not on the stage, Cody and his crony, Texas Jack, sat in Main Street saloons in their western outfits and told stories of the Wild West.

Arta and Kit, the two oldest Cody children, attended School No. 2 on King Street. The school principal was Mary S. Anthony, Susan B. Anthony's sister. In April 1876, Arta and Kit contracted scarlet fever. Cody, who was performing in Boston at the time, received a telegram from Louise requesting him to come home. He arrived just before Kit died. Much of the light in Cody's life went out when Kit, his only son, was buried in Mt. Hope Cemetery.

Cody tired of life on the stage and rejoined the U.S. Cavalry as chief of scouts. He moved his family to Nebraska, except for Arta, who stayed behind in Rochester to study at the Livingston Park Academy in the Third Ward. Cody was motivated to join the army because the Sioux were stirring up unrest in the Dakotas. Feelings in the country were elevated by the massacre of General George Armstrong Custer and his men at Little Big Horn. Cody gained some notoriety by killing the Sioux chief, Yellow Hand, in a duel.

At the conclusion of the Sioux wars, Cody went back on the stage for the remainder of his life. Annie Oakley co-starred with him in his new show. They performed for Queen Victoria in England, where Cody became a companion of Edward, the Prince of Wales. During Queen Victoria's Golden Jubilee, Cody and the Prince of Wales gave the Kings of Belgium, Denmark, and Greece a wild ride at breakneck speed through London in Cody's Deadwood coach, while being chased by whooping and hollering Indians on horseback.

In 1883, Cody and his wife returned to Rochester to bury their eleven-year-old daughter, Orra, next to her brother in Mt. Hope cemetery. Cody's Wild West show came back to Rochester every year to perform. In 1904, Bill and Louise returned again to Rochester to inter their oldest daughter, Arta, alongside her brother and sister. She died at the age of thirty-eight, just three weeks before she was to marry an army surgeon.

Cody did not manage his finances well. He had to sell a half interest in his show to James C. Bailey, the Bailey of Barnum and Bailey. Eventually, Cody had to sell the remaining half of the show and go to work for the Sells Floto Circus.

Buffalo Bill Cody died in Denver in 1917 at the age of seventy-one. His fans viewed his body in the Colorado capitol before he was buried on Lookout Mountain. Bill was a legend in his own time and was one of the last remnants of a wild frontier. He became a symbol of a West that had changed forever.

### Sam Patch's Last Jump

Sam Patch was born in Pawtucket, Rhode Island, in 1807. While in his teens, he lived with his widowed mother and worked in a local cotton mill. Patch became an excellent swimmer and jumper at an early age. He jumped from the bridge near the mill, but his biggest challenge was jumping from the roof of a paper mill 100 feet above the adjacent river. In his early twenties, he moved to Paterson, New Jersey, to work as a spinner in a cotton mill.

The first jump for which Patch gained notoriety was a seventy-foot jump off a cliff into the chasm near Passaic Falls in New Jersey. A crowd had gathered to watch the construction of a bridge over the chasm; Patch eluded the town policemen and jumped. He repeated the jump at Paterson in July 1828; the following month he jumped from a platform at the masthead of a schooner moored off Hoboken.

The ultimate challenge was Niagara Falls. On October 6, 1828, Patch made a seventy-foot jump before a small crowd from the lower end of Goat Island. He advertised that he would make a 120-foot jump on October 17. The platform on Goat Island was about two-thirds of the way up the surrounding banks. He took off his coat and his shoes, tied a handkerchief around his waist, and leaped.

Patch became a national figure, although he was only twenty-two years old. His income far exceeded that of a cotton spinner. He talked about jumping off London Bridge. However, High Falls in Rochester was much closer. The jump at the 100-foot High Falls was scheduled for November 6, 1829, and a crowd of 3,000 gathered to watch him. He sent off his pet bear first. The bear jumped successfully and swam to the shore of the River. Patch tied his handkerchief around his waist, waved to the crowd, and made his own successful jump.

Patch planned a higher jump for Friday, November 13, 1829. A platform twenty-five-feet high was erected on the rock above High Falls on the Genesee River. A crowd of 7,000 people came from all over western New York State to watch. He wore a black handkerchief around his waist. Some people observed that he did not seem to have his usual confidence that day. One spectator thought that he swayed when he climbed the platform, but it was explained that he had a glass of brandy to ward off the chill.

Patch made a speech before he jumped: "Napoleon was a great man and a great general. He conquered armies and he conquered nations, but he could not jump the Genesee Falls. Wellington was a great man and a great general. He conquered Napoleon, but he could not jump the Genesee Falls. That was left for me, and I can do it and I will."

Patch jumped, but his arms flailed, he lost control of his body, and he struck the River at an angle with his arms and legs spread apart. It was his last jump. The River was dragged for his body, but it was not found. On March 17, 1830, a farmer breaking the ice on the River to water his horse at Charlotte found Patch, who was identified by the black handkerchief around his waist. He was buried in a pioneer cemetery at Charlotte.

Sam Patch's death was the subject of many editorials and sermons, and it triggered the writing of many poems and songs. Nathaniel Hawthorne wrote about him, and William Dean Howells told Patch's story in a novel, *The Wedding Journey*, in which he referred to Rochester as "the enchanted city." The temporary marker on Patch's grave read: "Here lies Sam Patch. Such is fame."

## *Rattlesnake Pete's Cure for Goiters*

"Rattlesnake Pete" Gruber ran a saloon and museum at 8 Mill Street in Rochester from 1893 until his death in 1932. Pete was born in Oil City, Pennsylvania, one year before Colonel Drake discovered oil in nearby Titusville. He began his snake collection with rattlesnakes and spotted adders from the hills around Oil City. Native Americans from the Cornplanter Reservation taught him how to capture snakes with a forked stick, and Seneca medicine men taught him how to extract snake oil. He added guns and Indian relics to his collection and began to charge admission. He took his museum on the road to Pittsburgh, Jamestown, and Buffalo, prior to settling in Rochester.

In addition to his tanks of reptiles, Gruber's museum housed many of nature's oddities, including two-headed calves, four-legged chickens, and eight-legged lambs. His museum also contained memorabilia such as John Wilkes Booth's meerschaum pipe and the battle flag of Custer's last charge, as well as the first electric chair used in New York State and the skull of General Philip Sheridan's horse. Gruber was a good customer of taxidermists; his collection included a hairless cow from India and a 3,500-pound Percheron horse.

Gruber was bitten by poisonous snakes thirty-three times: twenty-nine times by rattlesnakes and four times by copperheads. On one occasion, he was unconscious for nine days and did not fully recover for nine months. He obtained his snakes from the Bristol Hills and from Pennsylvania. Gruber had many snake remedies, including poultices for blood poisoning. One of his most unusual remedies was reducing a goiter by wrapping a rattlesnake tightly around the sufferer's neck. He brought new meaning to the words, "The cure was worse than the ailment." Pete Gruber, an outgoing showman in a snakeskin coat and vest, was a Rochester institution.

## The First McCormick Harvester

In 1831, Cyrus McCormick, a blacksmith from West Virginia, invented a reaper that could harvest as much wheat as seven men harvesting by hand. McCormick moved to Washington, D.C., to apply for a patent for his invention. While in Washington, he met Brockport Congressman E. B. Holmes. McCormick had been looking for someone to manufacture his reapers, and Holmes told him that Brockport's Bacchus and Burroughs foundry had been manufacturing farm implements since 1828.

In 1844, McCormick moved to Brockport and contracted Bacchus and Burroughs to make 100 harvesters to his design. The inventor encountered problems with these first reapers; however, on Frederick Root's farm in the Town of Sweden, one of the machines became the first in the United States to harvest wheat. In 1846, McCormick ordered another 100 harvesters to be built at the small canalside shop of Dayton S. Morgan and William H. Seymour. McCormick was much more satisfied with the second 100 machines. One of these is on display in Henry Ford's Greenfield Village Museum in Michigan.

Although the Genesee region had been the wheat basket of the country in the late 1700s and early 1800s, the center of wheat production moved to the Midwest in the late 1800s. McCormick moved to Chicago and became a wealthy man manufacturing harvesters. Brockport was a center for the manufacture of farm equipment into the 1890s; however, the shift of wheat production to the Midwest was accompanied by the relocation of farm equipment manufacturing there.

Frederick Root, on whose farm the first grain had been harvested by machinery, invented a grain cleaner and separator. In 1851, William H. Seymour manufactured the automatic raking reaper, which he called "the quadrant platform." Seymour's old partner, Dayton S. Morgan, manufactured his line of Triumph reapers for twenty years until 1894 when his factory was destroyed by fire.

The Bacchus and Burroughs foundry was taken over by the Johnson Harvester factory that employed just under 500 people and turned out 6,000 machines during its peak year in 1882. That year the factory burned down, and manufacturing was moved to Batavia, which presumedly had a more effective fire department than Brockport.

### The Society of the Genesee

According to noted local historian and author Donovan Shilling, the original Society of the Genesee was founded in 1897 by Louis Wiley, who edited a weekly Rochester newspaper, *The Tidings*. Members were history buffs from the Rochester region and others who had a tie to the City. From 1893 to 1895, Wiley had been business manager of the Rochester *Post-Express*. He moved to New York City and within four years was named editor of the New York *Times*.

Shortly after he became editor of the *Times*, Wiley founded the Society of the Genesee and held the first annual dinner in New York City in 1899. Many of Rochester's movers and shakers were invited as well as notables from other areas of the country. Attendees included governors, diplomats, political leaders from Washington, D.C., and famous scholars. Over the years, Presidents William Howard Taft and Theodore Roosevelt attended the banquets, as well as presidential aspirant William Jennings Bryan and Rochesterian Major General Elwell Otis, who put down the guerrilla uprising in the Philippine Islands at the close of the Spanish-American War.

The dinners were elegant and memorable. Souvenirs were provided to members of the Society of the Genesee and their guests to commemorate the annual event. In 1911, the souvenir was a ten-inch blue-ware depicting the "High Falls" of the Genesee River. The scene on the plate showed a heavy springtime flow of water over the falls raising clouds of spume. A New York Central & Hudson River passenger train was shown crossing the downtown railroad bridge parallel to Central Avenue. Inscribed on the back of the plate were the words:

ROYAL DALTON ENGLAND
SOCIETY OF THE GENESEE
THIRTEENTH ANNUAL DINNER

The dinner committee for the annual dinner in 1930 included Dr. Kenneth Mees, Director of the Research Laboratory for the Eastman Kodak Company. The nominee for president of the Society of the Genesee for 1931 was Thomas J. Watson, president of the International Business Machines Corporation. Previously, Watson had been the Rochester Branch Manager for the National Cash Register Company.

The nominee for vice president of the Society was Clarence E. Barbour, president of Brown University and former president of the Colgate Divinity School. The guest of honor was Frank Gannett, publisher of Gannett Newspapers; the after dinner speaker was Kent Cooper, general manager of Associated Press. The annual toastmaster for the banquet was the Society's founder, Louis Wiley of the New York *Times*. Board members in 1930 included James Wadsworth, Jr., Frank E. Gannett, and Frank E. Tripp, who later succeeded Gannett at Gannett Newspapers.

The annual dinner the following year was on February 9, 1931, at the Commodore Hotel, where George Eastman was the guest of honor. Eastman received the congratulations of his fellow Rochesterians, his New York City friends, and Society of the Genesee members who now lived elsewhere. His good friend, Dr. Rush Rhees, president of the University of Rochester, was one of the speakers. Eastman was presented with an engrossed parchment scroll and a bound volume of autographed letters from his friends and colleagues.

The thirty-fifth annual meeting of the Society of the Genesee was held on January 23, 1933, at the Commodore Hotel in New York City. At 5:00 p.m., before the meeting, members drifted into the hotel's lounges where they had informal discussions about the deepening Depression, the problems generated by the dust bowl in the southern Midwest, and FDR's plans for addressing unemployment.

At 7:30 p.m., the Society's president, Elon Huntington Hooker called to order the meeting of 700 members and guests, including the mayor of New York City, and proposed a toast to the Society's founder, Louis Wiley, and to the pioneers of Genesee Country. The toast was followed by a five-course dinner. After dinner, the Society of the Genesee honored Edward Bausch, son of John Jacob Bausch, co-founder of Bausch & Lomb Optical Company.

Elon Huntington Hooker's address that evening was entitled "Memories of Carthage: Traffic on the Early Waterways" about the hamlet of Carthage, which had been a bustling port at the head of navigation on the Genesee River. In introducing the speaker, Louis Wiley observed, "Mr. Hooker has a rare skill of endowing historic events and facts with an atmosphere of romance and realism ... history becomes a living, vital thing, and Carthage, a community almost microscopic in size, takes on the allure of the celebrated city of the same name in ancient times."

As noted by Donovan Shilling, Hooker's address included these comments:

> A famous citizen who owned a farm in Carthage was Hiram Sibley, born in North Adams, Massachusetts, in 1807, who migrated, at sixteen, to the Genesee Valley. Between 1840 and 1850, he became interested in the electric telegraph and, with Ezra Cornell and others, consolidated the small existing telegraph companies into the Western Union. It is said that the first meeting for the consolidation was held in Carthage on the broad piazza of Elon Huntington's home.

The Society of the Genesee was a vital organization in its day. Eventually, interest waned and other events, such as World War II, had a higher priority in people's schedules.

In 1995, a historical writers group called the New Society of the Genesee was founded by William and Martha Treichler, publishers of the *Crooked Lake Review* of Hammondsport, and Donovan Shilling. The New Society of the Genesee is a less formal organization than its predecessor, and its members are not necessarily the movers and shakers of the Rochester region but are in some way involved with the writing of local history. Monthly luncheon meetings in the region have replaced the annual banquet in New York City.

The "reasons for being" of the New Society of the Genesee proposed by the founders are:

"WHERAS: We join together monthly ... to enjoy the fraternity and companionship of those also interested in local history and

WHEREAS: We all have a common interest in promoting through lecture, teaching, writing, and/or publishing our accounts of local people, places, or events and

WHERAS: We all reside in a geographic area of Western New York between and including the Finger Lakes and the Niagara Frontier and

WHEREAS: We all have a common link to the Genesee Valley and its tributaries and waterways and

WHEREAS: Our forebears did enjoy such an organization...."

## *The Rochester Subway*

In 1921, two years after the last barge passed through Rochester on the Erie Canal, the City of Rochester purchased from New York State the Canal right-of-way through the City and through the Towns of Brighton, Greece, and Pittsford. In November 1921, Mayor Edgerton signed the ordinance that authorized the construction of the Rochester subway. Construction was authorized to provide an interconnecting "belt line" for freight traffic for the five steam railroads serving the City and to remove interurban electric trolley cars from the downtown streets.

When the Erie Canal opened in 1825, many of Rochester's industries located along the waterway. The proposed subway was considered an inexpensive way to provide freight service to those businesses. Its route facilitated interconnections with the steam railroads and the New York State Barge Canal terminal near Mt. Hope Avenue on the east bank of the Genesee River. It was estimated that 20,000 freight cars a year would use the subway.

Four interurban railways had begun serving Rochester between 1900 and 1910: the Rochester & Eastern Rapid Railway, the Rochester, Lockport & Buffalo Railway, the Rochester & Sodus Bay Railway, and the Rochester & Syracuse Railway. The interurban cars were larger than city trolley cars and occasionally were operated as trains. They used the existing trolley car tracks and, because of their size, put pedestrians and other vehicles at risk. The interurban cars traveled faster than street railways and frequently derailed on sharp curves designed for slower speeds.

In 1912, nineteen fatal traffic accidents occurred in downtown Rochester. Main Street, on which many of the accidents occurred, was called the "Aisle of Death." Pressure to remove the interurban cars from city streets grew as the accidents increased. A roof over the canal downtown and an upper deck on the canal aqueduct over the Genesee River would be added when the subway was built. Traffic congestion downtown would be reduced considerably by the addition of a roadway (Broad Street) parallel to Main Street.

In 1920, City Engineer E. A. Fisher initiated plans to use the abandoned Erie Canal bed for an industrial and interurban railway. Per Andrew Lipman in "The Rochester Subway," his plan included:

• Constructing the covered portion from South Avenue to Brown Street

- Widening and deepening the canal bed and building new bridges at intersecting streets
- Constructing the overhead electrical system, interchanges, sidings, signal system, stations, and tracks

On November 22, 1921, the Rochester Common Council passed the ordinance that authorized construction of the part of the subway that connected the Buffalo, Rochester & Pittsburgh Railway west of Oak Street and the Lehigh Valley Railroad south of Court Street. In January 1922, Rochester paid the State of New York $1.5 million for the title to the Canal property.

Work began on the subway in May 1922. The Canal bed from the Genesee aqueduct to Oak Street was dug wide enough to accommodate four sets of tracks with an overhead clearance of seventeen feet. Seven old bridges over the canal were removed and cut up for scrap. Temporary wooden ones were used until permanent steel bridges were built.

Tracks for most of the rest of the subway were laid in an open cut. This included the section from South Avenue to the eastern terminus and from Oak Street to the western terminus. The Canal bed also was widened and deepened in these sections to accommodate up to four sets of tracks. Sixteen vehicular bridges and three footbridges were constructed at intersecting streets. Three subway stations were built downtown: Court Street station at South Avenue, City Hall station between Exchange and Fitzhugh streets, and a station at West Main and Oak streets.

The subway was completed in late 1927 at a cost of $12 million. Barely three years after it was completed, the interurban electric railways, with which it was connected, began to fail. On July 31, 1930, the Rochester & Eastern Rapid Railway went out of business due to competition from increased motor vehicle traffic to and from Pittsford and Canandaigua. In April of the following year, the Rochester, Lockport & Buffalo switched to buses, and, two months later, the Rochester & Syracuse ceased operation. This left the Rochester & Sodus Bay, renamed the Rochester Transit Company, to operate the nine-mile-long subway using cars from the old Sodus Bay line. Fortunately, use of the freight transfer facilities that supported the five steam railroads increased.

The subway generated deficits every year, which caused Rochester Transit to increase fares on surface lines to make up the difference. After 1929, the local trolley service, a subsidiary of New York State Railways, operated under the threat of foreclosure against the State-owned parent. Since the Rochester trolley lines operated at a profit, the City considered buying the lines; however, the 1930 valuation of $26.7 million exceeded the City's borrowing capacity.

During the 1930s, the City of Rochester's credit was burdened by welfare debts caused by the Depression. By 1938, when the Public Service Commission approved the purchase of the trolley lines by private investors, buses had become the preferred method of travel. The new privately owned company replaced the trolleys with buses, and, by early 1940, trolleys had disappeared from all lines except the subway.

After being considered a white elephant for most of its life, the subway experienced a boom during the early 1940s. Gas rationing and the shortage of automobiles during World War II doubled the number of passengers carried by the subway. In 1947, it transported over five million passengers.

City Commerce Commissioner Harold McFarlin was so optimistic that he recommended extending the subway northward to Kodak Park and southward to a more accessible suburban terminal. However, a significant drop in the subway's ridership in 1948 forestalled the suggested expansion. Two consultants who evaluated the economics of operating the subway recommended dropping passenger service and concentrating on freight service.

The resumption of the production of automobiles after World War II, and the public's love affair with cars was the beginning of the end for the subway. Construction of the New York State Thruway in the late 1940s and early 1950s, with connections at LeRoy, West Henrietta Road, and Victor, also contributed to the subway's demise. It operated at a loss of $48,929 in 1950, and its projected loss for 1951 was $56,000.

On July 1, 1956, service on the subway ended. It could no longer compete with buses, cars, and trucks. The subway was a good idea when it was conceived, but, with the exception of the World War II years, it struggled financially for most of its life. Part of the subway right-of-way along the Erie Canal bed is now an expressway (Route 490). For many Rochester residents, remembering the subway is a nostalgia trip.

## *Rochester's NBA Team—The Rochester Royals*

The Rochester Royals, Rochester's professional basketball team in the late 1940s and early 1950s, evolved from roots in semi-professional basketball. Les Harrison, organizer, owner, and coach, was an accomplished businessman who built his team through successful player acquisitions and trades. His teams played opponents from larger cities whose teams had better facilities and ample funding.

Harrison, a high school basketball star, organized and played on two semi-pro teams in Rochester, one sponsored by Seagrams and the other by Eber Brothers, a local distributor. Players were paid by the game, and players for the competition were encouraged to join the Rochester teams. On two occasions, the Seagram entry competed in the World Professional Basketball Tournament in Chicago.

For the 1943-44 season, Harrison changed the name of the Seagram team to the Rochester Pros, who played in the 4,200-seat Edgerton Park Sports Arena. He scheduled opponents with national reputations, including the Harlem Globetrotters, and began to recruit players from farther afield, such as from Notre Dame and Dartmouth Colleges.

In the pre-National Basketball Association days of the early 1940s, two leagues dominated: the American Basketball League (ABL) in eastern cities and the National Basketball League (NBL) in the Midwest, which was the stronger league. The NBL had franchises not only in major cities such as Chicago and Cleveland but also in smaller cities, including Fort Wayne, Oshkosh, and Sheboygan.

Harrison and his brother, Jack, could not find a sponsor so they proceeded on their own: "My brother and I mortgaged everything we could lay our hands on, and we got a franchise ... I think it was $25,000." Jack, a lawyer, was the legal advisor for the team. A competition was initiated to chose a team name. The winning entry was "Royals" because "what would be more fitting than this as a name for the team Les Harrison is going to send out to bring the crown to Rochester."

The Rochester Royals won the league title in their first season with players such as Otto Graham, later the Cleveland Browns quarterback; Chuck Connors, who subsequently starred on television as *The Rifleman;* and Red Holzman, who later was associated with the Boston Celtics. The Royals played 100 exhibition games in 1945-46 in addition to fifty-four league games.

The following two years, 1946-47 and 1947-48, the Royals won the division title but were defeated in the league playoffs. Rochester fans became accustomed to watching a winning team. The Royals attracted large crowds and sold out most home games. Guards Bob Davies and Bobby Wanzer and center Arnie Risen formed the core of the team.

The Basketball Association (BBA) was formed during the late 1940s by wealthy eastern owners who needed something to fill their hockey stadiums when their hockey teams were on the road. The BBA needed talented players and was willing to pay for them. NBL teams began to switch to the BBA. The NBL joined with the BBA to form the National Basketball Association (NBA) that had an eastern division principally including former ABL teams and a western division of mainly former NBL teams. From 1948-49 through 1953-54, the Royals won two divisional championships and finished no lower than second.

Due to an aging line-up and a new fast-breaking style of play in the mid-1950s, the Royals began to lose more than they won. Because of earlier winning seasons, the Royals had only low draft picks. Also, Rochester did not have a nationally ranked collegiate program, like Boston and New York, from which they could draw "territorial" drafts. In addition, the Edgerton Park Sports Arena ("a glorified warehouse" according to Harrison) did not measure up to major city arenas.

The move of City population to the suburbs did not help to retain ticket-paying fans. Televising NBA games, including Royals games, also hurt attendance. Rochester's NBA team was now competing with entertainment programs for television viewers. In the 1956-57 season, the Royals shared the War Memorial with the Rochester Americans hockey team that outdrew them two to one. The Royal's fan base began to shift from white collar to blue collar.

Ironically, the team's early success probably contributed to its downfall in Rochester. According to Bobby Wanzer, "I think what happened was that in the beginning we were in demand ... and I guess we had a lot of season ticket holders. And ... we could not build any new fans because we were sold out in the beginning, so I think what happened is that after a while people stopped trying to get tickets."

Eventually, Harrison could no longer afford the financial losses and looked for a buyer for the team. The team moved to Ohio and became the Cincinnati Royals. The NBA Board of Governors negotiated a contract with NBC and wanted to broadcast only from "major-league" cities. The Syracuse Nationals survived until 1963 in a smaller market than Rochester. In any case, NBA basketball would have left Rochester by then.

Kevin Cook observed about Les Harrison in "The Rochester Royals: The Story of Professional Basketball" in *Rochester History*: "He provided Rochester and Monroe County with a rich sports history. The memories his Royals left are still cherished by many in the community. But just as important, is the example he set for others by overcoming relatively humble beginnings to reach the pinnacle of basketball success. He was truly a hometown success story."

## Rochester as "Smugtown, U.S.A."

In 1957, Rochester newspaperman Curt Gerling published *Smugtown, U.S.A.,* a book that contained descriptions of and anecdotes about Rochester's movers and shakers of that era. In addition to discussions about the City's newspapers, politics, and society, Gerling included a chapter on "How to Get Ahead" and one on "Our Millionaires—and Where They Got It."

In the conclusion of his book, Gerling explains what he meant by "Smugtown":

> In a sense, "Smugtown" does not precisely describe the older residents of Rochester. For families of three generations or more, it is apt to be a matter of complacency and assurance. With the gifts of inherited family and/or wealth they are content to live in their carefully constructed spheres, unmindful of the criticisms or living habits of their counterparts elsewhere.
>
> It is actually the "Johnny-Come-Latelys" who are the smug. First, they have interpreted this complacency as smugness, this assurance as snobbery. They feel that "to belong" they must fervently embrace and perhaps ape those whom they have so greatly misconceived. Our newcomers who are smug by cultivation, rather than by choice, fail to recognize the one gift that we long-time residents have—that is, a sense of humor.
>
> We have that rare gift that enables us to laugh at our own weaknesses and foibles. We may not change them, but we are aware of them. Thus in our appreciation of ourselves, we, with justification, feel somewhat superior to those whose superficial concepts of our ways make them so much smugger than we are.
>
> This social complacency has, in some respects, trickled down and warped our concepts of proper busi-

ness conduct. We are amazed that someone not of our town, not on the "inside" of things, can achieve success without our direct aid. We are not annoyed when some fellow gives us a lesson in how to get ahead or makes a mockery of our carefully charted courses. We acknowledge his success, not with misgivings but astonishment....

In 1993, Curt Gerling's son, William C. "Bill" Gerling reprinted his father's book. In "Publishers Note," he observes:

*Smugtown, U.S.A.*—In the hearts of many, Smugtown will always mean Rochester. While the Rochester Chamber of Commerce has over the years promoted the city as the Flour City, the Flower City, Rochester Means Quality, and most recently as the World Image Center, the social psyche of the boomtown on the Genesee has always been smug. In the last 160 years, smugness has risen with the rise of the yellow box factory and its spin-offs.

*Smugtown, U.S.A.* will give its present day readers an almost scary window into the Community as it exists today and will serve as a primer of how Rochester works.... While America's urban problems of the last forty years have not passed Rochester by, many things remain the same in how Rochesterians deal with each other in their social and political environment.

In the last years of the 1980s and the early 1990s, Rochester's smugness has seemed to have gravitated away from those who have old Rochester money: those families which had the foresight to buy the original Kodak, Haloid, or IBM stock when members of the Watson and Wilson families were walking the streets of Rochester to fund their fledgling enterprises.

In the years since "Smugtown" became part of the language of Rochester, much has changed in the social, business, and political climate. For years, Rochester's stable economy was buttressed by a huge workforce at Eastman Kodak Company and the payment of the annual springtime bonuses. The Kodak workforce was augmented by employees of other home-based companies such as Bausch & Lomb, Lawyers' Co-op Publishing Company, Ritter Dental, Neisner's, Haloid, the Todd Company, Taylor Instruments, Gannett, and R. T. French.

Many of these firms were family or closely held and the product or service was invented in Rochester as well as headquartered here. While several of these firms still exist in Rochester and some still have their headquarters in "Smugtown," many have merged with firms from outside Rochester or faded from the scene, upsetting the tranquil, almost plantation mentality of the workforce.

Gerling's description of Rochester as "Smugtown" was not meant to be a criticism; it was primarily an insider's view of the city, told in a humorous vein. The topic of Rochester as "Smugtown" was picked up by national newspapers and magazines. Unfortunately, the impression that they gave of Rochester was not always flattering.

## *Rochester, "Our Kindest City"*

In "Our Kindest City," in the July 1994 *Reader's Digest,* John S. Tompkins commented, "Twice in half a century, surveys acclaimed Rochester, New York, as the most caring city in America. I went there to find out why." In 1940, a study was conducted analyzing the character of forty-three U.S. cities. Rochester was rated first in altruism. From 1990 to 1992, Robert V. Levine, chairman of the psychology department, California State University in Fresno and thirty-six of his students surveyed thirty-six American cities to "find where the most helpful people lived."

Levine observed:

> This city of 231,000, located on Lake Ontario and home to some of America's best-known corporations, is a throwback to a kinder, gentler America. It is the sort of place where, as happened recently, a post-office employee will come out to help an absent-minded person retrieve a bank-deposit envelope accidentally dropped in a mailbox; where a group of workmen reportedly replaced—for free— the fire-damaged roof of a neighbor who had spent years turning a wreck into a livable house; where a truck driver retrieved a child's doll from the street after it had fallen from a car—and returned it to the doll's heart-broken 2 1/2-year-old owner....

> As part of the research, the students pretended to accidentally drop something on the street, to need change, or to be blind or lame and in need of assistance. More people went out of their way in Rochester than in any other city. East Lansing, Michigan, and Nashville, Tennessee, were second and third.... I was irresistibly drawn there to see for myself. Ultimately, I traced the city's strain of generosity back to its earliest days and to one strong, determined man....

> Eastman firmly believed that part of the responsibility of having money was doing good works, and that

success in business and community involvement go hand in hand. He set an example that other Rochester corporations followed. By World War I, Eastman's participation in city affairs and his financial support of educational, cultural and social-service programs was so large that Rochester was called "George Eastman's town."

Residents give more money to United Way of Greater Rochester on a per-capita basis than residents of any other United Way region of its size.... There are more than 250 nonprofit volunteer organizations, filling every conceivable need—thirteen supply services to the blind, thirty-six provide food for the needy. More Monroe County lawyers volunteer pro-bono work then those in any other county in New York State. Rochester is full of people who are willing to help one another. ... and they're willing to bloom where they're planted.

Rochester may be known as "Smugtown, U.S.A." but it is a flower in the Flower City's cap to be known also as the "the most caring city in America." Rochester has a reputation to maintain.

## Rochester's Ties to Hollywood

As early as 1889, Thomas Edison ordered Kodak film to use in his experiments to develop a motion-picture camera. George Eastman perceived the potential of this development and obtained patents to protect his position in a future motion picture market. In December 1894, four kinescopes were installed for public shows in the Sibley, Lindsay, and Curr department store. In January 1896, Edison's latest version of motion-picture equipment, the vitascope, displayed full-sized motion pictures at Wonderland Theater on Main Street.

According to historian Blake McKelvey: "His [George Eastman's] energetic support of Edison's rights as the inventor of the basic machines in the motion picture field provided an occasion for the formation of the Motion Picture Patents Corporation and served to draw practically all American film users into his market." Eastman and Edison worked together on the development of motion pictures and became good friends.

Many Rochesterians have a Hollywood connection. Native Rochesterian Louise Brooks was an actress in Hollywood during the early days of the motion picture industry. She returned to live in Rochester in 1956 to do research at the George Eastman House for her book, *Women in Films.* Ingrid Bergman lived in Rochester inter-mittently from 1941 through 1943 during the association of her husband, Dr. Peter Lindstrom, with the University of Rochester Medical School. Audrey Hepburn's "significant other" later in life was from Irondequoit. She visited Rochester with him on numerous occasions.

Humphrey Bogart was the son of Dr. Delmont Bogart, a New York City physician, and Rochesterian Maude Humphrey, who was a well-known local artist. The Bogart family had a cottage at Seneca Point on Canandaigua Lake in the Town of South Bristol. Young Bogart spent his summers there.

Rochesterians Cab Calloway and William Warfield performed in movies. Calloway and his band were in *The Singing Kid* with Al Jolson, *Stormy Weather* with Lena Horne, *St. Louis Blues* with Nat King Cole, and *The Cincinnati Kid* with Steve McQueen. Calloway was also in the *The Blues Brothers* with John Belushi and Dan Ackroyd. Warfield performed the role of "Joe" in *Showboat,* in which he sang "Old Man River."

Rochesterian Garson Kanin's book *Born Yesterday* was made into a movie starring Judy Holliday and William Holden. Kanin also wrote eight screenplays, including four with Ruth Gordon: *A Double Life, Adam's Rib, Pat and Mike,* and *The Marrying Kind,* some of which starred Katherine Hepburn and Spencer Tracy.

The International Museum of Photography at the George Eastman House is involved in many ways with the motion-picture industry. The Museum, which has been a pioneer in restoring older Hollywood films and in replacing nitrate-base films with media that are more suitable for archiving, conducts a motion picture school for 15-20 international students each year in film preservation.

The George Eastman House conducts motion picture events and presents awards to Hollywood luminaries. The George Eastman Award, which is awarded every other year for lifetime achievement, has been awarded since the 1950s to many notables, including Lauren Bacall, Ingrid Bergman, Audrey Hepburn, Kim Kovak, Gregory Peck, James Stewart, Meryl Streep, and Martin Scorsese.

The International Museum of Photography collection includes:
- George Eastman's home movies and experimental films by the Eastman Kodak Company
- Early motion picture camera and projection systems
- One of the world's most complete collection of silent films
- An extensive collection of Warner Bros. motion picture stills
- Hundreds of Hollywood classics and early western movies
- The personal film collections of directors Cecil B. De Mille, Martin Scorsese, and Spike Lee
- Documentaries from Germany, Italy, France, the United States, and the former Soviet Union

The Museum's film archives include a motion picture collection of more than 23,000 titles from 1895 to the present. The Menschel Library houses thousands of books, magazines, catalogs, manuals, manuscripts, and advertisements documenting the art and science and cinema. The 535-seat Dryden Theatre of the George Eastman House highlights many series of Hollywood productions and offers free movies to senior citizens one afternoon a week.

The Eastman Kodak Theatre in Los Angeles, which opened in 2001, is the venue for the annual Academy Awards ceremony and many other Hollywood events. The Green Room in the Theatre contains photographs and memorabilia of George Eastman, who was a lifetime member of the Academy of Motion Picture Arts and Sciences.

## *How Xerox Invented the Personal Computer but Failed to Exploit It*

In 1973, over three years before Steve Wozniak of Apple Computer designed and built Apple I, Xerox's Palo Alto Research Center (PARC) created the first computer dedicated to the use of one person. PARC did more than design and build a computer. Its developers introduced a comprehensive system of hardware and software that changed the computing environment. They created an impressive list of "firsts" in digital computing:

- The first graphics-based monitor
- The first local area communications network
- The first "mouse" input device
- The first object-oriented programming language
- The first word processing program not designed for the use of experts

PARC developers called its computer "Alto" and its environment "personal distributed computing." They called it "personal" because it was designed for use by an individual and "distributed" because it was connected via a network to shared resources, such as printers and other computers.

PARC was unable to convince Xerox management to exploit the technology. PARC was a development and research center, not a manufacturing or marketing organization. The technology languished. Xerox failed to capitalize on its dramatic developments. Apple Corporation promoted the technology and became associated with the introduction of the personal computer. After Apple's initial success, Xerox introduced the Star computer but it was too late and too expensive. Xerox had missed the window of opportunity.

Xerox established PARC in 1970 as part of the company's plan to acquire or develop digital capability. IBM was entering the copier business, and Xerox knew that it had to expand into the computer business to remain competitive. However, Xerox did not want to take on IBM in large mainframe computers. Its goal was to compete with IBM in developing products for the "office of the future." In other words, it would develop and market equipment and systems to be used by managers and secretaries as well as production and sales personnel.

Peter McColough, chosen as founder Joe Wilson's successor as CEO of Xerox in 1968, decided to buy and expand an existing computer company rather than form a start-up. He approached Control Data Corporation, Digital Equipment Corporation, and the Burroughs Corporation, but no mutually beneficial agreements could be reached. In 1969, Xerox paid $900 million for Scientific Data Systems (SDS), a California-based company with sales of $100 million the previous year. Most SDS customers were in technical computing, but McColough planned to shift his new acquisition to commercial computing markets.

SDS had no independent development laboratory. Jack Goldman, who had succeeded John Dessauer as director of research at Xerox in 1968, recommended to McColough that Xerox establish a digital research and development center. McColough approved the request, and a talented team of scientists and engineers was assembled at Palo Alto to provide Xerox with future-oriented digital capability. Goldman chose George Pake, a highly regarded physicist with experience in both academia and industry, to establish and manage the new facility.

Both Goldman and Pake believed in hiring capable people and then following a "bottom up" rather then a "top down" approach to research. Overall goals were conveyed to the researchers, but it was left up to them to tell their managers what they had to do to accomplish them. After all, development of the "architecture of information" involved in moving to the "office of the future" was not immediately obvious to high-level managers.

Pake divided PARC into three components:
• The General Science Laboratory (GSL) conducted research.
• The Systems Science Laboratory (SSL) was responsible
  for broad "systems" research in engineering, information,
  mathematics, operations, and statistics.
• The Computer Science Laboratory (CSL) focused on
  computer systems.

Pake managed the GSL in addition to the laboratory as a whole. Bill Gunning, who had twenty years of computer science experience, was appointed to manage the SSL. Jerry Elkind, who was selected to head the CSL, had worked for NASA and for the computer consultant who had designed ARPAnet, the first nationwide computer communications network, for the Advanced Research Projects Administration (ARPA) of the Department of Defense. Bob Taylor, who had served as ARPA's chief administrator of computer funding, was named associate director of the CSL.

With the cost of mainframe computers and minicomputers exceeding $100,000, timesharing was a popular tool. Users at many terminals were connected to one central computer and shared its use. Computers were considered fast and people slow, so this was viewed as a good arrangement. However, it caused many computer scientists to work odd hours, such as the middle of the night, to gain access to the central computer. Developers' schedules were slaves to the computer's schedule. As the cost of computers came down with increased use of integrated circuits and microprocessors, an alternative to timesharing was sought. Taylor recommended a "one computer, one person" solution to the problem.

CSL computer scientist Alan Kay described a tool called FLEX in his 1969 doctoral dissertation that matched Taylor's concept. Douglas Smith and Robert Alexander describe it in *Fumbling the Future: How Xerox Invented and Then Ignored the First Personal Computer:*

> An interactive tool which can aid in the visualization of and realization of provocative notions. It must be simple enough so that one doesn't have to be a systems programmer to use it. It must be cheap enough to be owned. It must do more than just be able to recognize computable functions; it has to be able to form the abstractions in which the user deals. FLEX is an idea debugger, and, as such, it is hoped that it is also an idea media.

Kay proposed that PARC develop a FLEX-like computer called "Dynabook," which he referred to as a "dynamic media for creative thought." When the Dynabook project was turned down, he countered with a project called "interim Dynabook."

Interest in the project began to build within the CSL, and Taylor obtained approval to develop a computer that met the "one person, one computer" criterion. It was called "Alto." CSL scientist Butler Lampson described it as having an enhanced display monitor, being almost as powerful as a minicomputer, operating in a network of distributed machines, and being affordable. He referred to the use of such a computer as "personal computing." Computer scientist Chuck

Thacker contributed valuable ideas on developing it. Their goals were to make it both better and cheaper than a minicomputer.

Lampson and Thacker used some of the tools developed by Douglas Englebart, an early advocate of interactive computing, including an input device called a "mouse" and displays that could be divided into multiple "windows." Englebart's mouse was a bulky analog device that was converted into a digital tool and made smaller and more reliable.

Lampson and Thacker improved Englebart's displays. They used a technique called bit-mapping, which associated each picture element (pixel) with a specific bit of computer memory. Specific binary bits are programmed to be "on "(one) while others are "off" (zero); in combination the bits create a character on the screen and retain it in memory for later use. Unfortunately, this one-to-one relationship of pixels on the screen with bits in the computer's memory required a large storage capacity and therefore was expensive.

Another Alto innovation was multitasking, which allowed one processor to operate as many. A task was performed according to its priority. Multitasking slowed Alto down because the bit-mapped display used the processor two-thirds of the time, but it provided more functionality for less cost. In April 1973, after four months of work, the first Alto was completed. Ten Altos were built by the end of the year, and forty were completed by the following summer.

However, hardware alone does not make a computer system. Also needed were an operating system, programming languages, and application software. As the software became available, three functions were emphasized: communications, printing, and word processing.

PARC developer Robert Metcalfe's communications tool, Ethernet, did not use telephone lines but relied on local cable runs within a building. Ethernet connected an Alto to shared equipment, such as printers and other Altos. PARC also developed the xerographic laser printer. Laser printers were expensive, but sharing them reduced the cost to individual computer users.

Lampson and CSL scientist Charles Simonyi developed a word processing application called "Bravo" that allowed the word image on the screen to be the same as that output by the printer. This feature, called "wysiwyg" for "what you see is what you get," was not available on earlier word processing packages. Subsequently, a more user-friendly version, called "Gypsy," was developed. Alto was used successfully in an experiment at Ginn & Company, a Xerox textbook publishing subsidiary, to streamline the publishing process.

The Alto personal computer seemed prepared for takeoff. Thacker observed: "It was certainly from my own experience the largest piece of creative effort I have seen anywhere. And it was like being there at the creation. A lot of people worked harder than I have ever seen, or have seen since, doing a thing they all felt was worthwhile, and really thought would change the world." However, Xerox management made no attempt to translate PARC's developments into successfully marketed products.

In its defense, Xerox faced many challenges at the time. In 1972, the Federal Trade Commission (FTC) claimed that the company was monopolizing the plain paper copier market. The FTC accused Xerox of manipulating patent laws, setting prices that were discriminatory, insisting on leases over sales of equipment, and exploiting the market by using joint ownership arrangements with Rank in England and Fuji in Japan. In July 1975, the FTC discontinued the antitrust action. In order to comply with FTC demands, Xerox had to give up its patents, change its pricing policies, and allow supplies such as toner to be sold by other companies.

In late 1973, CEO McColough and president Archie McCardell, a Ford Motor Company financial executive who had joined Xerox in 1971, formed a four-person team to map the future strategy of Xerox. The team was headed by corporate planner Michael Hughes and included George Pake, who had been assigned to corporate headquarters after directing PARC for three years. The team evaluated four distinct strategies for Xerox and recommended the "office of the future" alternative. They suggested combining computers, copiers, and word-processing typewriters with PARC's innovations in communications, microcircuitry, and software. No action was taken on their recommendation.

Originally, Xerox research director Goldman thought that PARC's inventions would be brought to market by SDS. When SDS continued to lose money during the first half of the 1970s, he realized that another avenue was needed to capitalize on PARC's innovations. As the emphasis on financial analysis practiced by ex-Ford executives became prevalent at Xerox, Goldman's influence as the senior technical person waned.

In January 1973, Bob Potter became the General Manager of Xerox's Office Products Division, responsible for developing and manufacturing office products other than copiers. The division had few successes other than development of a popular facsimile machine. Potter wanted to move the division from Rochester to another location. Dallas and Silicon Valley were the favored locations.

Goldman lobbied strongly for Silicon Valley because PARC was located there. However, Dallas was chosen for strictly financial reasons, including lower costs for labor, taxes, and transportation. The financial types had won again; PARC was to remain isolated from the rest of the company. In Goldman's opinion, this decision had the greatest negative impact of any single decision on the future of digital technology at Xerox.

Potter visited PARC and observed the Alto technology, but he decided to concentrate on word processing. Although his background was in both technology and operations, he thought that PARC's ideas were too futuristic. Also, he was influenced by Xerox financial people, who emphasized short-term profits.

PARC developers were disappointed that the word "software" did not enter into Potter's plans for Dallas. They thought that products that were not programmable, such as Potter's electro-mechanical devices, would fail. Within a year and a half of entering the market, Potter's word-processing typewriter was out of date because of its display and communications shortcomings.

Xerox's Display Word Processing Task Force recommended that the new word processor be Alto-based. However, a team from Dallas recalculated PARC's estimates for the new product and concluded that the Alto would take longer to build and cost more than the estimates. The task force's recommendation was ignored. Next, Goldman proposed that a small entrepreneurial team be formed to produce a general-purpose workstation using the Alto. That proposal was also rejected.

The recession in 1974-75 impacted Xerox negatively. The company found that customers made as many copies in bad times as in good times, but they made them with existing machines. They did not buy or lease new copiers during a slowed economy. However, the greatest negative impact on Xerox was the staggering losses from the Scientific Data Systems acquisition. SDS lost $71 million in 1970-71,

$47 million in 1972, $45 million in 1973, and $42 million in 1974. Competing with IBM toe-to-toe for the "office of the future" was not working.

Combining the copier and the computer businesses in a functional organization grouped by design and manufacturing, marketing and service, and planning had eliminated the focus of the computer business. In effect, SDS drifted without a general manager. In July 1975, CEO McColough admitted that the SDS acquisition had been a mistake. No buyer for SDS could be found. Xerox took a write-off of just under $1.3 billion and left the computer business.

In 1975-76, the Office Products Division began to manufacture the laser printer developed at PARC; a patent was received for Ethernet; and the Systems Development Division (SDD) was formed to translate PARC inventions into products. Some PARC-developed products were finding their way to the marketplace. However, Xerox still was not prepared to exploit the advances made on Alto.

In 1976, PARC researcher John Ellenby was authorized to produce hundreds of Altos for use with laser printers within Xerox. He thought that at last technology transfer from the lab to the user was beginning to happen. In August 1976, Ellenby submitted a proposal on Alto to the Xerox task force determining new product strategies for the company. No action was taken on his proposal.

Ellenby was pleased to be asked to organize the 1977 "Futures Day" at which Xerox showcased its new products within the company. His team worked hard and thought they had made a strong case for proceeding with the Alto. By this time, McCardell had left Xerox to become CEO of International Harvester, and David Kearns from IBM had replaced him as president and chief operating officer. Ellenby was informed that Kearns had decided not to go into production with Alto.

In 1979, a Xerox investment unit contacted Steve Jobs of Apple Computer about a possible joint venture. Jobs requested and received a tour of the PARC facility. Larry Tesler demonstrated Alto for Jobs, who saw its potential immediately. He asked, "Why isn't Xerox marketing this? You could blow everybody away." Once Jobs knew that it could be done, he set out to duplicate it at Apple. He hired Tesler immediately and later Alan Kay, who eventually became an Apple Fellow. Most of the "look and feel" of the Alto that provided its ease of use eventually was incorporated into the Apple Macintosh and

Lisa. Xerox was amazingly open with its technology.

In 1978, Xerox combined the Office Products Division in Dallas with other non-copier units. General Manager Potter left to join McCardell at International Harvester as chief technical officer. In 1979, the Office Products Division was again made independent, and Don Massaro was hired from Shugart Associates to replace Potter as General Manager. Massaro, an entrepreneurial type, announced a new word processor, readied two facsimile machines for the market, announced PARC's Ethernet as a product, and started an electronic typewriter project within the first year. Soon he became interested in Star, a product that had evolved from the Alto.

He asked for $15 million to make and sell Star and was turned down. He scaled down his request and was turned down again. He proceeded on his own using his division's budget. Star's strength, like Alto's, was its "user interface," including the contents of the screen and the tools provided to work with the display. Star used icons, action-choice menus, and multiple screen windows along with electronic file cabinets, in and out boxes, and wastebaskets. Unfortunately, Star was designed to be used by managers.

Much of the software had already been designed when a decision was made to replace the processor. Hardware is usually designed before software, and compromises had to be made that slowed the speed of the machine to incorporate the new processor. It was the first personal computer to offer a bit-map screen, a laser printer, a mouse, combined text and graphics in the same document, and "what you see is what you get" word processing.

However, it had limitations in addition to its slow speed:
- Because it was a distributed system, it was more expensive than a stand-alone computer ($16,595 for the workstation, five times the cost of a stand-alone personal computer).
- It did not offer a spreadsheet.
- Its design was based on a closed architecture, not an open architecture, and suppliers could not make and sell components to be used with it.
- Its programming language was not available to the public (only Xerox employees could write application software for it).
- It was not compatible with other computers.

In April 1981, Star (Xerox 820) was introduced—eight years after the invention of Alto. It was not a successful product; however, the Xerox 820 was the first personal computer introduced by a Fortune 500 corporation.

Xerox's mishandling the introduction of the personal computer was a classic case of failing to capitalize on an opportunity. Ironically, the technology developed at PARC was exploited by others; Xerox did not receive the benefit of its labors.

An incredible body of talent had been assembled at PARC during the 1970s. Key PARC people seeded the laboratories of other companies; for example, Charles Simonyi joined Microsoft Corporation. Butler Lampson, Bob Taylor, and Chuck Thacker joined the Systems Research Center of the Digital Equipment Corporation. In 1984, they received the System Software Award from the Association of Computing Machinery for the invention of personal distributed computing. In 1987, President Reagan awarded George Pake the National Medal of Science for the notable accomplishments of PARC.

# *EPILOGUE*

## *Rochester in the Twenty-first Century*

### *Rochester 2010: The Renaissance Plan*
In 2000, Mayor William A. Johnson, Jr., initiated *Rochester 2010: The Renaissance Plan,* which he views as "The Passport to the Future." The Renaissance plan is comprised of eleven campaigns:

1. ***Involved Citizens***—Encouraging citizens to actively participate in shaping their community—"It is the policy of our city to engage the widest array of our citizens in the safety, upkeep and renewal of our neighborhoods and community, to provide opportunities for citizens to work together to plan for their collective future and to take actions to realize that future, to celebrate the positive aspects of community life and to support citizens taking responsibility for using these opportunities to enhance the community."

2. ***Educational Excellence***—Providing progressive, safe public education with an emphasis on lifelong learning and workplace preparation—"It is the policy of our city to support the highest quality educational and job-training opportunities for our citizens on a lifelong basis, to promote and support our public schools as a focal point of neighborhood activity and pride, and to encourage our citizens to take responsibility for using these opportunities to educate and prepare themselves for work, careers and responsible citizenship."

3. ***Health, Safety, and Responsibility***—Working with public health and safety organizations, encouraging citizens to improve their own welfare and that of those around them—"It is the policy of our city to support our citizens and families in leading healthy, safe, productive and self-determined lives. We support our citizens taking responsibility for helping to improve the health, safety, and welfare of themselves and those around them; developing and maintaining safe, clean, attractive neighborhoods that are free from public disorder and nuisances; and recognizing and celebrating examples of good citizenship and personal responsibility."

4. ***Environmental Stewardship***—Protecting parks, landscapes and wetlands for future generations and encouraging envi-

ronmental practices—"It is the policy of our city to maintain and enhance, through the individual and collective efforts of our citizens, businesses and governments, the overall quality of our environmental assets and resources (air, land, and water quality) our community's three great waterways (Lake Ontario, the Genesee River, and the Erie Canal), our unique and historic parks system, our open space areas and urban forest and our clean neighborhood environments."

5. *Regional Partnerships*—Fostering an open exchange of ideas and resources among Rochester and other regional governments—"It is the policy of our city to promote the concept of Rochester as the economic, social, cultural, transportation and institutional center of our county and region. We will seek out opportunities, plan and communicate effectively, and work together with other governments to develop solutions to our common problems, in a way that recognizes a collaborative neighborhood/ regional/global perspective rather than a city/state perspective."

6. *Economic Vitality*—Developing an environment in which business flourishes, jobs are plentiful, and technological innovation is encouraged—"It is the policy of our city to promote an environment in which businesses can develop and flourish; to develop a diverse local economy that supports quality jobs, produces new product, service and technology innovations and high-quality business and personal services; and to create a highly skilled workforce that embraces creativity and our rich entrepreneurial spirit. We will also promote and pursue the management of our community identity as a world-class city in which to do business, as well as a highly desirable place to live, work and visit."

7. *Quality Service*—Making public services affordable, reliable, and accountable, and encouraging citizen self-sufficiency to reduce the need for services—"It is the policy of our city to provide high-quality services, programs, information and infrastructure to our citizens in a way that is efficient, affordable, accountable and takes into account the diverse needs of our citizens, builds trust and understanding, is based on communication, partnership and collaboration, and, where appropriate, reduces demand for those services

by encouraging citizen self-sufficiency."

8. ***Tourism Destination***—Expanding Rochester's wealth of tourism attractions and activities to increase visitorship and elevate our standard of living—"It is the policy of our city to promote recognition of our city and region as a tourism destination that embraces a broad range of 'four-season' tourist attractions centered on our unique waterfront resources, recognizing especially the centrality of the Genesee River to the life of our community, along with arts, cultural, sports and entertainment facilities as well as our reputation as a supportive and innovative community, in a way that contributes to our community's local and national images as well as its economic vitality and growth."

9. ***Healthy Urban Neighborhoods***—Developing unique, interconnected neighborhoods and a variety of housing choices in a village-like setting—"It is the policy of our city to support unique, vital, interconnected urban neighborhoods which provide a variety of housing choices, accessible goods and services in a village-like setting."

10. ***Center City***—Transforming Rochester's downtown into a safe and exciting center for entertainment, nightlife, cultural venues, housing and restaurants—"It is the policy of our city to pursue recognition and development of our downtown as the region's 'Center City' to include an exciting mix of housing, specialty retail and services, restaurants, arts and cultural venues, entertainment and nightlife."

11. ***Arts and Culture***—Expanding our cultural heritage so that Rochester becomes renowned as a world-class cultural center—"It is the policy of our city to support and promote arts and cultural events, activities and institutions in a way that establishes our city as a 'world class' cultural center, contributing to our community's life, vitality and growth."

## *Examples of Organizations Participating in Planning Rochester's Future*
  • Economic development organizations

- Working groups of Rochester's leaders striving to keep the region's competitive edge
- Local alliances that are "Fighting for Rochester's Future" by addressing the topics of the economy, education, health care, public safety, and taxation.

### Ongoing Activities to Improve Rochester
- Continuing to develop the High Falls entertainment center
- Remodeling the Auditorium Theatre component of the Auditorium Center, venue for many concerts and plays
- Inaugurating the Canadian American Transportation Systems $42.5 million fast ferry between Rochester and Toronto in 2004. The 284-foot-long ferry takes less than two and a quarter hours to transport 774 passengers and 238 cars.
- Building a soccer stadium for the Rochester Rhinos
- Constructing a combined arts, education, and transportation center in downtown Rochester
- Enhancing recreational use of the Erie Canal
- Expanding and improving parks and hiking and biking trails

However, as important as infrastructure is, people are more important. Rochesterians remain civic-minded, volunteer-oriented, and conscientious givers to organizations, e.g. United Way.

Rochester has a rich history of philanthropy. Tom Galisano, founder and CEO of Paychex, Inc., is an example of a modern-day Rochester philanthropist. His gifts to the community include:
- $14 million to the University of Rochester
- $14 million to the Rochester Institute of Technology
- $5 million to Nazareth College
- $5 million to St. John Fisher College
- $5 million to Roberts Wesleyan College
- A gift to establish the Galisano Children's Hospital at Strong Memorial Hospital

As long as Rochester's people continue to strive in the tradition of the founders and achievers described in this book, our city will move forward and prosper. Rochesterians' response to the mayor's encouragement to "actively participate in shaping the community" will ensure that the city remains as vital and progressive as it has been in the past.

# BIBLIOGRAPHY

Ackerman, Carl W. *George Eastman.* Clifton, NJ:
Augustus M. Kelley, 1973.

Arrington, Leonard J. *Brigham Young: American Moses.* New York:
Alfred A. Knopf, 1985.

Balliett, Whitney. *Alec Wilder and His Friends.* Boston:
Houghton Mifflin, 1974.

Barnes, Joseph W. "Rochester's Congressmen, Part II 1869-1979."
*Rochester History, Vol. XLI, No. 4.* Rochester: Office of the
City Historian, 1979.

Beale, Irene A. "Amy Post, Anti-Slavery Woman." *Genesee Valley
Women 1743-1985.* Geneseo, NY: Chestnut Hill Press, 1985.

Belden, Thomas Graham, and Marva Robbins. *The Lengthening
Shadow: The Life of Thomas J. Watson.* Boston: Little, Brown,
1962.

Black, Sylvia R. "Seth Green, Father of Fish Culture."
*Rochester History, Vol. VI, No. 3.* Rochester: Office of the
City Historian, 1944.

Bragdon, Claude. *More Lives Than One.* New York: Alfred A. Knopf,
1938.

Brayer, Elizabeth.*George Eastman: A Biography.* Baltimore:
John Hopkins UP, 1996.

_____ . *The Warner Legacy in Western New York: The Architecture of
Andrew J. and J. Foster Warner.* Rochester: The Landmark
Society of Western New York, 1984.

Bringhurst, Newell G. *Brigham Young and the Expanding American
Frontier.* Boston: Little, Brown, 1986.

Calloway, Cab, and Bryant Rollins. *Of Minnie the Moocher and Me.*
New York: Thomas Y. Crowell, 1976.

Cantor, Dorothy M. *Claude Bragdon and His Relation to the
Development of Modern Architectural Theory.* Rochester:
University of Rochester, 1963.

Cantrell, John Bruce. "Garson Kanin." *Dictionary of Literary
Biography.* Chicago: Gale Reference Company, 1981.

"Carl Ferdinand Lomb." *Our Master Builders.* Rochester:
Rochester Athenaeum and Mechanics Institute, 1944.

Cazden, Elizabeth. *Antoinette Brown Blackwell: A Biography.*
Old Westbury, NY: Feminist Press, 1983.

Chappell, Eve. "Kate Gleason's Careers." *The Woman Citizen.*
Jan. 1926: 19+

Cherry, C. Waldo. "Eulogy, Hiram Haskell Edgerton."
*The Rochester Historical Society Publication Fund Series, Vol. 1.*
Rochester: Rochester Historical Society, 1922.

Cooper, Ilene. *Susan B. Anthony.* New York: Franklin Watts, 1984.

Crapsey, Algernon Sidney. *The Last of the Heretics.* New York:
Alfred A. Knopf, 1924.

Cross, Whitney R. *The Burned-over District: The Social and
Intellectual History of Enthusiastic Religion in Western New York,
1800-1850.* Ithaca, NY: Cornell UP, 1950.

Dessauer, John H. *My Years With Xerox: The Billions Nobody
Wanted.* Garden City, NY: Doubleday, 1971.

Doty, Lockwood R. *The History of the Genesee Country, Vol. IV.*
Chicago: S. J. Clark, 1925.

Douglass, Frederick. *Life and Times of Frederick Douglass.*
New York: Thomas Y. Crowell, 1966.

Edmonds, I. G. *The Girls Who Talked to Ghosts: The Story of Katie
and Margaret Fox.* New York: Holt, Rinehart and Winston, 1979.

Foreman, Edward R., ed. "Anti-Slavery Days." *The Rochester
Historical Society Publication Fund Series, Vol. XIV.* Rochester:
Rochester Historical Society, 1936.

____ . "Art and Artists in Rochester." *The Rochester Historical
Society Publication Fund Series, Vol. XIV.* Rochester: Rochester
Historical Society, 1936.

____ . "Some Rochester Inventions." *The Rochester Historical
Society Publication Fund Series, Vol. XIV.* Rochester: Rochester
Historical Society, 1936.

Fornel, Earl Wesley. *The Unhappy Medium: Spiritualism and the
Life of Margaret Fox.* Austin: U of Texas P, 1964.

Frank, Meryl, and Blake McKelvey. "Some Former Rochesterians of
National Distinction." *Rochester History, Vol.XXI, No. 3.*
Rochester: Office of the City Historian, 1959.

Gerling, Curt. *Smugtown, U.S.A.* Rochester: Plaza Publishers, 1993.

Hagen, Walter. *The Walter Hagen Story by The Haig, Himself.*
New York: Simon and Schuster, 1956.

Hambrick-Stowe, Charles E. *Charles G. Finney and the Spirit of
American Evangelism.* Grand Rapids: William B. Eerdmans,
1996.

Harvey, Bonnie C. *Charles Finney: Apostle of Revival.*
Ulrichsville, OH: Barbour Publishing, 1999.

Hinrichs, Noel. *The Pursuit of Excellence: James Cunningham, Son & Company.* Rochester: KMCEC Associates, 1964.

Hitchcock, H. Wiley, ed. *New Grove Dictionary of American Music.* New York: Macmillan, 1986.

Holl, Richard E. "Marion B. Folsom and the Rochester Plan of 1931." *Rochester History, Vol. LXI, No. 4.* Rochester: Office of the City Historian, 1999.

Huggins, Nathan Irvin. *Slave and Citizen: The Life of Frederick Douglass.* Boston: Little, Brown, 1980.

Jackson, Herbert G., Jr. *The Spirit Rappers.* Garden City, NY: Doubleday, 1972.

Jennings, Walter Wilson. *A Dozen Captains of American Industry.* New York: Vantage, 1954.

Kabelac, Karl S. "Kate Gleason, National Bank President." *Paper Money, Vol. XXXVIII, No. 3.* May/Jun 1999: 67-70.

Kerr, Laura. *Lady in the Pulpit.* New York: Woman's Press, 1951.

Klees, Emerson C. *People of the Finger Lakes Region: The Heart of New York State.* Rochester: Friends of the Finger Lakes Publishing, 1995.

_____ . *Crucible of Ferment: New York's "Psychic Highway."* Rochester: Cameo Press, 2001.

_____ . *Entrepreneurs in History: Success vs. Failure—Entrepreneurial Role Models.* Rochester: Cameo Press, 1995.

_____ . *Legends and Stories of the Finger Lakes Region.* Rochester: Friends of the Finger Lakes Publishing, 1995.

_____ . *More Legends and Stories of the Finger Lakes Region.* Rochester: Friends of the Finger Lakes Region, 1997.

Kneeland, Donald E. *Spirits of the Genesee/Finger Lakes Region.* Rochester: Lark Publications, 1984.

Lanni, Clement G. *George W. Aldridge: Big Boss, Small City.* Rochester: Rochester Alliance Press, 1939.

Lipman, Andrew David. "The Rochester Subway: Experiment in Municipal Rapid Transit." *Rochester History, Vol XXXI, No. 2.* Rochester: Office of the City Historian, 1974.

Lowe, Stephen R. *Sir Walter and Mr. Jones: Walter Hagen, Bobby Jones, and the Rise of American Golf.* N.p.: Sleeping Bear Press, 2000.

McKelvey, Blake. *Business as a Profession: The Career of Joseph C. Wilson, Founder of Xerox.* Rochester: Office of the City

Historian, 2003.

___ . "The Flower City: Center of Nurseries and Fruit Orchards." *The Rochester Historical Society Publications, Vol. XVIII.* Rochester: Rochester Historical Society, 1940.

___ . *Rochester: An Emerging Metropolis 1925-1961.* Rochester: Christopher Press, 1961.

___ . *Rochester: The Flower City 1855-1890:* Cambridge: Harvard UP, 1949.

___ . *Rochester on the Genesee: Growth of a City.* Syracuse: Syracuse UP, 1993.

___ . *Rochester: The Quest for Quality 1890-1925.* Cambridge: Harvard UP, 1956.

___ . "Rochester at the Turn of the Century." *Rochester History, Vol XII, No. 1.* Rochester: Office of the City Historian, 1950.

___ . *Rochester: The Water-Power City 1812-1854.* Cambridge: Harvard UP, 1945.

McNamara, Robert F. *The Diocese of Rochester 1868-1968.* Rochester: Diocese of Rochester, 1968.

Marouka, Susanne Keaveney. *The Architecture of Andrew Jackson Warner in Rochester, New York.* Rochester: University of Rochester, 1965.

Merrill, Arch. *Rochester Sketchbook.* Rochester: Gannett, 1946.

Miller, Basil. *Charles Finney.* Minneapolis: Bethany House, 1941.

Miller, Douglas T. *Frederick Douglass and the Fight for Freedom.* New York: Facts on File, 1988.

Morris, William H. *The Cunningham Car Made in Rochester.* Rochester: Institute of Fellows, Rochester Institute of Technology, 1986.

Mort, J. *An Anatomy of Xerography: Its Invention and Evolution.* Jefferson, NC: McFarland & Company, 1989.

Neuharth, Al. *Confessions of an S.O.B.* New York: Doubleday, 1989.

Noonan, D. P. *The Passion of Fulton J. Sheen.* New York: Dodd, Mead, 1972.

O'Reilly, Henry, ed. *Sketches of Rochester with Incidental Notes of Western New York.* Rochester: William Alling, 1838.

Palmer, Richard F., and Karl D. Butler. *Brigham Young: The New York Years.* Provo, UT: Charles Redd Center for Western Studies, 1982.

Parker, Jane Marsh. "How Men of Rochester Saved the Telegraph."

*The Rochester Historical Society Publication Fund Series, Vol. V.* Rochester: Rochester Historical Society, 1926.

Peck, William F. "Elisha Johnson: President of the Village and Mayor of the City of Rochester." *The Rochester Historical Society Publication Fund Series, Vol. VI.* Rochester: Rochester Historical Society, 1927.

Perone, James E. *Howard Hanson: A Bio-Bibliography.* Westport, CT: Greenwood Press, 1993.

Prichard, Peter S. *The Making of McPaper: The Inside Story of USA Today.* New York: St. Martin's Press, 1989.

Reeves, Thomas C. *America's Bishop: The Life and Times of Fulton J. Sheen.* San Francisco: Encounter Books, 2001.

Rhees, Rush. "The Gift and the Donor: James Goold Cutler." *The Rochester Historical Society Publication Fund Series, Vol. VII.* Rochester: Rochester Historical Society, 1928.

Rodgers, William. *THINK: A Biography of the Watsons and IBM.* New York: Stein and Day, 1969.

Ross, Ishbel. *Charmers and Cranks: Twelve Famous American Women Who Defied the Conventions.* New York: Harper & Row, 1965.

Sheen, Fulton J. *Treasure in Clay: The Autobiography of Fulton J. Sheen.* Garden City, NY: Doubleday, 1980.

Sibley, Hiram W. "Memories of Hiram W. Sibley." *The Rochester Historical Society Publication Fund Series, Vol. II.* Rochester: Rochester Historical Society, 1923.

Simon, George T., *Best of the Musicmakers.* New York: Doubleday, 1979.

Slater, John Rothwell. *Rhees of Rochester.* New York: Harper & Brothers, 1946.

Smith, Douglas K., and Robert C. Alexander. *Fumbling the Future: How Xerox Invented and Then Ignored the First Personal Computer.* New York: Morrow, 1988.

Solbert, O. N. "George Eastman." *Images—Journal of Photography of the George Eastman House, Inc. Vol. II, No. 8.* Nov. 1953.

Solomon, Martha. *Emma Goldman.* Boston: Twayne, 1987.

Stone, Desmond. *Alec Wilder in Spite of Himself: A Life of the Composer.* New York: Oxford UP, 1996.

Taves, Ernest H. *This Is the Place: Brigham Young and the New Zion.* Buffalo: Prometheus Books, 1991.

Tompkins, John S. "Our Kindest City." *Reader's Digest:* Jul. 1994, 53-56.

Untermeyer, Louis. *Makers of the Modern World.* New York: Simon and Schuster, 1955.

Warfield, William, and Alton Miller. *William Warfield: My Music & My Life.* Champaigne, IL: Sagamore Press, 1991.

Weisberg, Barbara. *Susan B. Anthony.* New York: Chelsea House, 1988.

Wessel, Helen, ed. *The Autobiography of Charles G. Finney.* Minneapolis: Bethany House, 1977.

Wexler, Alice. *Emma Goldman: An Intimate Life.* New York: Pantheon Books, 1984.

Williamson, Samuel T. *Imprint of a Publisher: The Story of Frank Gannett and His Independent Newspapers.* Toronto: George J. McLeod, 1948.

Wilson, Suzan. *Steve Jobs: Wizard of Apple Computer.* Berkeley Heights, NJ: Enslow, 2001.

Wolfe, Andrew. "Soldier Hero, Old Style: General Elwell S. Otis." *Saints, Sinners, and Salesmen.* Pittsford, NY: Genesee Valley Newspapers, 1971.

Woods, Clinton. *Ideas That Became Big Business.* Baltimore: Founders, 1959.

Zeltsman, Nancy, ed. *Alec Wilder (1907-1980).* Newton Centre, MA: Margun Music, 1991.

Zwierlien, Frederick J. *The Life and Letters of Bishop McQuaid, Vols. II and III.* Louvain, Belgium: Louvain Librairie Universitaire, 1926.

# INDEX

Achilles, Gertrude Strong, 104
Albany, 15, 17, 21, 22, 25, 50, 90, 99, 104, 209
Aldridge, George W., 63, 185-190
Algonquin Hotel, 78, 82, 83
Allan, Ebenezer "Indian," 13, 21
Alling, Joseph T., 97, 99, 188
Alsop, Joseph, 181, 184
AME Zion Church, 36, 170
Amhurst College, 96, 97, 100
Anthony, Daniel, 23, 38
Anthony, Mary, 27, 266
Anthony, Susan B., 14, 23-29, 38, 44, 100, 147, 236
Apple Computer Corp., 288, 294
Armstrong, Louis, 159, 160
Barry, Patrick, 3, 9, 14, 172-176
Basie, Count, 160
Batavia, 14, 130, 203
Bausch, John Jacob, 3, 15, 116-119, 273
Bausch & Lomb, 10, 118, 119, 135, 138, 273
Blackwell, Antoinette Brown, 39-47
Blackwell, Elizabeth, 43, 45
Blackwell, Henry, 43, 45
Blackwell, Samuel, 43, 45, 46
Bloomfield, 21
Bogart, Humphrey, 286
Born Yesterday, 81, 93, 94, 287
Bragdon, Claude, 179, 221-227
Brick Presbyterian Church, 237
Brockport, 15, 271
Buffalo, 17, 22, 53, 60, 104, 172, 208
Buffalo Bills, 11
Buffalo News, 58
Buffalo Sabres, 11
Burned-over District, 15-17

Calloway, Blanche, 159
Calloway, Cab, 157-162, 169
Canada, 35, 37, 38, 52, 53, 166, 173, 205
Canandaigua, 21, 22, 28, 129, 130, 204, 276
Canajoharie, 23
Carlson, Chester, 125, 149, 150
Carmer, Carl, 15, 16
Carnegie, Andrew, 59, 98
Carroll, Charles, 14, 19, 20, 130
Carter, Helen Strong, 104
Carthage, 52, 129, 130, 273, 274
Child, Jonathan, 49
Cody, "Buffalo Bill," 265-267
Corinthian Hall, 17, 35
Cornell, Ezra, 50
Cornell Sun, 59
Cornell University, 50, 59, 65, 142
Cotton Club, 160-162
Country Club of Rochester, 151, 152, 221
Crapsey, Rev. Algernon, 248-250
Crooked Lake Review, 274
Cunningham, James, 134-141
Curley, John, 72, 73
Cutler, James G., 99, 105, 179, 187, 191-193, 231
Cutler Manufacturing Co., 191, 192
Dansville, 21, 131
Dessauer, John, 125, 149, 289
Douglass, Anna Murray, 32
Douglass, Frederick, 15, 23, 31-36, 38
Douglass, Helen Pitts, 36
Eastman, George, 9, 15, 64, 99, 101-105, 107-114, 181, 182, 189, 273, 286
Eastman Kodak Company, 9, 15,

104, 109, 110, 112, 125, 135, 149, 181-184

Eastman School of Music, 76-78, 86-89, 102, 103, 112, 164-166, 169, 170

Eastman Theatre, 102, 103

Edgerton, Hiram, 189, 195-197

Edison, Thomas, 286

Ellington, Duke, 159-161

Ellwanger, George, 3, 9, 14, 172-176

Elmira *Star-Gazette,* 61, 62

Erie Canal, 14, 17, 33, 172, 275, 277

Fifteenth Amendment, 27, 28

Finney, Charles Grandison, 3, 15, 17, 40, 41, 45, 235-238

Fitzhugh, William, 14, 19, 20, 130

Folsom, Marion, 181-184

Ford Motor Company, 132, 133

Fourteenth Amendment, 28

Fox, Kate, 16, 38, 206-217

Fox, Leah, 17, 38, 207-209

Fox, Margaret, 16, 206-217

Fugitive Slave Law, 37

Galisano, Tom, 12, 15, 300

Gannett, Frank, 58-66, 273

Gannett, Inc., 69, 73

Garrison, William Lloyd, 23, 32, 33, 37, 40

Garth Fagan Dance Company, 10

Genesee Country Museum, 11

Genesee River, 9, 14, 21, 22, 52, 129, 275

George Eastman House, 10, 105, 111, 286

Gerling, Curt, 281-283

Gerling, William C., 282, 283

GeVa Theater, 10

Gillespie, Dizzy, 161

Gleason, James, 142, 146

Gleason, Kate, 142-148

Gleason Works, 141-146

Goldman, "Red Emma," 3, 218-220

Goodkind, Larney, 165, 166

Goodman, Benny, 79, 159

Gorham, Nathaniel, 21

Gosnell, Thomas, 264

Grant, Ulysses S., 36

Greater Rochester Visitors Association, 5,10

Greeley, Horace, 27, 45, 209, 210

Green, Seth, 52-54

Gruber, "Rattlesnake Pete," 270

Hagen, Walter, 151-156

Haloid Company, 15, 124, 125

Haloid-Xerox, 126, 150

Hampson, Thomas, 84

Handsome Lake, 90, 91

Hanson, Howard, 86-89, 166

Harper, Ida Husted, 29

Harris, Joseph, 175

Harrison, Les, 278, 279

Hawthorne, Nathaniel, 22

Henderson, Fletcher, 159

Henrietta, 39

Henry, Joseph, 90

Herz, Otto, 166, 168

Hill, David Jayne, 96, 180

Hines, Earl "Father," 159

Howe, Elias, 239

Howells, William Dean, 269

Hunt, Judge Ward, 28, 29

IBM Corp., 122, 123, 125, 149, 150, 288

Iroquois Confederacy, 90-92

Ithaca *Daily News,* 61

Ithaca *Journal,* 62

Johnson, Elisha, 129-131
Johnson, Jimmy, 90, 91
Johnson, Mayor William A., Jr., 4, 170, 297
Jones, Bobby, 155, 156
Kanin, Garson, 93, 94, 286, 287
Keating, Kenneth, 198-201
Kelsey's Landing, 52
Kilbourn Hall, 10
Kimball Tobacco factory, 135, 191, 231, 262-264
Koussevitsky, Serge, 87
Lake Erie, 16, 22
Lake Ontario, 9, 35
*The Last of the Heretics,* 248, 250
Lawyers' Cooperative Publishing Co., 5, 263, 264
*The Liberator,* 32, 33
Lincoln, Abraham, 50, 51
Lind, Jenny, 75, 209
Lockport, 14
Lomb, Carl, 119
Lomb, Henry, 15, 117-119
Lovejoy, Elijah, 33
Masons, 203-205
McCormick, Cyrus, 15, 271
McKelvey, Blake, 13, 19, 131, 132, 172, 193, 203, 250
McPartland, Marian, 84
McQuaid, Bishop Bernard, 251-253
Mees, Kenneth, 112, 272
Memorial Art Gallery, 10, 101
Mendon, 3, 240, 241
Miami *Herald,* 68
Miller, Mitch, 77-79, 81, 84
Monroe Community College, 10
Monroe County, 9, 10, 13, 21, 28, 63, 187, 285
Morgan, Lewis Henry, 90-92, 100

Morgan, William, 203-205
Mormons, 16, 17, 241-247
Morse, Samuel, 49, 50
Mott, Lucretia, 23, 38, 42, 45
National Cash Register Company, 121, 122
Nazareth College, 10, 162, 300
Neuharth, Al, 67-73
New Society of the Genesee, 272-274
New York State Thruway, 9, 277
Nineteenth Amendment, 29
*North Star,* 15, 33, 35
Oak Hill Country Club, 11, 104
Oberlin College, 39-42, 46, 238
Oliver, King, 159
Oneonta, 58
O'Reilly, Henry, 50
Oswego, 229, 240
Otis, Maj. Gen. Elwell, 177-180, 272
Ouzer, Louis, 78, 84
Pake, George, 289, 292, 296
Palmyra, 3, 16, 241
Palo Alto Research Center, 288-296
Parker, Ely, 90
Patch, Sam, 268, 269
Paychex, Inc., 15, 300
Phelps, Oliver, 13, 21
Phelps-Gorham Purchase, 21
Philippine Islands, 60, 61, 178, 179
Pittsford, 13, 129, 276
*Porgy and Bess,* 162, 169
Port Byron, 240
Post, Amy, 37, 38, 208
Post, Isaac, 37, 38, 208
Powers, Daniel, 55-57
Powers Block, 55, 56
Price, Leontyne, 162, 168, 169

Quakers, 37, 39

Red Jacket, 90

Renaissance 2010 Plan, 4, 297-299

Revivals, 17, 235-238

Reynolds Arcade, 15, 117

Rhees, Rush, 87, 95-106, 273

Roberts Wesleyan College, 10, 300

Robinson, Bill "Bojangles," 161

Rochester, 9-17, 21, 21-23, 25, 33-36, 40, 49, 50, 52, 55-57, 63, 64, 68, 69, 75-78, 87, 88, 90, 93, 97-103, 107, 109, 113, 114, 117, 118, 121, 124, 129-131, 134, 142, 145, 147, 151, 157, 162, 163, 165, 172, 173, 179, 181, 185, 195-197, 203, 208, 218, 221, 229, 236-238, 240, 252, 253, 256, 263-266, 268, 270, 272, 275-287, 297-300

Rochester, Nathaniel, 3, 14, 19-22, 130

Rochester, "Our Kindest City," 284, 285

Rochester Americans, 11

Rochester *Democrat and Chronicle,* 58, 64

Rochester Free Academy, 194, 195, 252

Rochester Knighthawks, 11

Rochester Institute of Technology, 9, 10, 98, 143, 147, 300

Rochester Museum and Science Center, 10

Rochester Philharmonic Orchestra, 10, 87, 170

Rochester Pops Orchestra, 162, 170

Rochester Red Wings, 11

Rochester Rhinos, 11

Rochester Royals, 278-280

Rochester subway, 275-277

Rochester *Times-Union,* 63, 64

Rochester's Ties to Hollywood, 286, 287

Rochesterville, 14

Rockefeller, John D., 115

Rome, NY, 14, 17

Roosevelt, Theodore, 97, 272

St. John Fisher College, 10, 11, 300

Schurman, Jacob, 59-61, 178

Schoolcraft, Henry Rowe, 90

Scrantom, Hamlet, 14

Selden, George B., 49, 108, 132, 133

Selden, Henry, 28, 49, 132

Seneca Falls, 23, 27, 35, 42

Sheen, Bishop Fulton J., 3, 254-261

Shilling, Donovan, 272, 274

Sibley, Hiram, 9, 15, 49-51, 77, 101, 102, 175

Sibley, Lindsay, and Curr, 48, 195, 286

Sinatra, Frank, 79, 84

Smith, Gerrit, 33

Smith, Joseph, 3, 16, 241-244

*"Smugtown, U.S.A.,"* 281-283, 285

Society of the Genesee, 272-274

South Butler, 43

Spellman, Cardinal Francis, 255-258

Spiritualism, 38, 206-217

Stanton, Elizabeth Cady, 23, 25, 27, 29, 38, 42, 44, 235, 237

Stone, Lucy, 25, 39-41, 43-45

Stone, Orringh, 13

Stone, Simon, 13

Stone-Tolan House, 13

Strasenburgh Planetarium, 10

Stromberg-Carlson, 138, 140

Strong, Henry Alvah, 108, 109, 113-115

Strong Memorial Hospital, 104, 300

Strong Museum, 11

SUNY—College at Brockport, 10

SUNY—College at Geneseo, 10

SUNY—Empire State College, 10

Syracuse, 17, 43, 60, 104, 280

Syracuse *Herald,* 60

Third Presbyterian Church, 236

Thompson, George, 23

Tonawanda Reservation, 90, 91

Town Hall, 166-168

Treichler, Martha 274

Treichler, William, 274

Tripp, Frank E., 65, 273

Tubman, Harriet, 36

Underground Railroad, 32, 35-37

University of Rochester, 9, 10, 51, 87, 95-106, 112, 162, 164, 300

University of Rochester Medical School, 104, 286

*USA Today,* 70-73

Utica, 16, 17, 64, 227

Vick, James, 9, 175

Waller, Fats, 161

Warfield, Thaddeus, 165

Warfield, William, 162-170

Warner, A. J., 229-234

Warner, J. Foster, 231

Watson, James Sibley, Jr., 77, 78

Watson, Thomas, 3, 120-123, 272

Webb, Chick, 158-160

Western Union, 15, 50, 51, 77

Whipple, Dr. George, 104

Wilder, Alec, 75-85

Wiley, Louis, 272, 273

Williamson, Charles, 19

Willys, John N., 63

Wilson, Joseph C., 124-127, 149, 288

Women's Rights Movement, 14-16, 35, 38, 40, 42, 45, 237

World Image Center, 9, 282

Xerox Corporation, 15, 124-126, 150, 288-296

Young, Brigham, 3, 239-247